Counselling Supervision

The *Counselling Supervision* series, edited by Michael Carroll and Elizabeth Holloway, has a clearly defined focus on counselling supervision issues and emphasizes the actual practice of counselling supervision, drawing on up-to-date models of supervision to assist, inform and update trainee and practising counsellors, counselling psychologists and psychotherapists.

Titles in the series include:

Counselling Supervision in Context
edited by Michael Carroll and Elizabeth Holloway

Training Counsellor Supervisors: Strategies, Models and Methods
edited by Elizabeth Holloway and Michael Carroll

GROUP SUPERVISION

A Guide to Creative Practice

Brigid Proctor

SAGE Publications
London • Thousand Oaks • New Delhi

SAGE Publications Ltd
6 Bonhill Street
London EC2A 4PU

SAGE Publications Inc
2455 Teller Road
Thousand Oaks, California 91320

SAGE Publications India Pvt Ltd
32, M-Block Market
Greater Kailash – I
New Delhi 110 048

British Library Cataloguing in Publication data

A catalogue record for this book is
available from the British Library

ISBN 0-7619-5978-5
ISBN 0-7619-5979-3 (pbk)

Library of Congress catalog card number 00-130555

Typeset by Photoprint, Torquay, Devon
Printed in Great Britain by Biddles Ltd, Guildford, Surrey

Contents

Foreword

For many years now Brigid Proctor, along with Francesca Inskipp, has led the way in practising, writing and training in individual and group supervision. There have been many speeches in British counselling and supervision conferences that begin with acknowledgement of these women as the first generation of educators and trainers in supervision. In the Counselling Supervision series, we wanted to position contemporary knowledge of group supervision, as it is generally practised, within the historical context of group theory and supervision in counselling as known in Britain and the United States. There was no doubt in our minds who should write this book and we were thrilled when Brigid Proctor agreed to take on the challenge. Brigid brings a passion and an enthusiasm that is contagious and invigorating. It is no accident that she should call her book *Group Supervision: A Guide to Creative Practice*. This book is in all aspects a creative venture. Brigid breaks down difficult concepts and presents them in imaginative and innovative ways and makes her years of experience as a group supervisor highly accessible to the reader. She speaks directly to the 'working supervisor' and we suspect her 'written voice' will become the 'internal supervisor' for many readers. The book blends an understanding of supervision with group counselling theories and individual supervision theories and illustrates these ideas across four case studies of supervision. These cases become the working material throughout the book and make supervisors' thinking and strategies concrete and practitioner-based.

In spite of the recent upsurge of books on supervision, particularly in Britain, it is surprising that not a single one is dedicated solely to group supervision. Perhaps it is partly due to the complexity of tackling this subject from a theoretical and practical stance with no substantial empirical base. Although in this book we have not directly corrected the paucity of empirical investigations on supervision, we are hopeful that the easy accessibility that Brigid brings to modelling the practice of supervision will be highly motivating to the researcher-practitioners among us. The book offers the combined experience, learning, reflection, reading and practice accumulated over many years as an individual and group supervisor. Further research and writings on group supervision would be a fitting memorial to Brigid's immense contribution to our field for she has written a gem of a book that anyone who does group supervision will want to keep close. Her love of supervision and talents in writing about it permeate this book, and we feel privileged to have worked alongside her as *Group Supervision: A Guide to Creative Practice* was born.

Michael Carroll
Elizabeth Holloway

Acknowledgements

As I reflect chronologically, this book owes most to experience starting a quarter of a century ago. The opportunity to work at the South West London College Counselling Course Centre introduced me to group working and learning. Discovering the meaning of co-operative work was personally and professionally transformational. For leading that exploration, I remain indebted to Gaie Houston and Thom Osborne. For coming out to play with supervision, I thank all the staff, and course participants whom I supervised. To my colleagues Robin Shohet and Ken Gray I am grateful for our work on formulating supervision frameworks.

Coming up to date, this book could not exist without my close colleague and friend, Francesca Inskipp. Our training together, and our formulation of it in Open Learning materials, has been a constant laboratory for model making. Long may that last. The other laboratory and consultation space has been my supervision and consultation with numerous counsellors and, more recently, with developed and developing supervisors. To all groups and individuals – thank you. Many of you deserve mention by name for your specific contributions. And, of course, to all the clients of all the counsellors, of all the supervisors. I suspect, but hope it is never the case, that they are sometimes an excuse for us to work and play together. I believe that collectively we have gone some way to relieving their distress and helping them 'live more resourcefully and to their own greater well-being' (BAC Definition of Counselling).

My gratitude to Brian, my husband, for helping me find order out of chaos, as my consultant; for protecting my space, as my carer; and both maddening and gratifying me as my illustrator. And, finally, a heartfelt thank-you to Michael Carroll and Elizabeth Holloway for asking me to write this book and being unfailingly encouraging, good-tempered and supportive editors.

For Naomi and her family group

Introduction

Developing a model

This book is intended as a practical guide for counsellors and psychotherapists who are interested in group supervision. It arises from experience in a particular context – the developing counselling and psychotherapy profession in the United Kingdom. It is time-specific. My experience spans the final 25 years of the twentieth century. Hopefully it will extend into the twenty-first century. Like most of my contemporaries, I learned how to supervise in a group through trial and error. I had had some minimum training in social work supervision many years earlier. When working on the Diploma in Counselling Skills Course at South West London College, I invented my way of offering one-to-one supervision to trainees who were learning to import counselling skills into their related helping professions. When economics made two years of individual supervision for each student impracticable, we decided, as a staff, to offer group supervision for the first year, followed by a year of one-to-one. Contrary to more usual thinking, we argued that if supervisees learned to use the group well, experience in that challenging environment would help them use their individual supervision economically, creatively and effectively. The results seemed to justify that assumption.

As my experience of supervision and of working groups widened, I became a trainer of supervisors. I found it difficult to communicate why I worked as I did and *how* I made judgements about good and bad practice. My trainer colleagues and I therefore wrestled into shape a framework for understanding the tasks of supervision in general. Subsequently, in writing Open Learning materials with Francesca Inskipp, we developed those frameworks further. Although we did not then name our thinking as 'a model', we now call it the 'Supervision Alliance Model' because it focuses on the 'why' and 'how' of making good supervision alliances at each stage of the process.

We then found that we had to grapple with writing intelligibly about group supervision. We had borrowed and developed various useful models in our group supervision trainings. We were able to demonstrate interesting and effective group supervision. We could give feedback to practising participants based on 'felt sense'. We had some clear frameworks to offer – how to set up ground-rules and working agreements in different contexts, for instance. We could offer a variety of useful maps which charted group development and suggest lots of ideas for using the group as participating co-supervisors.

However, there seemed to be significant gaps. On one training, I realized that I had no framework to offer which helped the participants understand why one might use a particular exercise. On another, I realized that I had no framework for thinking about the management of creative exercises and structures. Furthermore, we (Francesca and I) had not sat down and spelled out – or even identified – the skills of supervisors and supervisees who worked well in groups. Most particularly, we were discovering (the joys of co-working) that we worked very differently from each other. In analysing this, we recognized that, in addition to having different working styles, we habitually worked with counsellors at different developmental stages. Mine were usually experienced and, supposedly, moderately sophisticated at working in groups. Francesca's were usually trainees or volunteers. This realization was to be the clue to finding an important unifying centrepiece in what was becoming a coherent model of group supervision.

When we did begin to spell out the tasks, responsibilities, roles, and skills of a group supervisor, we were daunted. The task was so complex that I still wonder whether it would be better left inexplicit. However, the model seemed useful to numbers of group supervision trainees. Though complex, it is composed of a variety of component parts. These can stand alone for use in orientating oneself in one particular dimension. Hopefully, they are also clear and simple enough to act as an atlas, to be riffled through at times of confusion: which map do I need here, and to what scale? Does this group member need help in developing a simple skill? Should I have been thinking in terms of a concealed group preoccupation? What do I know that could help clarify this particular supervision issue at this stage of this session? What is our working agreement here? Do we need to review and update the ground rules?

Focus on counsellors and psychotherapists

Although I have supervised groups of practitioners whose work is not counselling, this book concentrates on the supervision of counsellors and psychotherapists. I have found that although many of the underlying ideas and practices transfer readily to other settings, there are certain tasks and ways of thinking that are peculiar to the supervision of counsellors or psychotherapists. When a model devised in the contexts of counselling is imported to other contexts without amendment, it can antagonize or confuse. Frameworks for thinking of tasks, for working agreements, for processes of group formation and participation, are potentially useful. If potential is to be actualized, ideas need to be translated into language and behaviour which is appropriate to the specific working culture and context. This is even true within the wider culture of counselling and psychotherapy. Words, models, assumptions are not always readily transferable across sub-cultures. Since I would like the Group Supervision Alliance Model, offered here, to be seen as relevant across a variety of theoretical orientations, that act of communication is enough to concentrate on in one book.

Underlying values

Although the subject of the book is group supervision, the processes described have wider application and implication. Counselling trainers may find it useful, as may supervisors of individuals. It incorporates the values I hold about education, co-operative enterprise, and professional service. It points up the relationship of these values to the kind of personal and social development which also acts therapeutically – for individuals, groups and wider systems.

References and glossary

In order to interrupt the text as little as possible, a dual referencing system has been used. Since the book is intended to be more practical than academic, references have been kept to a minimum. Authors who have been quoted or used as direct references are acknowledged in the text. Where a previous author has addressed themes which are similar or identical to those being discussed, footnotes refer the reader to the *Relevant Reading* section.

The glossary covers a wide variety of words. Some come from specific theoretical orientations and may therefore be unfamiliar to readers from other schools of practice. Some are everyday English words used in an unusual fashion. If you are puzzled by any word or its use, look in the Glossary – you may well find it there.

I The Group Supervision Alliance Model

1   Setting the scene

Dramatis personae

Group supervision is an enactment. For the most part, supervisor and group supervisees are on stage. However, off stage, there are at least two powerfully silent participants, and possibly one or two other influential players who may appear in the opening or closing acts, or at times of crisis (1). In setting the scene, it is worth taking time to consider each character in turn. Figure 1.1 represents these as stakeholders in the supervision.

Figure 1.1   *Stakeholders in group supervision*

The supervisee

Group supervision is the opportunity for each counsellor, in the role of supervisee, to make use of the reflective space reserved for her. She will not be able to use it for the benefit of her clients, or her own professional development, unless she can come to look forward to supervision as sufficiently safe and challenging. Additionally, it will be a major forum for the development of the 4 Cs – Competence, Confidence, Compassion and Creativity. Traditionally, supervision writing has been concerned with the supervisor – how to do, or improve, supervisor practice. This preoccupation mirrors societal and professional assumptions that 'the expert' is hierarchically more important than the 'learner', and needs help in becoming yet more expert. Too often, in my opinion, such books can begin to treat supervisees as 'them' (rather as some counselling textbooks tend to talk about clients). This can disguise the reality that supervisees are adult learners, most of whom are capable of developing their own 'internal supervisor'. In order to do so consciously, there may be information that can be spelled out before they ever enter supervision, and skills that they can learn or transfer to this new context.

Presenting clients or professional issues for supervision in an economic and accessible way is a skill in itself. To present in a group requires added courage and self-discipline. Using a group setting for reflecting and learning is also a specific ability. When starting in group supervision, supervisees may need to be reminded about some facts of group life, and encouraged to become aware, ahead of time, of some of the hopes, fears and expectations they habitually bring to group experiences. Most particularly, they need to be clear that in a group they will be (to greater or lesser extent, depending on the group agreement) not only supervisees but also co-supervisors. As such, they need a good deal of the skill and sensitivity that should be expected from supervisors. So, do supervisees, then, have the *information, skill, support and challenge* (Egan 1994) needed to enter actively and creatively into this group supervision alliance?

Much of this book is aimed at supervisors, but I hope it will be accessible and useful to group supervisees as well. While reading the case studies, which focus on supervisor practice and perspective, readers should also think about what would be happening for each supervisee in the groups.

The client

The client is one of the two powerful off-stage characters. Working well with the client is the heart of the matter – the counsellor is committed to practising to the best of her ability and the supervisor is employed to promote best work. In group supervision in particular, where the secondary satisfactions or hardships of group work can become centre stage, attention for the clients can be squeezed out. Would this client recognize himself, or the counselling issues being engaged with? Would that client experience group members as working to respect, understand, and help her? Will this supervision really result in helping them become more who they want to be and to act in ways which are resourceful and in their best interests? It will be salutary to think, in this book and during group supervision in practice, of the client's thoughts and feelings if he were a fly on the wall.

The supervisor

The supervisor is the person responsible for facilitating the counsellor, in role of supervisee, to use supervision well, in the interests of the client. His particular need is to have clarity about the task, so that he can be group manager as well as supervisor in a group. The role of group manager requires skills and abilities distinct from those of supervisor. Many will be transferable from other contexts. Some developed skills need to be left behind. The role entails sub-roles which may be in tension with each other. In addition to a clear map or understanding of the general tasks of supervision and their complexity, a group manager also needs:

1   An awareness of his own style, strengths and limitations in leading and facilitating groups. What abilities might he need to develop to do it better? Are his strengths as a supervisor well integrated with his abilities to engage supervisees in each other's supervision? Is he able to balance the needs of the supervision task with the needs of individuals and the demands of group building, maintenance and repair? The following chapter suggests three types of group supervision leadership, style and contract. The supervisor needs to have made suitable choices with regard to the style of group he intends to lead/offer and to communicate his choice clearly.

2   Access to maps of group task and process. The supervisor needs to have some understanding of how groups contribute or detract from the task of supervision and his ability as a supervisor. He will need to have ideas about how individual

members and the group as a whole can be helped and hindered by the presence of group forces (2). Cognitive frameworks add to understanding of group dynamics and processes but, importantly, they also need to help him manage confusing or difficult incidents in the group.

3   Increased awareness and trust in physical, sensory based processing. Counselling itself is a more physical activity than we realize. All thinking and feeling is rooted in and mediated by our sensory perception – seeing, hearing, touch, movement, smell and taste. In a one-to-one relationship, we can often process sufficient units of verbal and non-verbal communication in time to identify thinking and feeling – something which 'makes enough sense' to us to help us decide what, if anything, to say. A group, however, is almost always too complex in its units and levels of communication for processing minute to minute abstract thought. A group supervisor, I suggest, has to learn to trust his senses – to think in physical imagery – 'Who has the reins here?' 'Who is out in the cold?' 'Where have we got lost?' 'This is euphoric – we need to come down to earth.' 'I've lost the tune and the rhythm.' 'I was imagining a full-bodied bowl and suddenly it shattered.'

As we will see later, the amount of group skill required depends on the chosen mode of group. The supervisor needs to ensure that the particular supervision set-up he has chosen is well enough suited to his style and abilities as group facilitator.

The profession, the agency and the training course

Group supervision always takes place within a professional context – and often in the context of an agency, organization or training course. Most counsellors subscribe to a professional alliance which is codified in working agreements about ethics and good practice. The professional associations which represent and monitor this alliance for us are, collectively, another powerful off-stage character in the group supervision enactment. Organizational, agency and course managers who are responsible for managing the context of the group are influential characters at the outset. They determine the supervision contract and they may engage with supervisor and/or supervisees at times of crisis or transition.

When one is training supervisors (and perhaps supervisees), it is informative to ask them to do an exercise in which they take different 'stakeholder' roles and speak from those perspectives about the supervision process. Any conversation between a supervisor and a person speaking in role for some professional association (for instance BAC or UKCP) instantly reveals what heavy expectations those bodies have of their supervisors and how little supervisors feel supported or even informed by them. When, in addition, someone speaks on behalf of an organizational manager, expectations of the supervisor become greater, and perhaps conflicting. BAC may expect confidentiality of client material. Managers may be expecting to have feedback on how clients are progressing with their counsellors. If training courses are added into the exercise, tutors may be requiring, for example, that their trainees have a certain number of on-going clients. A placement agency may be concerned about waiting lists and create a policy of time-limited work. Although, back in real life, such an issue is not the supervisor's responsibility, he may be the person who becomes aware of such clashes, and who is at the centre – concerned for clients, trainees, the agency and proper 'professional' work. If group members are in contract with different agencies or courses, these differences are crucial to the focus of the supervision work.

So the profession, the client and any concerned organization, agency or training course are all stakeholders. Supervisor and supervisees need to be aware of these interconnections and know how and where they are accountable for the counselling work and the supervision undertaken.

Clearing the ground – models, orientations and frameworks

Terminology can be confusing in writing this complex supervision drama. In this book the word 'model' will be used in one way only – that is, to describe a comprehensive concept, or map, of supervision or of group supervision. The Supervision Alliance Model (Inskipp and Proctor 1993, 1995), which is referred to in the Introduction, and underlies the group model used in this book, is an example of this use of the word. Others are the SAS (Systems Approach Supervision) Model (Holloway 1995) or the Cyclical Model (Page and Wosket 1994). These focus on some concept which is central to the core beliefs on which the model is based and seek to map the process of supervision in its widest sense.

A model offers a mental map for ordering complex data and experience.

Within each model are specific 'mini-models'. In this book, the noun used from time to time to describe such a concept – a 'map within a model' – is 'framework'. So, the *framework of tasks of supervision* within the SAS Model (Holloway 1995) is the development of:

- counselling skills
- case conceptualization
- professional role
- emotional awareness
- self-evaluation

The *framework for tasks* within the Supervision Alliance Model sees the responsibility for supervisor and supervisee as:

- formative – the tasks of learning and facilitating learning
- normative – the tasks of monitoring, and self-monitoring, standards and ethics
- restorative – the tasks of refreshment

In Houston's (1995) model, the *tasks framework* is:

- policing
- plumbing
- (making) poetry

In Carroll's (1996) Integrative Generic Model the *task framework* is:

- creating relationship
- teaching
- counselling
- monitoring
- evaluating
- consulting
- administration

In this terminology, the well known Process Model of Supervision (Hawkins and Shohet 1989) (referred to later) would be a *framework for focusing* in supervision.

To distinguish these from the broad theoretical concepts, or 'schools' of counselling and psychotherapy practice which are often called 'theoretical models', I will refer to the latter as 'theoretical orientation'. It may well be that some supervisors describe their 'model of supervision' by the theoretical orientation in which they work, for example 'the psychodynamic model of supervision'. Carroll has pointed out (1996) that writers about supervision are increasingly moving away from 'counselling-bound' models to models based on social roles, developmental stages and so on.

One framework or map, within the Group Supervision Alliance Model, that will frequently be referred to denotes specific ways of conceiving the roles and responsibilities in group supervision. For ease, these will be described under types. You will read about Type 1 (or 2 or 3 or 4) groups. (The fuller name and description of each type will be given later in Chapter 3.)

As the founders of Neurolinguistic Programming quoted: 'The map is not the territory', and as Psychosynthesis has it, 'This is not the truth.' Models, maps, frameworks, orientations, types are the labels and descriptions devised to order and communicate our experience. In this book they are used as a preliminary. I would like the book to be useful in introducing, or re-introducing, you to the territory of group supervision. It can then be used not only to map (and encourage map-making), but also to guide and serve as a practical and psychological handbook.

The Group Supervision Alliance Model

Figure 1.2 maps the headings of the various frameworks within the Group Supervision Alliance Model. Each one is briefly described below and will be explored and illustrated in practice in subsequent chapters.

I   Professional alliances and contracts

Outer frame – the supervision contract

The supervision alliance is the outer frame within which group supervision is contained. Its binding agent is the stated contract, which specifies tasks, rights and responsibilities within a particular organizational, training or freelance context. It spells out,

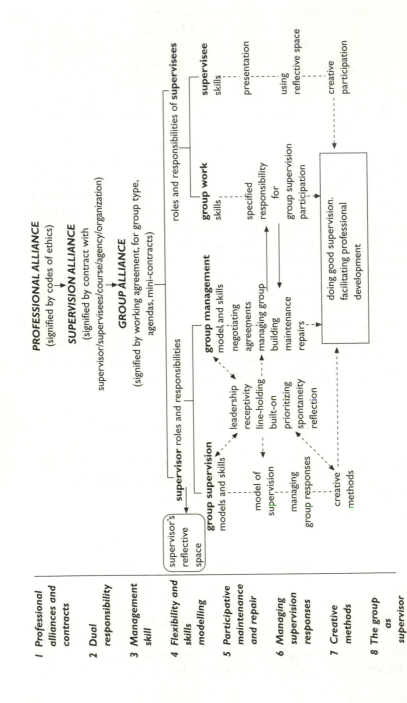

Figure 1.2   *Group Supervision Alliance Model*

for all active participants, responsibilities to the client and professional colleagues.

Group working agreement for an alliance

Within that, the group working agreement lays the foundation for
supervisor and supervisees to ally themselves in the group supervision task. Through negotiating and clarifying supervisor and
supervisee roles and responsibilities; ground rules; procedures
for working and reviewing; time management; and individual
learning aims, members of the group are actively engaged in the
ownership of the supervision enterprise. At the same time, they
are meeting and getting to know each other. Individually they will
be finding their feet in this new group. Collectively they will be
finding their shape and voice as a group.

This agreement acts as blueprint and container for supervisor
and group. Negotiated agendas for session work, and mini-
contracts for individual 'pieces' of supervision, continue the estab-
lishment of shared ownership. Individual learning aims gear the
work to personal and professional development. Planned reviews
and *ad hoc* processing ensure a continuing relationship with these
holding agreements.

2   Dual responsibility

The supervisor has a dual responsibility. She is responsible for
enabling and ensuring that good enough supervision is being
done in the group. This responsibility carries with it the care for
each individual's learning and developmental needs. It may also
carry managerial and training agendas, depending on the contract
with any course or agency involved. At the same time, she is the
leader in the group, at least at the outset. In her own style she
needs to set the tone for the development of a culture of intention,
empathic respect and straightforwardness – for a practical and
effective group alliance.

Supervisees have reciprocal dual responsibility. They need to
have, or develop, the ability to use supervision well. They also
need to develop skill and understanding in participating in group
supervision according to their specific group working agreement.

3   Management skill

Both supervisor tasks call for skilled management. Choices between appropriate but conflicting goals occur frequently. The supervisor needs to have clear and simple ideas for prioritizing what she wants the group to achieve in terms of the supervision task and in terms of the life of the group. This offers ground to stand on. Since so much happens every minute in a group, she will have to develop trust in her own spontaneity and the ability to reflect on the group in retrospect in the light of the models she is using. For this she will need her own support and consultation opportunities, appropriate to her own developmental stage as a supervisor.

4   Flexibility and skills modelling

The group agreement can range in style from members as active audience watching one-to-one supervision by the supervisor, to members as co-supervisors, with the supervisor as boundary monitor, ultimate buck-carrier and collegial participant. Depending on the agreement and the developmental stage of the supervisees, the supervisor will carry responsibility for inducting and encouraging them in their agreed roles. If she is to harness the group's resourcefulness, she will move between leading, following and line-holding. She will also be modelling and informing group members about those abilities for themselves.

5   Participative maintenance and repair

As the group develops there may be growing pains within the group or difficulties in relation to the wider context. These should not be mistaken for dysfunction unless other explanations fail. The supervisor carries responsibility for dealing creatively with 'family life' while maintaining supervision work. She has to support and challenge the group to engage actively in its own development, maintenance and possibly repair work.

6   Managing supervision responses

If the group is set up as one in which the supervisees actively co-supervise, there will be a further management task of helping them gear their responses appropriately. This may consist of holding attentive space, managing freeflow discussions or offering structures and exercises. In all work there will be varying elements of freeflow and structure, and the supervisor will be developing a sense of proper balance and timing. There are useful guidelines for good practice in managing group responses.

7   Creative methods

In order to access the group's collective good sense, she may want to employ creative methods that 'reach parts other methods can't reach'. In doing this, she will sometimes meet the unexpected and she needs rules of thumb to help her out until she can reflect more fully.

8   The group as supervisor

Developing good supervision work in a group, and providing a climate in which members grow in competence and confidence is, at least, challenging. The supervisor and, increasingly, the participants need to recognize that, at its best, a group is a great deal more than the sum of its parts. Potentially, the group *is* the supervisor. As a supervisor it contains not only the resources of supervisor and each group member, but, in embryo, the rich creativity of a complex living group system.

This model of group supervision is rooted in basic presuppositions that have proved more than an ideology – they seem to work in practice. They are borrowed and adapted from known and unknown gurus and mentors. Each time I write the list it is different – new presuppositions have been identified and added.

Relevant presuppositions

• It is possible and useful to clarify, progressively, what you are doing, why you are doing it and what you intend to happen as a result.
• You and your colleagues in supervision will be doing the best you can for yourselves at any one time and you are, in Carl Rogers' words, your own friend/s.

- Adult learners have the motivation and ability to co-operate with each other in shared learning and endeavour.
- They deserve information and the chance to know about and develop the requisite skills.
- This includes knowing their rights and responsibilities and believing that both will be taken seriously.
- Under these circumstances, they will usually take intelligent management of their own professional development.
- They deserve to be told the purpose of activities they are asked to engage in so that they can give or withhold informed consent.
- If they can trust that this is the case, they will increasingly be interested in taking some things on trust.
- Development takes place best in an atmosphere of inquiry, experiment and reflection.
- Anxious attention to rules can destroy such an atmosphere.
- Holding to agreed focus of the task, while respecting boundaries, creates space for inquiry, play and discourse.
- Functional and dysfunctional Child states and behaviour will surface in Adult group work.
- Individuals can have a playful and easy relationship with the 'unconscious'.
- The unconscious demands profound respect.
- A group is more than the sum of its parts.
- To the extent that a culture of empathic understanding, unconditional respect for each person and increasing honesty and authenticity is fostered, mutual trust can develop.
- To that extent each individual and the group as a system will experience freedom to be 'their best selves'.

The territory of group supervision

That is the overall map. Group supervision is a complex subject. Writing *about* it is not a medium that easily conveys the flavour of the experience. To convey this more directly, four case studies will be used in illustration throughout the text. For obvious reasons these cannot be 'real'. However, they are all true to actual incidents heard about or experienced by the author. They are chosen to illustrate:

- the differing backgrounds and starting points of group supervisors
- differing contexts

- differing group types and working agreements
- groups of counsellors in varying developmental stages
- a variety of ways of 'doing supervision'
- group transitions and turning points

In brief, the four case studies comprise:

- Case study 1: Ruth, a supervisor who undertakes to supervise trainees in year two of their integrative course as they start their practice in a variety of agencies.
- Case study 2: Carmel, who is employed by a voluntary agency. Her task is to set up a new group for volunteers who are mainly, but not entirely, students on differing counselling courses.
- Case study 3: follows Christine as she decides whether to supervise a team of counsellors who work for a large organization, including their manager who is also a counsellor within the team. It charts her subsequent experiences.
- Case study 4: opens with Martin being invited to set up a freelance group. It follows the process of setting up the group and his difficulties in enabling it to become established.

Each case study, and episodes within it, will be introduced when pertinent to the body of the text. The next chapter will consider the advantages and pitfalls of group supervision relative to one-to-one supervision, and will illustrate the reasons why group supervision may be chosen.

2 The group option

Why a group?

Developing the profession

I write about group supervision because I like it and believe it can often be the preferred option for supervisees, clients and the profession. It is a potent force in the development of a profession which must become increasingly flexible and adaptive to client needs and variety. One of the greatest dangers to the creative development of any activity is a closed system. Such a system relies on ways of working which are passed from a generation of the initiated to a generation of initiates, and the rites of initiation ensure both guardianship and exclusivity of 'the work'. Although the activity may develop tactically, in small ways, it is seldom challenged strategically.

In the UK, the art and craft of supervision has not traditionally been learned through formal training but has passed from supervisor to supervisee. Based predominantly on one of a number of particular theoretical orientations, a variety of traditional views were handed on, of counselling, psychotherapy and supervision. These closed systems are being challenged in several ways. There is an increasingly wide variety of on-going and short trainings available to prospective counsellors and psychotherapists. These trainings themselves can be part of closed systems – each with its own sectarian (or tribal) beliefs and assumptions. There is a move towards integrative and eclectic models (or, sometimes, conglomerations). As we have seen, supervision models are also increasingly integrative, as are many supervision trainings.

Group supervision offers practitioners from differing traditions the opportunity to mix and open their work to each other. In particular, where supervisees come from differing traditions and trainings, they gain from each other's varied training and expertise. Practice is also up for scrutiny. Anyone who has been in a group which includes members who are doing long-term work and brief therapy will recognize how challenging the conjunction is for both parties. Supervision groups can be a dynamic force in promoting flexible and varied practice that is geared more effectively to a range of clients and contexts.

In addition, group supervision increases accountability. Collusion – that is unspoken agreement not to notice certain facts of life – is possible in any supervision. However, a group has at least four or five chances for someone to notice what is culturally unmentionable.

Counsellor learning, stimulation and confidence

From the perspective of counsellors, there are many potential advantages over one-to-one supervision (1). Each group member has access to a wider range of practice. A trainee in individual supervision comes across, say, one ethical issue a term. In group supervision she would encounter at least four. She has 'second-hand' access to the clients of all her peers. Recall the list of trainee (and developing counsellor) learning tasks listed within the SAS Model:

- counselling skills
- case conceptualization
- professional role
- emotional awareness
- self-evaluation

A group supervisee has access to the style and ability of each other member of the group. That is a rich source of skill, conceptualization, and professional role management. The remaining two tasks are helped by other group resources.

Shared learning can be particularly stimulating – 'we can stretch, support and challenge ourselves, our supervisors and our colleagues in relationship around our work. Human beings seem to find this dynamic intrinsically pleasurable and satisfying of itself . . . [and] work done with joy is always likely to be of better quality than other work' (Clarkson 1998). For both trainees and experienced practitioners, group supervision can offer companionship in what is, by nature, a 'private practice'. The hunger for knowing more about 'how others do it' can only be realized in a supervision or training forum.

Variety of learning

Groups, too, offer a variety of learning opportunities. Counsellors and trainees learn to open their practice publicly. They practise sitting back and listening to others. They have time to think and reflect collectively. They have to interact with positive and critical feedback and learn to discriminate about what is useful in the responses and interventions of peers as well as of 'the expert'. Additionally, supervision groups encourage members to learn to trust their own perceptions while being open and receptive to differing views.

A group is the most effective forum for giving and receiving feedback about skill in communicating. I may feel empathic but do I come across like that? I may perceive myself as challenging – do others want more, rather than less, straight talking? My face may be rather inexpressive and this affects members of the group in different ways – I never knew that before. Emotional awareness and self-evaluation rely on accurate and varied feedback.

Skill and awareness in groups and systems

As a spin-off from direct improvement of counselling and supervision practice, group supervisees have an opportunity to experience in practice what is meant by such terms as group process, group development and group dynamics (2, 3). They can learn to comprehend the maps which have been developed for making the complexity of group life more intelligible. This will be of direct use in team working and any form of counselling group work. In addition, the better understanding of one complex system is readily transferable to other complex systems – families, organizations, cultures – in which counsellors will be personally and professionally involved.

With group understanding comes potential for increased skill in leading and/or belonging to groups. As we will see later, groups need leaders and members who have the ability for flexible role-taking. A good group encourages the development of leadership, assertion and receptivity at appropriate times. Feedback to members about their group skill will be sometimes spoken and often enacted. Most members will learn a good deal about their flexibility, appropriateness and their favoured and less favoured roles in the group.

Resources for the work of supervision

In another dimension, more participants mean more possibilities for doing good supervision. There is necessarily a range of attitudes, qualities and experiences present in a group. I am never more moved than when seemingly ordinary people begin to lay out their wares as they get to know and trust each other. The image I have is of them gradually pulling from their pockets little hints of handkerchiefs. Like a conjuror's trick, the hankies turn into silk scarves of differing colours and designs which, when waved, form patterns in a variety of tones and colours.

The variety of resources also means that it is less easy for the supervisor and any one supervisee to have shared blind-spots. Someone in a group is likely to keep in touch with the simple level and to take an advocacy stance for client, counsellor, or, perhaps, for other interested parties in the wider system – for instance, the client's partner or the counselling agency.

A greater number of members also allows the development of a wider choice of creative methods of supervision. By 'creative', I mean 'more than just talking' methods. These will necessarily include talking, but they can be deliberately designed to elicit information through our other human abilities. Creative methods tap into the richness of our outward and inward senses – of sight, sound, movement, smell, touch – and our mental ability to move swiftly in time and space. Talking alone will not elicit that quality of information, that ready access to the unconscious. Groups offer both wider choice and the richness of the group unconscious.

Harnessing difference

If group members can succeed in the task of doing 'good supervision', they will be able to weather anxieties about difference, and come to enjoy and celebrate variations in style, beliefs, emotionality, competence, experience, gender, class, ethnicity and age – to name a few dimensions of conscious difference. The forces of competition and comparison seem endemic in all of us who have been brought up in Western traditions in the twentieth century. An effective supervision group can harness these forces in the service of better practice. It will be a 'safe enough' place in which to acknowledge fear, anger, guilt and shame, and transform locked energy into sensitivity and potency of practice. It can be the collegial forum for acknowledging hope, love, and delight in the work, in clients and in one's own growing competence; and for acknowledging the need for mutual nurture. All these things can happen in the one-to-one or one-to-two supervision forum, but a group that achieves that safety and challenge has a special quality.

Economics

Last but, probably in effect, most telling, group supervision is an economic option. Employers can engage one supervisor to four or five (sometimes more) counsellors. Freelance counsellors can spread the cost of supervision while having more supervision time over all. Most accreditation calculates supervisory time using a ratio of hours over people. Most group supervisors and supervisees consider two hours of group supervision more valuable than, say, half an hour of one-to-one, so this ratio may change. However, even as the matter stands, groups are still a cheaper option.

Caveat

These are the potential advantages of group supervision. Skill and perseverance from supervisor and supervisees are required to realize that potential. Misused and wasted potential in a group can create boredom, anxiety and purposelessness which is more damaging than the ineffectiveness of poor individual supervision. Here and in subsequent chapters I will suggest that careful forethought, initiation and building of a group working alliance are the essential foundations for a good working group.

Group or one-to-one?

In discussion, counsellors who have experienced both good individual supervision and effective group supervision are clear about the relative advantages and disadvantages (4, 5). Individual work allows for 'special time' – a whole hour (or whatever) for oneself – when most of one's working time is spent in giving special attention to others. It luxuriously offers a unique relationship, which may progress from mentorship through colleagueship to an internalized special relationship.

Groups allow for the stimulation and excitement of co-operative enterprise. The supervisor is not the only and ultimate authority.

Members of the group may hear things better from peers than from the 'authority'. They may also offer each other mutual respect and begin to attribute to the group the skill and expertise which in individual work can easily accrue only to the supervisor.

Not only . . . but also . . .

Supervision in groups need not replace the advantages of one-to-one supervision. Many counsellors experience both, either alongside each other, or at different times in their counselling career. Trainees and volunteers often have no choice. Where choice is possible, individuals can take responsibility for doing an audit of their current developmental needs and designing a supervision package to meet them. A designer package might include, for instance, one-to-one peer supervision, and a led group, or a monthly peer group and fortnightly individual supervision.

What size makes a group?

Is supervision which consists of two supervisees meeting with one supervisor 'a group'? How many is the maximum number for group supervision? These questions are unanswerable. Reframed, they become more manageable. If I am working with two supervisees, are there ways of thinking about group working that could help? The framework, offered in the next chapter, for thinking about contracting group roles and responsibilities is highly applicable to pair supervising. Other frameworks for 'thinking group' *may* be more useful than 'thinking individual' with a couple, as will systemic thinking about working with couples in any context. If group frameworks help you, as supervisor, make sense of interactions and processes, and, more importantly, build the climate for a working alliance which is more, rather than less, than the sum of its parts, use them.

The optimum numbers for a group, depending on the time available, are probably four, five or six. These allow for variety and for intimacy. Reframing the question about the upper number for group supervision, I would ask: Is this the only supervision these members are having? What are you contractually offering them? Does it accord with your and their responsibilities as specified by Codes of Ethics and Practice? What amount of time will each member get for their reflective space? If it is an additional opportunity to other supervision, what is your working agreement with members for the times they are not 'it' (the presenting supervisee)? Are your roles and responsibilities, and theirs, deliverable within the constraints of time and task? If the answer to the last question is 'probably yes', then careful thought needs to be given to how to create sufficient safety for honest presentation and feedback. The frameworks offered here will be helpful, but possibly not sufficient for thinking about that unless the supervisor uses the group as audience to one-to-one supervision.

Who and when

Supervisor readiness and development

Supervisees may have little choice about what supervision they are offered, or required to have. Supervisors usually do have choice. They can choose to accept an invitation to supervise a group or to seek an opportunity to do so. They can choose to supervise individuals, or groups, or both. Opportunities to group supervise may occur in a variety of ways and at varying stages of a counsellor's supervisory career (6, 7). Each supervisor will be aware of at least some transferable skills and understanding when agreeing to manage her first supervision group. Through formal training, or informally, through self-training, mentorship and apprenticeship, she will have the responsibility of identifying her strengths and shortcomings and intentionally building her confidence and competence.

Contexts and givens

Training course groups

In most cases the decision to supervise trainees or established counsellors in a group may lie with an organization, agency or training course. In fact, it is probably true to say that for most trainees and volunteers, their first experience of supervision will be in a group. For courses (and for the trainees undertaking them) group supervision costs a great deal less than individual supervision. Not all courses take responsibility for offering any supervision. Some leave supervision entirely in the hands of a placement agency or a private supervisor. However, when a course does offer supervision, trainees working together in a group can benefit from all the factors mentioned earlier.

Case study 1 – Ruth

Ruth was an experienced psychodynamic counsellor/psychotherapist who worked as a student counsellor. A counselling Diploma course was set up in her college. The course director had informally consulted with Ruth during its preparation. Subsequently, he invited Ruth to become an internal course supervisor to a group of second-year students. Ruth had previously supervised three individual students who had been in placement in the University Counselling Service and had had good feedback from them. She was pleased to be asked to supervise a group on the course. For her, it was an opportunity for a new experience and further professional development. She had had no formal supervision training, but determined to apply for a course in the following year.

The context and the group

The course identified itself as predominantly psychodynamic in orientation, but in the first year there was a strong counselling skills component which emphasized the person-centred core conditions and introduced students to the Egan skills model. Ruth felt concern that the course could be a bit of a mish-mash and she was glad of the chance to help trainees develop in the psychodynamic tradition. In order to equip herself better, she sat in on some skills practice in the first year and read handouts and feedback sheets on trainee's practice sessions. This led to some interesting discussions – indeed arguments – with the skills tutor. She found them stimulating and, through reading and discussion with like-minded colleagues, she arrived at a clearer understanding of how psychodynamic skills and practice differed from and complemented the basic counselling skills approach.

At the same time, Ruth contracted a separate monthly consultation space for all her supervision work. To date, she had taken her individual supervision work haphazardly to her counselling supervisor whenever she wanted to talk about it.

This course had decided to offer in-course supervision in a group when trainees began counselling practice. The director thought this would ensure that trainees were helped to integrate the course learning with their practice. Ruth was aware that this was her brief and she took seriously her responsibility to understand the implications. She also realized that this supervision of a group would require more preparation and reflection than her individual work.

Agency groups

Agencies, too, often offer group supervision to their workers, who may be employees, self-employed or volunteers. Agencies differ greatly in their expectations of group supervisors and the clarity with which they communicate. Any supervisor needs to familiarize herself with agency policy and clarify the extent to which there may be managerial, training and appraisal responsibilities. Specialist knowledge will be desirable if the agency offers specialist counselling. The counsellors, trainees and volunteers in these settings often come from a variety of training backgrounds. The supervisor will need sufficient understanding to be empathic with the basic ideas and assumptions of a variety of models. She also needs to have developed her own ideas about basic good practice that she can share with the group. Otherwise, she may find herself and her group becoming unhelpfully confused.

Case study 2 – Carmel

Carmel had been appointed as a new supervisor in a voluntary agency. She had recently completed supervision training. She had supervised a number of individual counsellors, mainly trainees. She had previously run a supervision group of telephone counsellors for a voluntary agency. This was her first counsellor supervision group. She had a Diploma in Person-Centred Counselling and was currently doing an Integrative Psychotherapy degree. Her own supervision had offered her a variety of experiences. She had had a number of one-to-one supervisors who had been person-centred in varying degrees. In connection with her degree course, she had sought out a psychodynamic supervisor for variety of experience, and was also in an integrative supervision group. At the interview, she observed that she thought she was well enough equipped to handle the needs of a group of individuals with differing life experiences, who were undergoing different trainings. She had not worked in this particular agency before, but had experience as a trainee in working with a similar client group. She was one of three applicants for the post.

The context

She was to be group supervisor for four new volunteers, three of whom were on different counselling courses and one of whom was a social worker. The agency used trainees from different Diploma and Degree courses to undertake a large proportion of the counselling work. In addition, it had a few volunteers, usually with related 'professional' backgrounds, who had undertaken the basic specialist counselling training offered by the agency. When volunteers or trainees were offered a counselling appointment, they were asked to abide by the Statement of Policy, Practice and Ethics to which the agency works. This emphasizes that the counsellors in the agency seek to offer the basic person-centred 'core conditions' of a helpful counselling relationship:

- empathic understanding;
- judgement-free respect for the uniqueness of each client within their cultural background and context;
- authenticity – a responsive, open counsellor engaging with each unique client in order to help him or her 'live more resourcefully and to own satisfaction' (BAC definition).

It also states that individual counsellors have differing resources and trainings. An intake worker will meet with clients initially and allocate clients as appropriately as possible.

Agency policy

The agency works to the BAC Code of Ethics, supplemented by some specific agency requirements. There is a clear description of administrative practice. This includes a description of the responsibilities of the manager of the agency and of the accountability required by volunteers to the manager. It also describes the responsibility of the agency supervisors to the clients, the counsellors and the agency. This entails some managerial duties such as checking that the counsellors are keeping records, handing in completion sheets, etc.

It also specifies the supervisor's responsibility to disclose to the manager any reservations about a counsellor's competence or ethical practice. The supervisor is responsible for organizing one individual appraisal session with each supervisee after four months' supervision. Any reservations should first be raised there, and the manager informed if the counsellor's practice does not subsequently benefit from the feedback. Any ethical issue, which might have implications for the safety of the client, counsellor or agency, must immediately be shared with the manager.

There are several interesting aspects of Carmel's situation. First, the agency, over the years, had created a full and clear working contract with its supervisors. Some supervisors do not like to undertake any managerial responsibilities. Carmel was clear from the outset what this post entailed and was prepared to manage the overlap between managerial, consultant and training supervision. She was clear about agency policies and also about its basis for practice. She, and the manager, judged that her specialist knowledge was sufficient, although it rested on her experience as a trainee. The manager probably considered that her concern to work integratively was the more important qualification. The task of supervising new practitioners from differing backgrounds, in what would be the first supervision group for most of them, would be formidable. Carmel was well aware of her normative and formative responsibilities, that is, her responsibilities for both monitoring and developing quality of practice. She took comfort in the clear way in which they were spelt out. She knew that, in theory at least, the agency would back her up in case of difficulties.

For agencies, as for courses, the decision to do group supervision is usually an economic one. However, it clearly has advantages in developing and maintaining 'house style'.

Group supervision of a team

A third context in which group supervision has obvious advantages is when a team of counsellors work for a particular organization or service (8). As with volunteers in an agency, 'house style', organizational policies and specialist expertise can all benefit from the open sharing of work. But teams have an on-going life together. Group supervision can help team working, but it can also reflect day-to-day tensions and unresolved dynamics.

Case study 3 – Christine

Christine had been invited to apply for the post of group supervisor to a team of counsellors providing an Employee Assistance Service to hospitals within an NHS Trust. She had worked part time in a GP's surgery for several years. She was currently freelance. She worked with private psychotherapy clients and was also on the books of two Employee Assistance Programmes whose clients were offered a maximum of eight sessions. In addition, she was a tutor on an Integrative Counselling Diploma based on a relational model. She worked as a group supervisor for a team of volunteer counsellors within an addiction agency.

The context

Although all members of the team were trained counsellors, the service they offered had a wider remit than 'pure counselling'. It was sometimes considered that advocacy with the employee's manager might be a more suitable intervention than counselling. At other times, offering information, or resources within or outside the Trust was considered a more economic option. The team worked on different sites and was managed by a former mental health nurse, Maria, who had trained as a psychotherapist. She had been largely responsible for pioneering the scheme. The service was always under threat both from lack of resources, and because Maria's immediate manager did not give the service high priority.

Over a five-year period, the service had had an effect on the culture of the Trust, and it was extensively, and intensively, used by a wide range of employees – cleaners, managers, nurses, doctors, porters. The team had fortnightly case-study groups with the service manager and peer supervision without the manager on the alternate weeks.

The stress of the work told on manager and counsellors alike. Various team issues blew up, and a consultant was engaged to do team development work. One of the outcomes of this was a recommendation that the team should have group supervision with an external supervisor once a month. Both manager and counsellors were pleased with this idea and it was decided that the new supervision group would take the place of one peer group and meet for two and a half hours monthly.

At this point, a question arose as to how an outside supervisor should be appointed. This decision mirrored the difficulties and trust/mistrust issues which existed between manager and counsellors and among the counsellors themselves. It was decided that manager and/or counsellors should recommend two or three candidates and that all members of the team would meet and interview any who were interested. In the event, only two candidates expressed interest – Christine and a psychotherapist who had worked as a group supervisor within the Health Service. At interview, he was clearly geared to long-term psychotherapeutic work and he was unwilling to supervise counsellors who were not necessarily engaged in that kind of work. He made it clear to the manager that he did not think that such a 'hybrid' service was workable, or even ethical for counsellors to be offering.

The role

Christine felt challenged by the prospect of working with this team and, in her interview, questioned both manager and counsellors. By the time the interview was over she had ascertained that:

- the group could be considered a consultative or (as some of the counsellors called it) a clinical supervision group;

- the case-study group would in effect be a managerial supervision group in which policy decisions would be made and on-going managerial support and appraisal would be offered;
- the manager in role of counsellor would also be a member of the new supervision group;
- the supervision would be reviewed after the first six months to see if it was satisfactory to both parties;
- supervision would take place on one of the service sites.

Christine had also divined that everyone in the service wanted an external supervisor but that manager and counsellors had differing hopes of what the supervision would achieve.

Consultation and decision

Soon after the interview she was offered the job. Before deciding to accept, she discussed the situation thoroughly with the supervisor development group (see Chapter 11) to which she had belonged for two years. She doubted the wisdom of the service manager attending the supervision. She knew very little about the culture and practice of the service. It seemed to have grown in response to needs as they became apparent, and much of its practice was passed on verbally rather than being written down. In talking with her group, she identified that, organizationally, it seemed to be at the extreme limits of a family-stage organization. The members knew each other personally, expected to have personal relationships with each service member, worked to a mainly oral tradition and took turns to take various informal roles within the team in a largely unconscious way.

For the purpose of delivering a service to clients, she judged that the team was predominantly working well – otherwise she would not have considered accepting the job. However, she suspected that service objectives, priorities, philosophy and administration needed to be more clearly articulated and contracted into by counsellors as they joined the service. Extent and boundaries of autonomy and accountability probably needed to be spelt out and mutually understood. From her own experience, she knew how hard this was to achieve when everyone was working flat out, when the service was continually under threat and when the team was probably always in some apparently unmanageable dynamic.

Her tendency to think as a consultant about the service was clear to the other members of her development group. They questioned whether she would not be better offering her services as consultant? She decided that a clear supervision space for the team, should she be able (and enabled) to achieve it, was probably more immediately useful. Reflective space seemed a scarce resource for everyone. In any case, she had not been invited in any other role. She decided to accept the post on a six-monthly, renewable basis. She stipulated that supervisor, manager, and group would clarify an appropriate organizational contract for the supervision within the first few meetings. Meanwhile, she, as supervisor, would carry no managerial responsibilities. She asked Maria, the manager, to be aware of keeping her colleague and manager roles and respons-ibilities as distinct as possible. Although she still had doubts, she decided to 'go with the flow' for six months. The discussion in her group reminded her that she would need to discipline herself, let alone the team members, to create a holding environment within the supervision group, for each counsellor and his/her clients.

Christine was an experienced practitioner and supervisor. Like Carmel she knew the difficulties which might lie in store for her and the team. She believed in the working ethos of the service. She respected the team and appreciated the difficulties under which they worked. She welcomed the opportunity to work with experienced counsellors. Her faith in the creative power of group supervision had grown through her experience of leading and belonging to supervision groups. She realized that she would have to ask for a clearer definition of the boundaries of her responsibilities and of the manager's role in the group. She thought it well worth agreeing to work together for six months while creating a viable contract. She was glad the appointment would be reviewed at that point.

Freelance groups

The remaining context in which groups are common is freelance practice. Counsellors who are practising independently appreciate the chance to develop regular colleague relationships. Supervision is a requirement for all counsellors in the UK if they belong to a professional association. They are free to choose the supervision they prefer, as long as it is available. Experienced supervisors often initiate groups. However, counsellors may initiate a group and invite someone to be its group supervisor.

Case study 4 – Martin

Martin, an experienced supervisor and psychotherapist, was approached by Felicity to ask if he would consider running a supervision group for experienced counsellors. Her motivation was her wish for collegial contact. As a freelance counsellor, she felt increasingly isolated, having been out of training for three years.

Martin was interested in the idea. Although he had supervised many individuals at all stages of practice and run groups in agencies, he had never run his own group. It seemed an appropriate challenge at this stage of his development. He was a transpersonal psychotherapist who had remained active and interested in further training. Much of his original training and further development had been done in group contexts. It was a milieu in which he felt comfortable and at home.

Setting up the group

He suggested that Felicity should canvas her network for prospective participants and said that he would do the same. She already had one person in mind. He had been on her training course and they had stayed in contact. After talking to Felicity, and discussing the matter with his own supervisor, Martin realized that they had not thought through various issues. He suggested that they independently draw up some criteria for group membership and then get together to see if their criteria made a good enough match.

His criteria

Theoretical orientation – basically humanistic assumptions. Otherwise, a mix desirable for cross fertilization.
Context – freelance or employed (or a mixture). Hopefully experience of long- and shorter-term work (e.g. employee, student or primary care work).
Experience – equivalent of two-year full-time practice, post qualifying.
Gender – mixed – preferably at least one other man.
Numbers – four or five.
Cultural/ethnic diversity – to be actively sought.

Her criteria

Must be experienced – three or four years post training.
Can call themselves counsellors or psychotherapists but must do some long-term work.
Have some interest in spirituality/transpersonal work.
A mix of men and women.
Must see the group as a serious commitment.

Comparing lists, Martin noticed that his list was the more functionally based of the two. Felicity was interested to see the two lists, and agreed with Martin's criteria. She made the point that she wanted to be sure that the group would be one where transpersonal perceptions could be safely discussed. She herself was trained in psychosynthesis and had asked Martin to lead the group because she knew that he had transpersonal training.

After some months of talking and negotiating about possible meeting times, Martin had recruited:

- a woman supervisee of his who was a Relate-trained counsellor and in addition did freelance couples work and individual counselling;
- a male student counsellor from a college at which Martin was a trainer.

Felicity recruited:

- her ex-training colleague – a man who worked as a freelance psychotherapist and was also developing organizational mentoring;
- a woman who worked entirely freelance and was delighted to have the opportunity to work in a group; her practice included doing time-limited work for a national Employee Assistance Programme when called upon;
- a woman counsellor in a GP practice who also had a small private practice.

The Relate counsellor was Indian by birth and Hindu by religion. The student counsellor was Jewish by birth and religion. Felicity was a practising Anglican and the others practised no formal religion, though both were interested in transpersonal work. Martin was a long-time meditation practitioner and was interested in Buddhist thought, but had no formal religion. He felt pleased that, through perseverance, the group was heterogeneous culturally and sub-culturally. Felicity was privately more concerned about whether the group would be sufficiently homogeneous. She feared that, instead of the group being mutually supportive, she might find herself in unequal competition with the variously experienced participants.

Felicity's and Martin's experience is a reminder about the responsibilities of setting up a group. In a course, a team or an agency much of the initiating of the group is routine. The members are in place – at most decisions have to be made about group composition and the extent of members' choice. A later chapter will look specifically at peer groups, a context in which group expectations and criteria of membership are crucial to satisfactory group formation.

Counsellor preference

These examples have focused on the supervisor and on the context of the proposed group. Imagine that the information had focused on each prospective supervisee. In the first two cases, what might the trainees and volunteers have understood and anticipated about the supervision group they would find themselves in? What might the team members in the NHS be thinking and feeling about the new venture? Were the widely assorted members of Martin's and Felicity's group wholeheartedly looking forward to meeting each other and working together?

Some counsellors have learned to fear and dread group situations – frightening or shaming experiences in school, home, the workplace may have fed into that fear. The work of one-to-one counselling is a safe interpersonal working forum for those who feel like that. Training may have offered remedial group experiences, or it may have reinforced their suspicion of groups as a learning medium. For such counsellors, one-to-one supervision will be the preferred option unless or until they are 'exposed' to a group that has a remedial, or even transformational, effect. On the other hand, there are counsellors who have largely lived and thrived in groups. Despite inevitable setbacks, they have had enough rewarding experiences that they enjoyed and were stimulated by. They may fear the one-to-one as potentially intense and exposing, whereas in groups there are places to hide as well as places to shine. Most people, however, will approach a new group with a mixture of anticipation and anxiety (3).

It is this variety with which each group supervisor is confronted. Having appreciated the context and the proposed contractual obligations, he meets several human beings gathered together. If they begin to enjoy their meetings and do good work together, they will have wrought some everyday magic, based on skill, good judgement, and wise understanding. Facilitating the magic will, in the first instance, be the responsibility of the supervisor.

3 A typology for supervision groups

Creating a typology

Not all styles of supervision group require the same degree of group-work skill and confidence on the part of a supervisor. In this chapter, we will look at a framework for identifying four different types of supervision group (1, 2). In practice, they are not clearly distinct from each other. Initially, Francesca Inskipp and I identified two of them by becoming familiar with each other's group style and realizing the differences. We had imagined that we both worked in a similar way to each other. Since each counsellor's experiences of group supervision are limited, one may tend to believe that what one knows is what 'it is'. When we undertook informal research with other practitioners, we realized that there was another distinct style which neither of us had used or been exposed to. We therefore postulated three supervisor-led types, and identified a peer group as a fourth distinct type.

We then reflected on our experiences as supervisor and as supervisee in the light of these identified types. We could see instances where our automatic style and assumptions had been appropriate, and other situations where another group arrangement might have been more useful. In offering this framework to an extensive number of supervisors, on training courses and in groups or seminars, it has seemed to be a useful and recognizable formulation. It is offered here as a help (a) in identifying roles and responsibilities in a group; (b) in clarifying the overall contract between supervisor, counsellors and agency/course; and (c) in creating appropriate working agreements and ground rules ('good manners') for the group, both between supervisor and group members, and amongst group members.

In a *Type 1*, or *Authoritative Group*, the supervisor is responsible for supervising each participant in turn. The members' role is that of supervisee, with the responsibilities that that entails. Their other major role is that of audience to the supervision. Participation is limited and is ancillary to the supervision which is being given. In other words, supervision *in* a group.

Table 3.1   *A typology for supervision groups*

Inskipp and Proctor	Adapted from Eric Berne
Type 1 Authoritative Group Supervision The supervisor supervises each supervisee in turn and manages group. Supervisees are primarily observer/learners.	Supervision *in* a Group
Type 2 Participative Group Supervision Supervisor responsible for supervising and managing group; also for inducting and facilitating supervisees as co-supervisors.	Supervision *with* the Group
Type 3 Co-operative Group Supervision Supervisor is group facilitator and supervision monitor; supervisees also contract to actively co-supervise.	Supervision *by* the Group
Type 4 Peer Group Supervision Members take shared responsibility for supervising and being supervised.	

Type 2 is the *Participative Group* – the supervision equivalent of Berne's therapy *with* the group. Here the supervisor takes prime responsibility for supervising each supervisee. However, he also actively teaches and directs group members in co-supervising each other to a greater or lesser extent. From the outset, the members of the group know they are expected to be active in responding to each other; and that they will be helped and challenged to do that.

Type 3 is the *Co-operative Group* – otherwise supervision *by* the group. In this type, the members, from the outset, agree to be active co-supervisors. Each supervisee will take a great deal of responsibility for identifying what he wants from the group, and even how he would like to be supervised. (We will look at options when thinking about creative work in supervision.) The supervisor, while still holding overall responsibility for the supervision work and for the well-being of the group, will take a less active leadership role.

Type 4 is the *Peer Group*. In this there will be no permanent supervisor who holds overall responsibility for the work of the group, or for its well-being (3, 4). Formal leadership may be rotating, according to an initial agreement or it may be organic – moving from person to person. It may even become unofficially vested in one member. Nevertheless, the initial agreement will be that all participate equally in the role and responsibilities of both supervisee and supervisor. There will need to be shared understanding of the extent of accountability for each other's work in the absence of a designated supervisor.

Horses for courses – groups for troupes

This typology of groups is not hierarchical nor is it suggested that any type is intrinsically better than another. They *can* be seen as leading on from one another in a developmental manner, but this need not be the case. Very experienced psychotherapists may enjoy belonging to an authoritative (that is, Type 1) group which has the excitement of a master class. Participants may prefer different kinds of groups at different times. In addition, supervisors may feel more suited to one type than to the others. Certain contexts may call for a particular type. Experienced counsellors who work independently and have learned good 'group manners' in other settings will benefit from the active exchange of a co-operative (Type 3) group. Some trainees, on the other hand, may *prefer* the safety of the 'spectator' role in a Type 1 group but *benefit* more from a well-run, participative (Type 2) group.

For a supervisor who 'finds herself' running a group more by chance than by choice, and who feels very under-experienced and under-confident, Type 1 may be the preferable option. For an experienced, laid-back supervisor, a Type 2 group can feel very bossy and busy. Many such have made the mistake of thinking that experienced counsellors can work co-operatively in a Type 3 group only to discover that, although experienced in counselling, the participants had never learned to work co-operatively in groups. Such groups may need to be re-negotiated as Type 2 groups – starting that way and gradually moving into a co-operative group would have been a much easier option. Undoubtedly, being a member of a well functioning co-operative group is an excellent foundation for being in a peer group; and also can act as a consciously undertaken apprenticeship for becoming a supervisor.

This then is one map with which to approach group supervision. Each type has in common that it can be set up well or badly. A well working group of any sort is preferable to a badly working group of any sort. There are guidelines for good practice which have been hinted at earlier. These apply across the board. Similarly, there are roles, skills and abilities which are needed by group supervisors as enhancements to those of an individual supervisor. These will differ somewhat according to the particular type of group.

Type 1 – the authoritative supervision group

If we look at Type 1 – the *authoritative* type, or supervision *in* a group – what would be good practice? Such a way of working is not so dissimilar from individual supervision. Supervisors in training have said that there is a major leap between being a *counsellor* and becoming a *supervisor* – what could be called a paradigm shift in understanding and learning (5). The basic attitudes and abilities and the knowledge and good judgement have a deceptive similarity. However, in recent years, trainers of counselling supervisors seem to agree unanimously that to be a good supervisor it is not enough to be a good and experienced counsellor. (It is, in my mind, desirable – even essential – as a basis.) Others (Carroll 1996) argue that supervision can be seen as a distinct profession from counselling or psychotherapy; that it has more in common with supervision of other professionals who are not counsellors than with the job of counselling. That argument is not pertinent here – it is used only to suggest that having learned about individual supervision, supervising *in* a group is not so very different. There are added responsibilities but it requires no paradigm shift. That shift is required when setting up participative and co-operative groups.

Good practice by the supervisor of a Type 1 group will be the same as is called for in his particular model of individual supervision. Generic principles might be:

- clarity of purpose;
- shared agreement as to roles and responsibilities;
- scrupulous regard to context and other 'stakeholder's' expectations;
- engagement with and knowledge of the supervisee's style, learning needs, agendas and frames of reference;
- security in his own current beliefs and assumptions about good practice;
- an ability to undertake any managerial and administrative tasks which may go with a particular context.

Further, I would add:

- an inquiring and curious mind that checks out his own and the supervisee's assumptions against what actually seems to happen in practice.

These raw ingredients go to make up the supervision cake. An absence of any one ingredient will create an impoverished version. However, the *method* of mixing and cooking is what makes the cake good, good enough, or plain awful. For me the method for good practice, in that respect, requires a commitment to establishing the person-centred core conditions (6, 7); and a culture suited to an adult learner – what, in *this* setting is 'not too hot, not too cold but just right'.

One-to-one but a group arena

Principles of good one-to-one supervision are basic but not entirely sufficient. There is, necessarily, a more complex set of relationships with a group of supervisees than with one. So a supervisor setting up an *authoritative* supervision group will need to find some way of discovering the necessary information about each member of the group. This entails a set of initial decisions. Will this knowledge be elicited in the group or in a private interview with the supervisee? How much of a one-to-one relationship is it useful to establish with members? *Useful*, in this context, would mean what would help the supervisor and the supervisee to do good supervision together. This Type 1 supervisor does not need to think too long and hard about the effect of these decisions on the power relationships in the group. These will only become of interest if members are expressing dissatisfaction with each other or with the supervisor. The main power relationship is one-to-one and serially.

As each member brings a case for supervision, the supervisor will need to be aware of that particular supervisee's ability to use the supervision offered and of the effect that sharing her work publicly in a group will have on that supervisee's reflective space. A supervisee will, at times, experience exposure and possibly shame within an exclusive one-to-one supervision. Exposure will be felt differently in a shared relationship. Criticism and negative feedback from supervisor to counsellor has to be appropriately crafted. After all, forthright feedback of any sort is not of use in itself; only in so far as it aids the counsellor in the development of better practice – more skilled, more empathic, more honest, less rigid or whatever. The supervisee will also have to have space to give feedback as to the usefulness of the supervision – and again the supervisor will need to be aware of the differences between giving and receiving feedback in the private space of individual supervision and the public space of a group.

The audience, too, needs to have some clear instruction as to what is expected of them. In my mind, the distinction between good and bad practice in an authoritative group is whether the participants know what is allowed and expected, or have to

discover by trial and error. There are painful stories about participants in trial-and-error groups. Some have struggled for months
to discover how to win rewards (the approving smile), or to avoid
punishment (the irritated frown). Some have spoken their minds,
only to be told that what to them was their unique thought was
'parallel process', which they had never been helped to understand. One woman stayed silent and (to her initial relief) was
not noticed, but when a man in the group was rebuked for not
speaking, she began to imagine she must be invisible.

Supervisee as Parent, Adult and Child

So the authoritative Type 1 supervisor is not exonerated from the
responsibility of being basically sensitive to the implications of a
group as opposed to an individual forum for supervision. Such
sensitivity seems to come naturally to many parents of several
children – they know, or learn, how important are fairness,
explicitness and psychological protection as opposed to over-
protectiveness. So, too, do good class teachers. The difficulty for
many supervisors lies exactly in the proposition that group supervision is 'adult learning'. Adults *should* have learned to take
care of themselves. To treat them as children is patronizing and
disrespectful.

However, this is not the whole truth. A group setting is 'restimulating' to most of us. As we first enter it, we are back in the play-
ground or the classroom on the first day. Or we are joining an
established 'gang' whom we imagine know each other well. As
we may have done then, we will fall into accustomed family roles
or 'newcomer' behaviours. The most grown-up of us will be
comparing ourselves and the others – favourably or unfavourably
according to our habit.

The good authoritative group supervisor will make an alliance
with the Adult in each group member, but will also be sensitive
and respectful to the Child (8). I have heard of feedback –
apparently grateful – on 'how much as adults we are treated in
this group' – only to learn later of considerable private agony and
shame. Relentless assumptions about Adulthood are not, in my
opinion, good modelling for developing counsellors, nor for established ones. A Type 1 group supervisor must establish a safe forum
for honest reflection on counselling practice and relationships. To do
this he must become increasingly aware of how each group member
learns, reacts to feedback and can be encouraged to disclose
thoughts and feelings, which are embarrassing or distressing.

In addition, the familiar format of teacher and audience – in this case supervisor and audience – may tend to encourage, or re-activate, passivity and dependency. The supervisor may have to take more care than in individual supervision that each member understands their 'Parental' responsibility for their own work and practice. The supervision offered will need to take particular account of encouraging – or challenging – the supervisee to think for herself and explore her own assumptions and actions. Demonstrating how to encourage the move from learned dependency to less familiar self-responsibility will be a skill needed by the counsellor in the counselling relationship back at the ranch.

Case study 1 – Ruth

Type 1 group

Like many supervisors, Ruth's anticipated type of group supervision was that which she had been offered in training. That had always been of the Type 1, or supervision *in* the group variety. Since then she had experienced only individual supervision supplemented by case discussions at work. During her training, she had felt extremely inhibited with one supervisor and found herself being less than honest in what she presented. Another supervisor had related more warmly with individuals and made good use of the group. She determined that she would engage the group-as-audience and be mindful of the trainees' needs for support and encouragement.

Meeting, inducting and clarifying a working agreement

She arranged with the tutor that she could meet her group for an induction session before they began their second year and their counselling practice. Five trainees had been allocated to her group. She ascertained that only one of them so far had a placement organized. She spoke with them all in turn in the group, exploring with them what their intentions were for finding placements. She emphasized that the course expected them all to have found a placement by the start of the following term. (She was not unaware of the difficulties this presents for trainees, but she was clear that her responsibility was confined to offering support and reminding them of the contract with the college.)

She gave them copies of two forms which she used with her individual supervisees. One was a personal information sheet with basic relevant details about the trainee, which she asked them to fill in and return for her records. To this was attached a copy of the administrative contract which she had drawn up with the college. To induct them into the way that supervision would be offered in the group, she gave each a pro forma sheet with simple headings. She explained that she expected them to fill one out for each client, giving her one copy and keeping one for their own supervision file. She expected them to make a brief note each time they brought the client to supervision. This would be a reminder of their supervision.

She asked each trainee what, if any, had been their experience of supervision and what their expectations were. She explained that she saw supervision as an opportunity for each person to have time each week to present a client in her/his own words. She would offer supervision with particular emphasis on the processes of transference and counter-transference. She would also be focusing on building respectful and empathic relationships with clients and on particular interventions which counsellors made with clients. In other words, she would be helping them apply their learning from the first year and increasingly encouraging them to make practical sense of their second-year, psychodynamic training.

After each bit of supervision work, she would ask the members of the group to comment briefly. As time went on, she would expect them to begin to notice how the experience of the 'audience' might reflect what might be happening in the counselling relationship – the parallel process – but she would not complicate the task at the outset. Her initial aim was to give them the support they needed as they started their practice. She would ask for feedback after the first three sessions to find out if the supervision was being helpful.

Ruth had developed her method of supervision through 'sitting with Nellie'. She had reflected on her experiences and formulated her own principles of good supervision practice. She reminded the group of their contract with the college. She gave clear instructions as to the purpose of the supervision and how it would be done and to the role and responsibilities of supervisor and supervisee. She gave all members space to talk about their expectation of supervision. She held the reins firmly, but allowed space for supervisees to clarify what she was expecting of them and to talk about themselves in relation to the supervision task. She had promised a review opportunity. She had engaged with the Adult of each member and reminded them of their Parental responsibility for their own practice. She had not openly acknowledged the probable presence of anxious Child, but her clarity and respect would probably serve to offer safety and containment.

So, in summary, good practice in a Type 1 group supervision will comprise:

- the making and maintaining of a clear, open and explicit working agreement;
- suitable induction;

- the ability to communicate in a 'Target' manner, that is, to speak to the Adult, the Child and the Parent of each counsellor;
- sensitivity to the effect of the group environment on individual participants.

Type 2 – the participative group

In supervisor training, counsellors experience two major 'paradigm shifts' in thinking and practice. As we have seen, the first is moving from the frame of 'counsellor' to that of 'supervisor'. The second is when they begin to practise running a Type 2 or Type 3 group. An experienced individual supervisor will be called upon to start 'thinking group'. An experienced group worker of any sort – a teacher, trainer, youth worker, group therapist – will have to remember to focus on supervision, to think of supervising *with* a group and all that entails.

Task, maintenance and individual

Immediately there will be three distinct fields for attention – Task, Maintenance and Individual.

Figure 3.1   *Fields for attention (Source:* Adapted from Adair 1987)

In Figure 3.1 each field overlaps with the other, so 'juggling' with all three is probably an inappropriate metaphor. The *task* of supervision requires that the reflective space of each participant be jealously guarded and preferably enhanced. For supervisees, this is the still centre of their learning. Creating, maintaining and, where necessary, repairing, the *group alliance* and relationship allows this to happen with increasing reliability. If each *individual*, in the role of supervisee, is receiving rewarding supervision, their active investment in the group will be high. Investment will also depend on their confidence in their own and each other's active and increasingly skilled participation in their role of developing co-supervisors. This describes a cycle of positive reinforcement.

The supervision *task* will be affected adversely if there are interpersonal issues in the group or if the *group* is stuck in a misalliance of some sort. *Individuals* will be more or less consciously preoccupied with group issues and their openness to supervision or their responses as co-supervisors will reflect those preoccupations. Of course, in a Type 1 group, such undermining group dynamics may be present, but because the individuals are given their turn of undivided attention from the supervisor, the destructive effect is, at best, limited and, at worst, unacknowledged. In a participative group, preoccupying interactions, which interfere with the joint tasks of supervising and being supervised, cannot be ignored. They lead swiftly to a cycle of negative reinforcement.

If cooking a cake is an appropriate metaphor for managing a Type 1 group, creating a banquet might be an appropriate metaphor for a participative group. Each part of the process of preparing, cooking and serving a meal is interdependent with the others. Pre-planning is essential – with regard to menu, ingredients, time, task, etc. – but what receives attention at any one time depends on unique circumstances. There is never any doubt as to the task – in that case, the production of a meal with several courses; in the case of group supervision, the production of several bits of good participative supervision work which blend into a satisfying whole.

The underpinning skill for both crafts is the same. Fritz Perls would call it flexible gestalt formation. Rather than serial, convergent thought, the group supervisor, as the cook, needs to develop the ability for allowing whatever needs attention to come to the fore, be attended to and then fall back as the next field for attention emerges. Table 3.2 offers a summary of some of the calls on the attention of the supervisor, listed under the four headings of task, maintenance, individual and overlapping. Perhaps it might be better *not* to see them spread out in such a way – the lists are formidable. Subsequent chapters will offer frameworks of aids and abilities for co-ordinating satisfying group supervision feasts.

Not just frills but unique resources

A participative supervisor may have to offer a good deal of induction, education and training. Supervisees will have variable past experiences of groups, and equally variable skill in being

Table 3.2   *Tasks of the supervisor in participative and co-operative groups*

All the tasks of individual supervision, plus

1   Tasks of managing the supervision work
   - negotiate working agreements with the group
   - hold the time structure
   - ensure that each member has opportunity to present
   - hold the boundaries and focus – task, process, individual
   - model/teach skills of responding, focus, feedback
   - introduce and manage creative structures to deepen understanding
   - review and re-negotiate group working agreement and individual learning

2   Tasks of building, maintaining and repairing group alliance
   - set up structures to help members get to know each other
   - show empathy, respect, authenticity
   - build a climate of co-operation
   - have simple models of group process in mind to make sense of events
   - help members explore tension and conflict in values, theories, styles
   - recognize when group needs to struggle with issues – allow the right to fight
   - enable the repair of breakdowns in communication
   - help the group reflect on factors which help and hinder good supervision
   - facilitate members leaving and new members joining

3   Tasks of supporting and challenging individual supervisees
   support and challenge individuals to, increasingly:
   - manage their own learning and development
   - identify what to bring for supervision
   - present in ways that give access and are effective for their own learning
   - give clear feedback
   - be open to feedback and discriminate what is useful
   - appreciate their own strength and style
   - become aware of accustomed style and role in the group and develop flexibility
   - develop the ability to monitor and manage issues of power, comparison, competition

4   Tasks which overlap
   helping the group:
   - hold the boundaries between counselling and supervision
   - acknowledge, respect and use variations in competence and style
   - develop the shared ability for playfulness and creativity
   - become more aware of conscious and unconscious processes

supervisees, let alone co-supervisors. They may not be ready or able to take shared responsibility. If they were, the group would probably be set up as a co-operative (Type 3) group. It is therefore particularly important that they understand the essence of participation, at the outset in theory, and, increasingly, in practice. The supervisor – having made the paradigm shift spoken of earlier – needs to communicate that members are not just frills added on to the expert supervisor. They are the rich resource which makes this group more than the sum of its parts.

It can be helpful for the supervisor to announce an intention to be bossy in the interest of induction and training, so that potential richness can show and be harnessed. Bossiness may take the form of careful management of a 'structure' or of interrupting in order to ask a recipient if they are finding some feedback useful. It might show in making suggestions for role taking, or in encouraging forthright responses. Making the purpose of such leadership clear heralds respect for, and trust in, the participants. Its exercise must be balanced by a ready appreciation of each participant's openness to playing this supervision 'game' (in the traditional, not the psychological, sense of that word). Counsellors, like ordinary people, are often fearful of joining in new games until they have a sense of the rules and of the reliability of the umpire. They can also be surprisingly distrustful of assertions that their contribution is wanted and considered valuable. Once again, the process of induction into the *task* interweaves with the development of a fruitful *group alliance* and communicating and modelling respect and empathic understanding of each *individual*.

Case study 2 – Carmel

Type 2 group

Carmel's agency was having a fresh intake of counsellors and increasing the overall numbers of volunteers. Her new group was to consist of four members:

- Kate, a mature woman, who was considering early retirement from social work and was wanting counselling experience in order to have extra strings to her bow;
- Stephen, a young man, who was on the second year of a person-centred counselling course, having previously worked in personnel;
- Farah, a woman who had been a teacher and was doing an integrative counselling course while her two children were small. Her course was based on a combination of person-centred and Gestalt practice.
- Mary, a woman graphic designer, who was on a different integrative course which combined Egan skills practice with person-centred and psychodynamic theory.

For three of them, any type of supervision was a new experience. Kate had supervision in her work. Latterly, this had mainly consisted of case and caseload management.

Forethought and preparation

Carmel had already discussed her readiness to supervise a group with her supervision consultant and she now used her consultation to reflect on the new information. She noted that the participants were mainly new to supervision, but that all but one had a background in professional 'people-work'. She decided to float the idea of a participative (Type 2) group. As we know from her biography, she had had supervision training and was currently in an integrative supervision group on her degree course. She felt quite daunted by the amount of setting up and induction work, so, with the agency, she negotiated an initial session with the supervisees before they started working with clients. She wanted to remind them about the overall contract they were in together and she anticipated a good deal of exploration and negotiation in making a participative working agreement.

Carmel was pleased that she had a contract which spelt out her roles and responsibilities as far as the agency was concerned. It defined the lines of communication and accountability between her and the manager and between her and the supervisees. It took into account wider professional accountability – in that case to BAC and its Codes of Ethics. The supervisees had access to this agreement in written form. A good deal of the initial ground clearing had been done for her and for them, and she felt well held by the agency.

Meeting each other

She met with the members of her new group, introduced herself and invited them to take a few minutes each to introduce themselves. She wrote four headings on a flip chart as a suggested format:

Course or working background
One thing about me in my previous life
One thing about my current life which is not counselling related
One thing you would probably not imagine about me

The list produced some rather apprehensive laughter. She introduced herself first, using the headings and taking care not to disclose anything which was too dramatic or which might inhibit the group members or induce undue competitiveness. The group seemed to relax and begin to engage with each other. She then offered a simple exercise to help them talk about their experience and/or expectations of supervision. She had prepared for this by bringing a variety of attractive and unusual objects – shells, fossils, stones, buttons, etc. – which she laid out on a table. She invited them each to pick an object which attracted them. When they had done so, she asked them to say what their object might tell them about their hopes, fears and expectations of group supervision. They all did this, addressing the question in a variety of serious and jokey styles. The way in which they joined in the exercises confirmed to her that a participative group would be suitable for these four trainees with wide and differing life experiences.

Agency contract

Having focused on the task of group building in the first third of the session, she had designated an hour for affirming the agency contract and preparing the ground to create a group working agreement. She went through the main points of the agency's supervision policy in order to clarify its meaning in practice. The process of doing that also gave her and them valuable information about each other and their context. That part of the contract was non-negotiable. If she accepted the job and they had accepted the placement, they were all agreeing to that contract and it was her responsibility to monitor that it was respected. Tasks, roles, responsibilities were clear and agreed at that level, but 'how' the group would undertake those tasks was in the hands of each supervisor.

Working agreement

The 'how' was the focus of the working agreement that Carmel made with the group. She had brought with her a written description of the type of group she hoped they would engage in (Type 2). She spoke to the outline, emphasizing the key points. She was asking them to accept responsibility for using the group to the best of their ability for their own counselling supervision. She was also asking them to take shared responsibility, with her, for becoming co-supervisors of each other. She would actively manage their contributions on occasions and would initiate exercises in order to help them contribute usefully to each other's supervision.

They divided into pairs to talk over these ideas. On returning, there was an atmosphere of apprehensive eagerness. Mary raised a reservation about there not being enough time for proper supervision, and there were some murmurs of assent. Carmen acknowledged this anxiety, promising to make sure that supervision remained the priority.

She then gave them some suggested ground rules which she asked them to consider before the next meeting, when they could use them as a basis for setting up a group working agreement. Meanwhile she asked them to brainstorm what they wanted from her and each other in order to use the supervision group well. There was some mutual laughter as they realized the conflicting enormity of their expectations.

Supervision work

The last half hour she kept for thinking about starting work with clients. She encouraged them to discuss their expectations about meeting their first clients, to raise any anxieties and ask anything they wanted. She also gave them a sheet suggesting headings for recording client work and identifying what they were pleased with in the interview and what they might be worried about.

If a participative group is set up well, the supervisees will have understood that they are expected to develop the ability to be effective co-supervisors under the leadership of the supervisor. They will increasingly appreciate how to balance active participation with skilful listening and attending to the presenting supervisee. They will be learning from each other and from the supervisor a variety of ways of presenting their work, and they will become more adept at knowing what they want from the group and from the supervisor.

This description is a still snapshot, not a moving picture. Developments and difficulties will be touched on elsewhere. Nevertheless, if a group does not bear any resemblance to the snapshot, it is likely that it has not been set up well enough or appropriately. If participants are unsure about their roles, their power and their worth as participants, it may be because the purpose of the group has not been clearly enough communicated in the first place, or revisited sufficiently as the group becomes established. The supervisor may have pressed on to impose participative work when supervisees were reluctant. They could even be hostile to each other, the supervisor or the assumptions behind initiating that type of group. The whole idea of supervision may be new and difficult and an authoritative Type 1 style might have been more appropriate. Since the task is supervision, and the centrepiece of the work is the reflective space for each supervisee to bring her client work, the type of group must serve that purpose.

Type 3 – the co-operative group

Spot the supervisor

An objective observer who dropped in on an on-going supervision group at an undetermined stage of its life together might find it hard to discern if it was an advanced participative (Type 2) group or a fully fledged co-operative (Type 3) group. If it were the latter she might find it difficult to discern from casual observation what the supervisor's responsibilities were meant to be. In both cases she could probably identify the supervisor, but in a co-operative group he might sometimes appear influential in his contributions, and at other times hardly speak at all. He might act as progress chaser or process observer from time to time. He would probably contribute later, rather than sooner, to a particular piece of work. The participants would also appear authoritative, at times very authoritative; leadership might change hands discernibly. Presenters might be highly proactive, requesting specifically what they wanted from the supervision and how they wanted the group to work. Time-keeping would clearly be a shared responsibility. Interaction between members would be spontaneous. If interchanges were usefully vigorous and disputative, then if it were not Type 3, it would be a very established Type 2 group that was spilling over into a different contract with each other.

A group of colleagues

The co-operative group will have been set up as a conscious group of colleagues. The supervisor will carry full supervisory responsibilities – he, not the group members, will be ultimately accountable (in so far as this is possible) for the counselling work which the members bring to supervision. He will carry responsibility for confronting ineffective or unethical practice if he discerns or suspects it. He will be answerable for allowing a group to have become unsafe or ineffective for its members, as will supervisors in Type 1 or Type 2 groups. However, in this group, he will have suggested to the members that they share these responsibilities, and will have checked out that they are prepared – that is are willing *and* able – to do that. He will exercise his responsibilities largely by monitoring the supervision work done in the group, adding his contribution when he has something worthwhile to say that has not already been said.

That is why an observer might not guess immediately who the supervisor was – his contribution would be no more authoritative – perhaps less – than other members. He should ensure that reviews happen at regular intervals, in accordance with the original agreement. However, he might chair the group in deciding how it should be done, rather than conducting it himself. Another exercise of his responsibility might be in letting the group stray from an apparent purpose or time boundary – how can they ever manage their own work if they are always held to the straight and narrow by a supervisor?

Nevertheless, since he carries overall responsibility, he must always be prepared to step in if he is not able to 'trust the process' – even if in so doing he risks being more paternalistic than is comfortable. And when is it responsible to let group members be frustrated and angry, or warm and cosy – and when is it not? This then is the complex role of supervisor in a co-operative group.

If a group is not well set-up as a co-operative group, and if the members experience aimlessness or frustration and anxiety for much of the time, the supervision work will not be well done. Abrogation of leadership can promote a *laissez-faire* group, engaging in 'fight or flight'. This is especially the case when members are not as 'good' in a group as their experience as counsellors suggests. The supervisor may not realize this, or may be reluctant to acknowledge it to himself or the group.

Case study 4 – Martin

Having gathered four additional prospective members, Martin and Felicity decided that neither would interview them. One or other knew each applicant fairly well already. Martin was clear that he did not want to set up hierarchical expectations that it was 'his' group. Felicity saw herself as the initiator but wanted no special role once the group was set up.

They agreed that Martin should send out some basic administrative information; he also suggested that he should write an outline of how he anticipated his role and responsibilities in the group and what he expected of group members. This had been an afterthought – having spoken with other group supervisors at a conference he realized how differently they all ran their groups. He wished he had drawn up this position statement before recruiting, and feared that some of the participants might not like what he had written and would drop out at the last minute. He anticipated running a group akin to a Type 3 co-operative group. He wrote the following draft agreement and ran it past Felicity. She said it sounded interesting.

Suggested group agreement

As group supervisor I will take responsibility for leading and monitoring the supervision work of the group.

I will endeavour to enable the development of a safe and challenging atmosphere for the group to work in.

Each member will take responsibility for the work they bring to the group and for saying what is wanted from the group.

As experienced counsellors, I trust members to offer respect and understanding to each other and to contribute their thinking and expertise as co-supervisors.

The group will meet for three hours fortnightly and members will be asked to make it a top priority.

There will be a review of the supervision after three months.

All five participants did come to the first meeting. They agreed the draft statement on the nod and there was no discussion or negotiation. At the first three-monthly review, three members expressed strong and varying dissatisfactions with the group and its work. The main gist of these was that they wanted Martin to be less laid back, and to give more of himself and his expertise as a supervisor. He said he would think about this feedback.

The difficulties in the group had surprised him from the start, and he had arranged regular consultation with an experienced group supervisor. The feedback he received at the review seemed to be more than 'normal storming' (see Chapter 6). He realized that he had based his expectations on people having had the same amount of group work in their training that he had experienced and offered as a trainer. He decided to take their complaints at face value, and negotiate a stronger leadership role – in building the group, in being a more authoritative supervisor and facilitator of supervision, and in monitoring members' interventions. He also asserted his wish that the group would become more self-managing over time. The group subsequently stayed together until the second review, when external circumstances led to the departure of one of the original members. The rest were still together two years later, by which time an observer would have described them as a Type 3 group.

In addition to overestimating the group skills of his supervisees, Martin probably failed to realize the extent of their unexplored differences – professional, cultural and personal. Felicity had recognized them, but specifically decided that she wanted no leadership responsibility. If Martin had negotiated (or taken) stronger leadership, he could have openly acknowledged differences and chosen to explore them when he considered there was sufficient safety in the group. As it was, the group moved into 'fight or flight' and their potential as co-supervisors could not surface. Instead of a leader-full group, a leadership vacuum developed.

Determinants of choice of group type

These three examples – Ruth, Carmel and Martin – illustrate factors which influence supervisors to set up a particular type of group. Figure 3.2 maps some of those influences. Each supervisor brings to the task a more or less developed model of supervision. This will be influenced by theoretical orientation and by personal experience of supervision and the experience of others – mentors, colleagues, supervisees. He or she will have some models or frameworks of group task and process – also influenced by

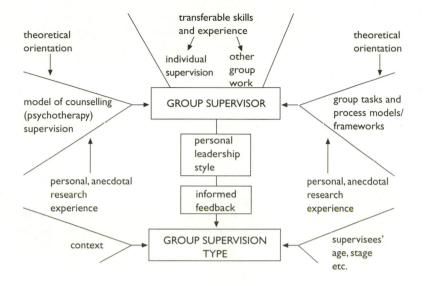

Figure 3.2 *Determinants of group supervision type*

theoretical orientation and experience. Each will have a blend of transferable skill and experience – as supervisor and as group leader or member.

From this amalgam, each needs to identify his or her potential ability as group supervisor and facilitator, and his or her preference and suitability for differing styles of leadership. This personal knowledge, supplemented by feedback from peers or mentors, is one major determinant. Contextual factors – the setting of the group, any agency/course requirements for supervision, the 'age and stage' of the prospective supervisees – are the other major determinant. From these a prospective group supervisor can identify suitable type options and settle for one. As we have seen, this may be a firm choice, or one which is tentative until he or she has met group members and made a more informed assessment of their needs and abilities.

Type 4 – the peer group

The observer of a well-working peer group would be puzzled until she realized there was no one supervisor. No identifiable member would always lead or be the most authoritative. Everyone would appear expert at different times.

If the group were *not* well contracted, she might decide it was a support group or even a discussion group. A purposeful peer supervision group which 'counts' as proper supervision for the purposes of some professional membership, should be clearly identifiable. The form and structure of the group may be predictable or variable but it will include the reliable provision of reflective space for each practitioner in the group. It should be a supervisor-full group, since each member has agreed to be one of the people to whom the others are accountable for competent, confident, creative and ethical practice. How accountability is managed must be specified in the original agreement. The limits and realities of responsibility will be refined over time, as will the ground rules for the management of the work.

The group may arrange for a visiting consultant to act as participant observer, to help the group review and reflect on the quality of their work together. Some of the members of the group may have additional supervision – one-to-one or in a supervisor-led group. For others it may be their only supervision, though preferably not their sole regular professional development opportunity.

Self/peer-accountability

A peer group demonstrates, most graphically, a truth which is often forgotten or overlooked. In the end, we are all self-accountable; and we should never be *only* self-accountable. No amount of 'expert' supervision can detect practice which we determine to hide (other than live supervision at all times). However new and ignorant we may be as practitioners, we may have skills which our best supervisors do not possess. Conversely, however experienced we are there will be different perspectives and newly devised practices which could enhance our work. Once we are qualified and have some experience, we are all colleagues. Some of us may choose, or be invited, to develop some extra abilities – to supervise others. But we are only taking a role – invited by our colleagues. We are not more, or other, than they. A peer group speaks this particular truth clearly.

A led supervision group speaks other truths. First, if we are to feel safe to disclose our work in a group, it is important and time-effective to have someone who will take responsibility for preserving our reflective space. Second, it is a treat to have someone take responsibility for managing our precious supervision time. And third, it is comforting to imagine that he, or she (or someone better, somewhere else), has greater expertise than we do.

II Managing supervision groups

4 Agreements as friends

Permission to manage

Running supervision groups is a managerial enterprise. Table 3.2, which listed the tasks of the participative and co-operative group supervisor, shows that the need to manage is self-evident. I encounter many supervisors who are confused about this. Their empathy and respect for the client in their counselling work probably screens them from the reality of their overall management of the counselling *alliance* and each counselling *interview*. When they become supervisors, these counsellors – who are often excellent managers in other areas of their lives – take on a kind of pretence that that is not what they are doing. Administrative management is acknowledged, but *appearing* to take charge is felt to be disrespectful and unempathic (1, 2). Covert management may work (just) in individual supervision, but it is unhelpful in setting up group supervision.

The person-centred tradition tends to support this confusion, by assuming that groups can be expected to find their own collective way forward. They often do, given time, but supervision is usually time-limited and has clear agreed agendas to be pursued. Psychodynamic and action-oriented humanistic traditions can also support the confusion. Practitioners can encourage the 'acting out' of stereotyped group behaviour in the belief that people (being their more primitive selves) are being themselves in habitual ways that might not otherwise 'show'. There is even a belief that if people know what is expected of them, they may be passively compliant.

The task of supervision is to help counsellors achieve best practice – in general and with particular clients. Leadership is needed to clarify rights and responsibilities and develop trust so that they can reveal their work in a rounded manner. Most groups, however carefully set up, wittingly or unwittingly expose primitive behaviour. Managing need not discourage spontaneity nor shared ownership of the supervision enterprise.

In training supervisors, my colleagues and I have learned to make explicit our underlying assumption that management is necessary and inevitable. This permission – demand, even – always seems to be received with relief. The issue is not *whether* to manage, but *how* to take leadership of the variety of management tasks and processes so that group members share ownership of their supervision. This chapter focuses on structural aids to participative management. The following chapter focuses on development of skill and ability in participative leadership.

Structural aids

Contracts and agreements can be structural aids for engaging group members and other parties to the supervision (3, 4). They are, by nature, mutual arrangements. The words imply shared consent. One of the parties to a contract or agreement will take leadership in initiating the agreement. Both, or all, have responsibility for maintaining it.

The example of Martin's group agreement is a reminder that an agreement is only such if all parties have given informed consent. In supervision in general, prior experience is a prerequisite of informed consent. A new supervisee cannot understand that particular alliance. The best she can do is imagine it in the light of similar or reported experience. A group supervision agreement will always be based on a presumption of good-will between supervisor and group members. Egan (1976) suggests that it is important to invite group members to act into their more trusting self, rather than into their least trusting self, unless or until they have evidence that it is unsafe to trust.

Contracts and working agreements cannot ensure trusting participation. Nor can they ensure shared understanding of tasks, values, priorities and good practice. However, declaring or negotiating them is an opportunity for clarifying and amending intentions and expectations.

Both Ruth and Carmel thought that setting up a group contract and agreement would be onerous, time-consuming and complex. They arranged a specific session to cover all the items they wished to raise. Carmel, in addition, understood that it would be an opportunity to get to know each other, create a culture of participation, and discover if the group was ready for a participative working agreement.

These specific agreements can be viewed as rods for the back. Supervisees can experience them as such if they are dealt with ponderously. The word 'contract' has binding implications. I prefer to use it only for the formal arrangements with agencies, courses or employers. The term 'working agreement' is more friendly – an encouragement to view working arrangements as flexible friends. In the busy life of group supervision, think of them as like the walls of a bouncy castle. They hold the boundaries in a springy way, and generate energy. In order to do that, they need to be well constructed and reliable. They also need readjusting in the light of experience.

The Russian frogs

A series of working agreements can take the strain of management from moment to moment. I imagine them as a nest of Russian dolls. I had a beautiful gift of Russian frogs which I now use in training and in supervision groups. Since this chapter is about making friends with contracts and agreements, using that image will perhaps speed the transformation of contractual frogs into agreeable princesses (or princes).

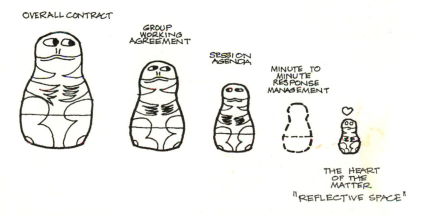

Figure 4.1   *Structural aids for management*

In Figure 4.1, the *supervision contract* is the outside holding frog, which determines the shape that all other agreements will have.

Within that is the *group working agreement*, which incorporates the roles and responsibilities that the group members and the supervisor will take. It is primarily an agreement about the *Type* of group – authoritative, participative, co-operative, peer. It incorporates shared ideas about 'good manners' and about how the work will be done – the procedures and ground rules. Within that again, is the *session agenda*. This will have been outlined by the working agreement – the shape of a session will not have to be renegotiated each meeting. The specific session content and timing must be agreed and the agenda determines priorities for the session. Within that is the agreement with each supervisee about the management of his bit of 'work' and his reflective space – the series of *mini-contracts*.

You may notice that there is a 'shadow' frog in Figure 4.1. The supervisor has to make minute-by-minute judgements about one major responsibility. Keeping clear reflective space for each counsellor is the heart of supervision. The supervisor shares, but cannot abrogate, the responsibility she has to client and counsellor. Only a fraction of supervision time is available to each counsellor to present his work. The supervisor has a continuing responsibility to enable each member to spend the rest of the time fruitfully. Balancing these two responsibilities, from minute to minute, is an aspect of group and task management that cannot be contained in a separate agreement. The shadow frog is 'the space between', supported by the working agreement, the session agenda and the counsellor's mini-contract. Within those, it remains fluid and flexible

Big frog, or supervision contract

The supervision contract defines the group supervision task in its professional context. It delineates, more or less specifically, the roles and responsibilities of supervisor and supervisees within professional Codes of Ethics (5, 6), and agency, organizational or freelance policy. Case study 2 (Carmel) illustrates a situation that was carefully thought through to be helpful and holding for all parties, including clients. The case study of Ruth indicates that she had an administrative contract with the training course. She was clear about her formative aims. We do not know if she had an assessment role or if she had thought about her relationship to any agency supervisors that the trainees might work with. As with individual supervision, incorporating these issues in the contract would help to clarify her responsibilities if she had reservations about the quality of a trainee's practice.

For group purposes, most of these overt or covert responsibilities are common to all participants. They exist apart from individual contracts with differing training courses or agencies. They set the non-negotiable boundaries of responsibility – for confidentiality, record keeping, monitoring, assessing. They determine the 'mays' and the 'musts' . Carmel *might* choose to share a reservation with the manager at any point; she *must* inform him of any ethical issue with safety implications. The supervisees *may* keep all kinds of private notes for their own learning and information. They *must* keep agency notes and hand in completion sheets.

Dynamic implications

This contract has increased significance in a group setting, as opposed to individual supervision, for at least two reasons. One is the effects on the dynamics of the group of the shared 'outside rules'. Members will react differentially – taking them for granted, anxiously complying, deliberately testing or flouting – according to their accustomed style. Remember, too, that at the point when these 'rules' have to be clarified and taken seriously the members are often new to the situation and new to each other. Some part of their psyche is likely to be back at home or school again. Their reactions will have a knock-on effect on their fellow siblings or 'class members'.

The second significance is that non-compliance with a 'must' after the supervisor has made a clear purpose statement is a lively group issue. In a Type 2 or 3 group, peer responsibility for supporting and challenging each other to respect the contract may have been openly negotiated. In a Type 1 group, the supervisor alone is faced with the decision of when and how to address any non-compliance.

Case study 1 – Ruth

When the group started supervision work, members used Ruth's proforma as a basis for presenting clients and making supervision notes. One member, Pieter, did not complete one for his clients on two consecutive occasions. Ruth asked him why that was. He replied that he almost always had difficulty in meeting deadlines for any kind of writing. Ruth was tempted to explore the meaning of that behaviour in Pieter's life in general or for working in this group. Mindful of the early stage of the group, and because the trainees needed help and support with their clients in the time available, she decided to restate what she *required* from the group members. She explained why things must be done that way, emphasizing her shared responsibility with Pieter's agency manager for the quality of his work, and for supporting him if anything went wrong. She invited the others to say, briefly, how and when they filled out the sheets.

Must or may? Enforcing requirements

Pieter took this seriously, and usually completed his sheets. From time to time he would backslide, and later in the life of the group Ruth expressed her frustration. Pieter said, sheepishly, that he was working on the issue of failed deadlines with his counsellor. Ruth acknowledged that, and reiterated that filled sheets were a 'must' not a 'may' in this supervision group. At the following review, Pieter said that he had felt relieved and grateful not to have been 'publicly analysed'. He doubted if he would ever be the best deadliner in the world, but he was finding that he felt less shamed and resentful when challenged about his 'habit'.

If contractual requirements are made specific from the outset, and reiterated periodically, confusion can be prevented. Unclear requirements elicit potentially destructive games-playing in a group. On the other hand, when clear agreements are misunderstood, ignored or flouted, there will be a knock-on effect in the group. The other group members would notice Pieter's failure to 'keep the rules' and mark how Ruth dealt with the issue. They would have noticed, equally, had she let the issue slide. They would have drawn covert conclusions from her action *or* inaction.

Group members had no formal responsibility to Pieter in this respect. They were onlookers to a little interpersonal drama. A Type 2/3 supervisor would have had an added decision to make – challenge the behaviour herself or wait until a group member drew attention to it? In making this choice, she would be weighing the *task* elements (and the *normative* responsibilities) against the *group* development and *individual* power element (the *formative* responsibilities) (Tuckman 1965; Inskipp and Proctor 1995). There are no 'right answers' in such situations. It raises management choices and each choice will have expected and unexpected consequences. Action or inaction *is* managing. The responsibility to maintain the overall contract is affected by the particular working agreement.

Frog 2 – the group working agreement

A great deal has already been said about creating agreements for the particular type of group that the supervisor is proposing. Ruth took responsibility for determining the style of her group. Carmel and Martin took leadership in proposing roles and responsibilities they envisaged as suitable and productive for their group in its setting. Both were open to tactical alterations and original suggestions, but strategically they had both decided on the basic type. The type which is adopted influences the necessary ground rules for the group (7).

Table 4.1   *Constituents of a group working agreement*

Functional arrangements	Interpersonal ground rules	Individual learning agenda
Time	'Good manners' as:	Course requirements
Place	supervisee	Learning gaps:
Time management	developing counsellor	counselling skills
arriving	co-supervisor	conceptualization
left overs	group member	professional role
supervision slots	Confidentiality for:	self-awareness
processing, etc.	clients	self-evaluation
Reviews	members	group skills
Presenting options/musts	agencies	Continuing professional
Note-keeping, records, etc.	courses, etc.	development

Table 4.1 indicates the component parts of an agreement. There are three major components. The first deals with the structures and arrangements for fair and effective conduct of the supervision – the functional arrangements. The second deals with agreeing ground rules for individual and group behaviour which will best support members to carry out their responsibilities to themselves, each other and the wider contract. These are the interpersonal ground rules (the 'good manners'). The third relates to the learning agenda of each supervisee.

None of these elements will be agreed once and for all. In a participative or co-operative group they flow, initially, from the supervisor's knowledge of necessary basics and the present understanding and experience of the participants. Over time, they should be reviewed, and probably altered, as they become more 'real'. At the outset they may have been made in the shadow of rather fearful imaginings. Any new or different rules will be formulated in the light of members' shared experience of behaviour and protocols that help or hinder them in role of supervisee and co-supervisor.

Dynamic reactions

If discussing the overall contract stimulates primitive attitudes to outside rules, negotiating the functional ground rules stimulates other primitive attitudes. These include thoughts and feelings about:

- fairness
- trust
- getting enough, or too much
- freedom to opt out
- control and the right to insist on inclusion
- responding to the moment
- having firm rituals
- little and often
- less frequent and luxurious space

Negotiating good manners, in its turn, unearths needs:

- for protection
- for challenge (often within carefully formulated limits!) and stimulation
- for risk
- for safety
- for closeness
- for separateness
- to 'be myself'
- for others to be as I want them to be

If the supervisor can encourage an atmosphere of empathy, respect and authenticity, the process of negotiation prepares for and begins the supervision *task*. At the same time, the process builds a *group working alliance* which is founded on the shared wisdom and experience of the members (8). If, in addition, the supervisor refrains from getting too caught up in the nitty-gritty, he can help the group acknowledge the primitive forces at work, with acceptance and humour. In that case, he will have made allies in the job of harnessing group energy in the service of good supervision.

Case study 2 – Carmel

Notes after the second session

Whew! I'd been warned, but what intense anxiety. I nearly got terminally caught in bureaucratic wrangling. F wanted to present every week; S wondered what would happen if his client hadn't shown; K suggested he could talk about general issues, but he didn't like that at all. M cut across and said she had no idea how to talk about her case and I found myself reminding her about the handouts I had given them.

I said that I intended that they should each bring client work each time they had some to bring, but that they could choose whether to use the time if they had a 'no show'. K promptly wondered what would happen if someone had no client for several weeks. That did me – I delivered a lecture on trust and self-responsibility. I can see now that K is being an alternative leader – not surprising with her experience. And I don't feel too confident, that's for sure. I do *not* want to compete with her. Must beware not to automatically speak after her.

After that M, who seemed reassured by remembering the handout, said in a rather simple way, 'Couldn't we say people have the choice for the first few weeks and see how it works out?' and to my relief everyone agreed. We then had the same kind of wrangle over how long they could spare for checking in at the start and for reflecting at the end. K wanted plenty of reflection time, M and F feared they would not have enough time for their client work. By this time I was beginning to chill out. I could see the pull of freedom v. responsibility; group v. individual, etc., etc. This time round, they reached some satisfactory conclusion without a lecture from me – I just held to having some little time to meet and part.

Asked K to make a note of the decisions for checking against other's recollections next week – very briefly! The discussion of the ground rules was less energetic. They asked me about what one or two of them meant, and suggested one or two extra. We agreed that we would have a review of ground rules and of arrangements on October 30th and that we would allow half an hour. I checked if they were agreed about working to them meanwhile, and they groaned' yes' impatiently. So we had a good laugh and a break for a pee and started supervision work – with M! I *didn't* raise the issue of how we would decide who went first!

Table 4.2 shows the amended ground rules that Carmel distributed at the next session. Over time, if the group becomes an

Table 4.2   *Carmel's amended ground rules*

Ground rules

Following our initial meeting and discussion, I drew up these ground rules. They include the things you said you wanted (or didn't want). They also include items which I think are important for you to begin to take responsibility for. They are aspirations, not rules. But if we agree to them it means we can support and challenge each other if we are not respecting them. It may be there are some which are unnecessary and others which you may want to add. We will review them at our first review – they may make better sense to you when we have worked together. Their object is to help us develop a group which uses and offers supervision that is helpful and enjoyable.

As supervisee:
- preparing for supervision – what do I need to talk about? (either using the sheet of questions or preparing in your own way)
- presenting in a way that helps you, me and the group connect with you and/or your client
- becoming aware of what you want and could get from supervision
- being open to feedback – i.e. listening before replying, clarifying if unclear
- learning to decide which feedback is useful and which is not
- saying no if you do not want to work in certain ways or if you do not want feedback

As trainee counsellor:
- recognizing what you are good at
- noticing what you need to learn more about
- becoming aware of when and how you are unhelpful to clients
- geting feedback to see if you are accurate

As group member:
- listening carefully to others
- seeking to understand before disagreeing
- respecting each person for who they are and what they bring to the group
- maintaining absolute confidentiality of clients and group members within the agency contract
- being as honest and open as you are able about anything that makes it difficult for you to use supervision well
- being your more trusting self unless you have good reason not to trust
- monitoring your competitiveness and noticing if it helps or hinders supervision

As co-supervisors:
- supporting each other in learning and practice
- learning to give honest and useful feedback
- being open to new ideas and ways of working
- increasingly being aware of differences in training and understanding
- clarifying when you do not understand

As supervisor: I undertake
- to abide by the ground rules
- support and challenge you in all the above
- to manage the supervision work
- to share my experience and understanding in the service of good supervision and practice
- to lead the group in developing as a helpful forum for supervision and as a development opportunity for self and peer supervision

organically working system, the rules may well be forgotten. They will need to be part of the review process when the group re-evaluates. Meanwhile, they serve to act as a transitional protector – 'I do not want any feedback now, thank you,' (Ground rule – *It's OK not to accept feedback when you want to reflect on your session*). Alternatively, they can encourage truth – 'If I were your client I would be quite afraid if you said that to me' – because *honest feedback, if requested or agreed to*, is a part of that particular group's interim working agreement.

Individual learning aims

If the members are to share some of the formative responsibility for each of the others as counsellors, they need to know what each of the others wishes and needs to learn in the way of skills, understanding or personal development. The supervisor, too, will begin to know the strengths and difficulties of each supervisee, as with individual supervisees. These personal agendas can form part of the early negotiation, and be reviewed periodically.

Little by little

Negotiating these issues – arrangements, ground rules and learning agendas – not to mention clarifying the overall contract, can be too lengthy a process. Group members need and want supervision urgently at the start of a new group. Allowing the agreement to build up over time is often better than rushing it through. People will have more attention for it in small bites; it can continue to be a group-building process and it becomes more real as supervision gets under way. However, it takes discipline to persevere.

Case study 3 – Christine

Christine was preparing to meet the team members of the NHS Trust Employee Assistance Service for the first time as a supervision group. She was very uncertain what type of group to initiate. She knew that all the members were experienced counsellors, meeting regularly in case study and peer groups. At least one of the members had been an individual supervisor in a previous job. She also knew that they differed in the way they worked and probably in their view of best practice. She would have to discover how effectively they could co-operate as co-supervisors. In addition, she was unsure what effect the presence of their manager, Maria, would have, as fellow supervisee. She hoped that they would be able to become a well-working Type 3 group but knew that she could not presume on their wish or ability for that at this stage.

She decided to suggest that they worked with each other for three sessions in a loose working agreement. Meanwhile, she would take responsibility for managing the time and work, consulting with them as she went along. Each week, they would spend half an hour exploring aspects of their contract and working agreement. On the fourth meeting, she would take responsibility for pulling the strands together and offering a draft contract with the organization, and suggested arrangements and ground rules for their work together. Meanwhile, they would all have had plenty of opportunity to present clients or work issues for supervision.

Everyone appeared relieved that she was taking leadership of the overall process. They stressed their need for time for client work which they felt often got squeezed out by organizational issues. Christine raised the question of Maria's role in the group. She said that she would be glad of the opportunity to learn about agency policy which Maria's presence would offer. She stressed that she did not want to seal her into her managerial role. Maria replied that she wanted to be considered an ordinary member of the team while in the group. Christine noticed some tension in the group during their exchange. A quarter of an hour had already gone so she decided to stick to her interim agreement at all costs. She could see no clear outcome of 'going into' the dual role issue at this stage, when she knew so little about the team dynamics.

Instead, she asked them to brainstorm assumptions about 'good group manners' when working together in supervision. She used a flipchart to write down their responses:

- respect
- understanding
- not butting in
- being honest
- confidentiality outside the team
- having breaks
- being patient when we have 'off days'
- not stereotyping each other

She asked if these would do as an interim set of ground rules, and they agreed. She then asked them to brainstorm their worst fears, and again wrote them down:

- being told what to do
- wasting time wrangling and arguing

- never being told what to do
- weeping
- people storming out
- not being given any supervision time
- people arriving late, leaving early or going over time

Using 'over time' as the cue, Christine said she now wanted to move to supervision work. Could they agree to arrive and finish on time, weep as much as they liked, and be self-disciplined about arguing and storming out? Meanwhile, she promised to tell people what to do and never interfere. The group broke for ten minutes amid laughter before getting down to client work.

How much of the group working agreement needs to be written down is arguable. There are no formal sanctions for violating good manners or due process. The agreement is a guardian, not a ruler. Writing helps people become clearer about what they are creating. However, it also serves to make intentions into rules, so it can encourage some bureaucratic anxiety. More importantly, it is disempowering if agreements are made and then ignored or not referred to again. For members of the group to experience their co-supervision as belonging to them, for them and their clients, the agreement must be taken seriously.

Frog 3 – the session agenda

When I asked supervisors for Golden Rules for doing group supervision, one said *'Do not be intimidated by time.'* Time is amazingly elastic and, for group supervision, it usually needs to be. In the Table 4.3 there is a list of possible agenda items for each session.

Getting there and endings

Supervisees vary in the time they take to 'arrive'. Even if members agree to 'focus in' prior to coming together, there is still the flutter (or rasp, or silence) of being together. 'Check-ins' or 'check-outs' commonly exceed their allotted time. *Group maintenance* easily slips into *task sabotage*. Yet good work is usually done when there is a buzz in the group. Lack of interpersonal contact makes it

Table 4.3   *Options for session agendas*

---

1   Coming together
  • brief personal check-in
  • update from last session's clients
  • raising issues leftover from previous session/s
  • space for one member each session to review caseload/professional development, etc.

2   Agenda building
  • bids for time
  • emergency requests
  • supervisor/managerial issues
  • time decisions

3   Presenting
  • may include contracting, exploring, focusing, deepening understanding/ awareness, new ideas, plans for next client session, etc.
  • likely to include contributions from, and issues arising for, other members
  • possible identification of parallel process
  • debriefing – presenter and members
  • time for recording/note-taking
  • relaxing and taking breath

4   Two, three or more presentations as above

5   Review of session
  • individual learning needs
  • group maintenance needs
  • identifying themes
  • review of session process
  • plans/requests for next time

Source: Developed from Inskipp and Proctor, 1995

difficult for supervisees to share their work if they feel vulnerable about it. Review, or processing time, at the end of a group is also highly valued and allows for conceptualization of learning. Preserving time to process requires determination.

An agreed agenda at the start of the session allows for some acknowledgement of these facts of life, and an opportunity for a shared commitment to time management. It ensures that leftover issues can be brought back. It allows for adjustments because of unforeseen circumstances – a bereavement, for instance, or a special issue about an agency. The frog of the working agreement is substantially containing – the agenda cannot incorporate much which is outside that – but the use of this session's time is also unique. Realistic agenda-making can go a long way to relieve the intimidation of time.

The littlest frog – the heart of the matter

So, finally, to the central management task, to which all other tasks are servant. Each individual piece of supervision (of client work or related professional issue) is what the group is about. Later chapters will offer guidelines for involving group members in that task. The supervisor can forget to engage the supervisee in identifying *her* wishes for the session if he is too keen on involving the group, or pursuing his own agendas for the counsellor. Her own formulation of her supervision issue must be the starting point.

The mini-contract

There is a refreshing amount of new thinking about contracting in counselling and psychotherapy, and much of that discussion is useful in relation to contracting with supervisees (Sills 1997).

Contracts can be 'hard' or 'soft'. They can specify if the supervisee wishes to 'know what to do', 'understand what is happening', 'lay out the story', etc.; or, in a 'hard' contract, that she will determine precisely how she is going to raise the issue of, for example, ending the counselling work with a particular client. In the case of group supervision, mini-contracts can allow a supervisee to identify her own present state of vulnerability, eager curiosity, playfulness or distress, and suggest what kind of responses she would like.

While the supervisor is not bound to limit his interventions to these requests, such information gives many clues as to the most suitable way of using (or silencing!) other group members in a suitably protective, supportive or challenging way. If he wants to pursue a totally different agenda to that specified by the supervisee, the mini-contract made with her at the outset of her 'session' allows him to make that explicit and to indicate if his agenda is negotiable or non-negotiable.

Mini-contracting is enabling and empowering for supervisee, supervisor and group members. It signals the start of full attention to that particular supervisee and her client or issue. It marshals group members to lay aside previous preoccupations in a busy session. It encourages the supervisee to take responsibility for thinking about what she is hoping for, and why she is giving priority to this issue. It offers navigational aid to the supervisor in determining how the group can respond in the most useful way. It acts as a check on how helpful and satisfying the session was for the counsellor. In all, mini-contracting is a powerful management aid in fulfilling the central supervision work.

Chicken or egg?

Does the heart sustain the body, or the body protect the heart? The frogs can be ranked from the smallest to the largest, as well as from largest to smallest. If the reflective space of each supervisee is the heart of the matter (and most supervisees have no doubt that it is), then management of the *session* is crucial to preserving the heart. The way that the supervisor *protects the reflective space*, or else actively manages (or supports others to manage) it, is the immediate containing process. Unless the *working agreement* and *mini-contract* offer clarity of ground rules, and of individual and group priorities, each supervision intervention has to be made on the hoof with no coherent strategy as guide. Such arbitrary day-by-day and minute-by-minute choice-making is confusing and disempowering to supervisee and group; at worst it can be crazy-making. It is also hard and unprotected work for a conscientious group supervisor.

The shadow frog

The shadow frog in Figure 4.1. represents absence of specific contract. It is the 'space between', in which the supervisor often has to decide for himself, as each supervisee presents, how to use group resources in the service of supervision work and the development of each group member. It signifies that on-the-wing decisions are bounded by the 'shape' of the prior agreements and current mini-contract, but, within that, have a life of their own.

Focus, boundaries and creative desperation

So far, the word *boundaries* has not been mentioned, although 'management of boundaries' is often high on lists of 'supervisor abilities and skills'. The outer frog, *the overall contract*, puts down boundary markers which pervade every managerial choice in group supervision. By clarifying the parameters of the supervision task – the shared professional accountability, the professional and organizational ethical imperatives – a pale is established which defines what lies 'beyond the group supervision pale'. The *working agreement* defines what behaviour and priorities lie within this *particular* group pale. In turn, the *session agenda* and *mini-contracts* sketch out the 'pale for the day'. There are numerous boundaries around each piece of supervision work.

However, to over-emphasize the ability to keep boundaries can stimulate an attitude of wariness and mistrust. Rigorously excluding all that is beyond the pale may foster an anxious, even mildly paranoid, mind set. The *ability to keep focus* can be equally demanding and perhaps more rewarding. It includes the skill of stating priorities and holding to them and calls for respect and discipline in the pursuit of agreed aims. The mind set that the formulation of *focus within boundaries* seems to generate is one for which I do not think there is a good English word. A state of continuing mild optimism is the nearest I can get to the hopeful counterpart of anxiety. Whatever that state is called, it fuels vigorous engagement with competing aims. That can lead to creative leaps in the face of firm containing boundaries of time, task and other agreed realities.

So, in conclusion . . .

Group supervision – especially in a participative or co-operative group – is a formidable management task. Different supervisors will manage in widely differing styles. Different groups of supervisees will interact in surprisingly different ways when co-managing their own and each other's supervision. Negotiating agreed aims and a shared working culture contributes to clarity of task and focus, to forging a unique group alliance, and to encouraging individuals to own and use their power and influence creatively in the shared work.

To return to the *normative*, *formative* and *restorative* supervision tasks, negotiation emphasizes the shared responsibility for ethical practice – the normative task. It facilitates identification of individual learning needs for self and other – the formative task. The respect, empathic engagement, honesty and purposefulness called for provide the conditions for the 'facilitative environment' of Rogers (1961) and Winnicott (1965). That culture and environment is an optimal atmosphere for learning and development. It can provide a safe play space for shedding old habits and trying new ways of being in, and experiencing, the world of counselling and supervision. It is restorative and often therapeutic.

5 Skilful group allies – supervisor and members

The craft of the supervisor

Working with a group is a craft. Like any craft, it is based on skilfulness which is apparent but not always identifiable. For instance, everyone knows that a group supervisor needs to 'know about group dynamics'. It is not always recognized that they need to know how to use their 'knowledge' in the service of the task of supervision. As we saw in the previous chapter, many group supervisors run good groups without realizing they are skilful managers. That chapter offered structural aids to management, and this one has reference to craft. It attempts to make visible what is 'obvious'. It refers particularly to working in participative or co-operative groups. If it indicates need for a bewildering array of skills, it is because that is what good participative group supervisors have. There may be other skills not mentioned here. Access to other people's groups is limited and the task of 'modelling' group skills calls for systematic research. For starters, what appear to be useful are the following abilities:

- to borrow and create increasingly useful maps as aids to comprehension;
- to use them in making rapid choices among conflicting priorities;
- to move smoothly between intentional states of leadership, receptivity and assertiveness;
- to audit one's transferable assets and temporarily shelve those that are inappropriate;
- to licence movement, spontaneity and physical imagery;
- to allow 'gestalts' to form, be addressed and relinquished;
- to run rapid self-scans;
- to be rooted and grounded in unselfconscious respect, empathic understanding, authenticity and clear intention;

- to welcome and enjoy diversity;
- to be inventive in ways of engaging groups in supervision;
- to welcome 'the enabling unconscious' and sensory awareness;
- to treat every personal and group process with respect and curiosity;
- to reflect, regularly and in company, on group task and process;
- to use these abilities to become an informal (or formal) researcher.

Many of these abilities will have been well developed in other contexts (1, 2). The trick of licensing them and adapting them in a new context must also be a skill. The list suggests that some supervisors will temperamentally be better suited to work in participative groups than others. The advantage of a Type 1 group is that it does not require the range of flexibility and can therefore be an enabling forum for supervisor and group member. Nevertheless, flexibility is always desirable, and can be learned.

Using maps for making sense of groups

Figure 3.2 (p. 55) suggested the varied influences on prospective group supervisors. They include style and ability, theoretical model, experiences in groups, previous training in group work, counselling and teaching or related disciplines. From these the supervisor will garner information on how to initiate a supervision group, and how to structure it. She will have to decide how to create the atmosphere she considers best suited to good group work, how to maintain it and, when necessary, re-create it. She will also have to decide how to keep tabs on the development of each individual in the group. When the group is established she needs to have her own private comprehension of unexpected happenings.

Compared with individual supervision, or supervision *in* a group, participative and co-operative groups present the challenge of *participation management*. When group members are actively participating in each other's supervision, personal interaction is greatly increased. The lively system that is the group will be engaged in subtle balancing processes. These processes are mediated through individuals, although the individual participant, when 'speaking for himself' (or 'holding his own peace') will almost always be expressing something on behalf of the 'felt sense' of the group.

Private hunches about group processes and dynamics are necessary but not sufficient to help create, maintain, and effect running repairs in the group. This depends on using tentative understanding and developing skill to help group members work as a group. Routinely, they will need help to grow in self-management and participation. More or less frequently, the supervisor may need her understanding to decide when and how to trouble-shoot. The following two chapters offer maps which have proved their worth in these respects and illustrate how they are practically helpful. Using these, or other frameworks, to help the group work well requires skill.

Transferable assets for roles

For all the various tasks spelled out in Table 3.2 (p. 47) there is a corresponding role. In a single session, the group facilitator may need to take the role of negotiator, teacher, trainer, model, conciliator, umpire, director. This is quite apart from additional 'ordinary supervisor' roles such as monitor, evaluator, assessor, colleague, counsellor, consultant. Luckily, the skills that go with the roles will almost all have been exercised elsewhere, at some time or another – as mother, father, sister, brother, friend, counsellor, trainer; in everyday life or in previous work or play roles. Some may be immediately transferable. Others may need adjusting to a new context.

Shelving assets

Sadly, some well learned skills and mental sets may need to be abandoned, or at least temporarily suspended, in favour of new ways of thinking and therefore speaking. We are familiar with the need for counsellors to suspend advice-giving in the early stages of becoming a counsellor, however wise and skilled their advice. The new group supervisor needs to suspend his ability to hold long reflective pauses and to give undivided, one-to-one attention. Long pauses are unlikely, at the outset, to encourage participants to risk engaging with each other. Undivided, one-to-one attention is based in the idea of 'thinking individual' and may have to be suspended when the supervisor needs to 'think group'. When new skills and mind set have become unselfconsciously incorporated, the shelved abilities can take their place back in the tool kit. The supervisor will be 'thinking group' and will have a range of options in response to this particular silence in this group at this moment.

Flexibility

Active leadership

Movement in and out of such varied roles in response to changing moods and events in the group requires considerable flexibility of behaviour. Luckily, roles can be grouped. Table 5.1 illustrates three main headings under which behaviour-for-role can be grouped.

Table 5.1   *Behavioural flexibility for group supervisors*

Active leadership	Proactive Aggression
Purpose- and preference-stating	
Telling what and showing how	
Setting up and managing structures	
Intervening to move action/communication	
Assertion	**Proactive assertion**
Negotiating	
Managing agreed time and boundaries	
Line holding	
Staying in there	
Saying No	
Receptivity	**Proactive compliance**
Openness to mood and flow	
Following initiatives	
Sensitivity to timing	
Self side-lining	
Listening	

Source: Adapted from Gilmore and Fraleigh 1980

Many roles call for *active leadership*. Gilmore and Fraleigh (1980) call this *proactive aggressivity*, a term which more usually denotes 'hostility'. It derives from the latin for 'to go forward' and it entails being prepared to act to change one's environment, including other people and their thoughts, feelings and actions. Teaching is *aggressive* in this way. It seeks to alter the furniture in other people's minds. As counsellors and supervisors we seek to influence others (even though that may be an uncomfortable thought). Our safeguard is that we seek to facilitate change in accordance with stated values and ethics.

Creating working agreements calls for leadership. It entails firmly holding the conch and being prepared to influence others in a chosen direction, even if they are initially reluctant. This ability will be needed in many of the group supervisor tasks listed earlier. It is mediated through communicating with visible purpose. A leader needs to make plain if some specified behaviour is a *requirement* (a 'must') or a *possibility* (a 'may'). (The trade name for these is *purpose-stating* or *preference-stating*.) She needs to signal intentions by movement and tone of voice as well as verbally. If she means to influence she must first attract attention. She will only do this well if she knows what she wants to happen and has made a decision to 'go for it'.

Receptivity and assertion

In balance with the ability to lead, the facilitator needs to be prepared to 'go with the flow'. This is different from 'going along'. It requires being receptive and freely following the initiative of one group member, or trusting the group mood of the moment (in Gilmore's terms this is proactive compliance). She will only feel free to do this trustingly if she can be suitably assertive when she feels or thinks that the task – either the task of supervision or the task of group maintenance – is not being well enough served.

Assertiveness is the ability to restate priorities, to speak in opposition to the flow, to stand firm within agreements. It is not wresting the leadership back (that would be moving back into active leadership). Like a dam in a stream, assertion leaves the initiative energy – the active leadership – with the blocked stream.

In the example of Ruth (case study 1), her strength was active leadership. The other side of that coin was that it took time for her to trust the group to be at all self-managing – receptivity to others' leadership is not necessarily required in a Type 1 group. It may also be that she denied herself the opportunity to develop assertiveness in that context. If the group seemed to be 'straying', she probably moved swiftly back to active leadership. Christine and Carmel, in negotiating their participative working agreements, called on all three ways of being – leading, receptivity and assertion. However, active leadership was the 'lead behaviour'.

Figure 5.1 suggests the balance, of the three ways of being, required by different group types. From Type 1 to Type 3, the need

Active leadership	Receptivity	Assertion

Type 1 – Authoritative group
Contracting, inducting supervisees, doing the supervision

Type 2 – Participative group
Contracting, inducting as supervisees and as co-supervisors, structuring for
participation, group facilitation

Type 3 – Co-operative group
Contracting for co-operation, enabling task and group, encouraging initiatives,
asserting normative responsibility

Type 4 – Peer group
Contracting shared responsibility for leadership and supervision, co-operative
engagement

Figure 5.1   *Role flexibility for group supervisors*

for active leadership dwindles, to be replaced by assertiveness
and receptivity to other's initiatives. The ability to move smoothly
and appropriately between active leadership, engaged receptivity
and calm assertiveness is the mark of a group supervision craft-
worker. 'The leader who knows when to listen, when to act and
when to withdraw can work effectively with nearly anyone, even
with other professionals, group leaders or therapists, perhaps the
most difficult and sophisticated group members' (Heider 1986).

Rooted in core conditions

If the supervisor is successful in both leading and encouraging
participants to supervise each other well, it will be because her
intentions have been understood, engaged with and trusted by
participants and the group as a whole. It is a provocative, if
familiar, working hypothesis that this will happen to the extent

that she has shown genuine respect to each member of the group, has listened and answered empathically, and has had the intention of openness and honesty in relation to the task of supervision (Rogers 1961). To this should be added the extent to which she has been straightforward and simple about the shared task. These attitudes have been broken down into constituent microskills, which we can identify and develop, by choice (3, 4). There are probably far more as yet unidentified, which we learn by chance, or not at all.

Gestalt formation

When comparing the facilitation of a good group session to the preparation of a satisfying feast, I wrote that the basic skill for managing such complex events was flexible gestalt formation. A whole literature has been devoted to this process (for example, Perls, Hefferline and Goodman 1972; Sills, Fish and Lapworth 1995). It is the trick of allowing successive highlights to come to the fore, be addressed and then fall back into the welter of material from which they emerged. 'Addressing' means focusing on the emergent highlight and meeting the need which has lit it up for attention. Having sufficiently satisfied that need, the next trick is to let it go and be willing and able to address the new emergent highlight. As various group events occur, the facilitator needs to let a gestalt form, a highlight emerge, focus on addressing it to the best of his ability, and then let it go so that he is free to address the next highlight.

Prioritizing

Highlights emerge from a welter of events, but not from chaos. We will have already been mentally striving to map events, in order to bring them within our range of understanding. When a highlight emerges, perhaps in the form of a lively interchange, each person in the group will have some ready map from which to name it. One group member might think, 'He's being domineering again.' Another might conclude, 'That put me in my place.' The supervisor might wonder if the group was moving into a 'storming' phase. In order to make choices about priorities – how to be and what to do at any one time in the service of the most immediate goal – the supervisor needs a system of comprehension which becomes her own and serves her well.

For instance, in the early stage of a group's life, would it be appropriate to encourage a participant to 'digress' into some personal material which is holding the group members' keen attention, when the group has, so far, been rather 'buttoned up'? Would it perhaps be better to hold strict time before the next presentation? That emphasizes firm boundary holding and getting the supervision done at all costs, while risking the tentative flowering of the group. Or perhaps one should emphasize shared responsibility by drawing the groups' attention to the choice? The cost would be interrupting the moment, creating self-consciousness and spending time in the process. Such moments are frequent, particularly in the childhood of a participative group. Which is the priority at the moment, by what criteria and in the purpose of which objective?

Self-scanning and spontaneity

In individual supervision most interactions can rely on having space. The habitually reflective supervisor will have set up a climate of slow and deliberate communication, at least for some of the time. Her supervisee will either share this pace by temperament or have moved towards it through acclimatization. In groups, unless or until the group members have achieved a well-working respect and rhythm, the supervisor will not be allowed reflective space. A stimulating or worrying event will probably produce a spate of reactive responses – or a long, inhibiting silence which will call to be broken at all costs by some anxious member.

There are many worthwhile objectives in view at any one time, and a multi-levelled communication in process. The supervisor will be hard put to be reflective *and* to participate helpfully at the same time. She has to trust her instincts. Afterwards, in some calm space, she can reflect on the meaning of what she chose to do, what her intentions were and what the consequences. I suggest that 'good instinct' is the result of a two-stage process. Stage one is running a lightning scan of one's experience – sensation, hearing, vision, imagining and images, self-talk, involuntary movements. Stage two is acting on that 'because it feels right', or rapidly adjusting one's intention. This differs from acting on a conscious theory. That requires more reflective space. For any group work, the facilitator needs to develop the art of rapid scanning deliberately, and at first self-consciously. The ability to notice his own reaction, run an instant internal scan and trust himself to move into action or hold confidently to inaction, will often take precedence over the more thoughtful and considered approach.

Movement and physical imagery

Facilitating individual counsellors to act in concert as a supervising group is akin, I imagine, to conducting an orchestra. Both are highly physical activities. Videos of group supervision show a great deal of interactive and reactive body movement. Supervisors move around in their seats, eliciting or resisting eye contact; engaging and sitting back; encompassing the group with a sweep of eye or hand, or gazing fixedly at one person, with head and shoulders forward. Groups, when working well, can look like a dance and sound like a melody. When something happens to break the flow, it is as if participants come up for air. If the 'movement' appears completed, they will spontaneously start to shift, stretch, breathe explosively, laugh, chatter, move their chairs back. If the work was interrupted by a member or members becoming self-conscious – assertively breaking the mood, becoming stuck or impatient or otherwise out of synchronicity – other vigorous reactions follow.

To have 'something to hold on to' when experiencing some impulse to action at such moments, the facilitator must license his ability to think in active physical imagery. He might say to himself, 'Yes, we need to let off steam', or 'There's a lot still to do – I don't want them to get out of hand', or ' I want to keep their noses to this grindstone', 'I don't want to let her off the hook at this point.' 'He's broken the spell again – he did that last week too – should I follow him – he may have got on to something we haven't – if we get on with the work we may freeze him out? Oh, listen, they *are* freezing him out – will he put up with it? Shall I let them ride, or pull on the reins?'

Reflective practitioner and informal researcher

Having made such decisions on the hoof, the group supervisor needs to monitor those interactions which stay in mind as problematic, troublesome, curious or exciting. Spontaneity differs from impulsiveness. Good instinctive moves are usually distinguishable from anxious impulses when reflecting on the event in retrospect. This will particularly be so if one's own impression is supplemented by feedback from other participants. At the risk of teaching supervisors to suck eggs, I reprint a version of the Reflective Cycle – Figure 5.2 – to suggest how naturally reflection flows from working spontaneously in the group with the help of self-scanning and physical imagery.

Figure 5.2   *Version of the Reflective Cycle*

Reflecting on what worked well, when and why, in the light of useful frameworks (5, 6), improves existing maps – 'He kept interrupting and I thought he was challenging me. On asking him what it felt like for him in this group, he said that although people pretended to accept him, he had never felt as if he belonged. Suddenly the whole feel was different.' In addition, fresh frameworks or hypotheses about group interaction can arise when practitioners are aware that their existing maps do not seem to accommodate certain recurring events. 'Perhaps it would make more sense to think in terms of participants' assumptions, rather than my assumptions of how and why they might be behaving.' By looking beyond familiar maps, supervisors can become informal researchers in what is insufficiently mapped territory. How the supervisor finds his own reflective space and who is there to support him will be the subject of Chapter 11.

The craft of the participative group supervisee

The responsibility of the supervisor includes training and inducting supervisees. Skill, time and management are required to balance this considerable teaching role with all the other supervision tasks. Trainees and counsellors who have not been in group supervision previously may not be willing or able to take responsibility for working participatively. Even when they say they are, they are unlikely to understand what is entailed.

Self-conscious incompetence

Like supervisors, supervisees will have transferable assets. If they are new to group supervision, and possibly to counselling practice, it does not mean they are new to the world. They may well have lived more life than their supervisor. Uneven facts of life make joining a new group, for a new purpose, tricky. Familiar hierarchies are overturned. The task is a new one about which the rules and criteria for success are unclear. Presenting for supervision requires exposing quite personal information – how you relate with another person. This is something everyone has done all his or her life. Undertaking it formally and self-consciously creates anxiety.

Trainees especially may dip into a hole of self-conscious incompetence. 'Not getting it right' is uncomfortably close to being an inadequate person. Experienced counsellors may have been working on their own, with only one familiar supervisor to share their work. A group triggers self-consciousness. Comparisons are inevitable, and the counsellor may feel the need to defend and explain practice that had been taken for granted.

Refer back to Table 4.2 (p. 68), Carmel's amended ground rules. These indicate the range of roles, skills and abilities she asked of group supervisees. For a supervisee there are skills of presenting work and using supervision well in a group forum. For a trainee (or practising counsellor) there is the task of taking public responsibility for learning and change. This includes making good use of colleagues' ideas and practices. For a group member, 'good manners' consist, at least in part, in being honest about some things he or she would generally choose not to say; and hearing things from others that might feel quite humiliating. In addition, group members are asked to monitor some usually self-protective mechanisms. For a co-supervisor, there is another whole bag of responsibilities to share and skills to learn.

Forewarned is forearmed

It has not been usual until quite recently to prepare trainees for supervision (7, 8). Yet it does not seem appropriate for the group supervisor to have to do all the induction and preparation – the group is for doing supervision. The plea here is for trainers to take increasing responsibility for ensuring that their trainees can use group supervision well. This means giving them clear information about what is expected of them. Second, it means giving them an opportunity to think beforehand about the implications of working in a group for supervision. In addition, I hope that supervisors and trainers will increasingly support and challenge new and experienced counsellors to take responsibility for preparing themselves and recognizing what is required.

Could it be possible that, without realizing it, supervisors can take pleasure in mystifying the process? Putting grown adults into an arena with which they are unfamiliar, but in which the stakes are high, is potentially infantilizing. By being asked to behave in different but unspecified ways, they, like victims for brainwashing, are stripped of their familiar trappings and are thrown back on their 'stress' behaviours. Anxiously determined to maintain some identity, they may become stroppy or watchfully compliant with what they imagine is acceptable behaviour. Watching them struggle their way through it and making theories about their difficulties can be quite a boost to the ego.

Nevertheless, no amount of prior information can be a substitute for the experience of getting to know each other and taking risks in working together. It is a question of how much information, how many 'maps' and which ones, are useful for them to have available. Some people learn gloriously by being thrown in the deep end. For others, who may be highly functional once they know what is expected of them, learning without first having adequate information can be restimulating to the point of terror.

Case study 2 – Carmel

As Carmel approached 30th October, she was aware she was taking the coming review very seriously. The group had met five times since their initial session. The session arrangements made for arriving and processing seemed to work well. The ground rules had seldom been referred to after initial amendment by the group. When she looked at them again they appeared formidable.

She recognized that, at the time she composed them, she was feeling overwhelmed by the amount of ground clearing and preparation which was needed. By writing down the responsibility she wished the super-visees to share, it had felt less of an onerous job for her. At the review, she decided to check what they had really thought and felt about them (if they had read them at all, she thought ruefully).

She still had a heavy sense of urgency. A year seemed so little time for them to develop as safe and effective practitioners. The group sometimes seemed a distraction rather than an aid. She wondered if a Type 1 group would have been easier and more economical of time.

The week before the review, she alerted the group and asked them to do some homework in preparation.

Table 5.2   *Review preparation*

Are the session arrangements working well for you? Are there any changes you would like?

Referring to the ground rules:
As supervisee how would you rate yourself against the items there?
• What would you like to do better?
• What are you satisfied with?

As trainee counsellor:
• Name one skill/ability in your work with clients that you feel good about.
• Name one thing you want to learn more about/do better.

As group member:
• Does the list make sense to you?
• Does anything need changing?
• On the list, what do you find easy and straightforward to do/be?
• What do you find hardest?

As co-supervisor:
• Do you still want to take that responsibility?

As supervisor:
• Am I respecting my undertaking?
• Is there anything more or less you want from me?

She checked that they all had copies of the ground rules and reminded them that they had scheduled half an hour.

Kate wondered if they could do the review in that time. Stephen thought the group was going well enough and wondered if they needed a review. Mary inclined to agree with him. Farah thought it would be useful. Carmel pointed out that it was non-negotiable. She promised to do her best to see they kept time and asked the same of them.

During the week, she sat down and asked herself how each member of the group was doing – including herself. Her general impression was that they were so varied in their group and supervisee skills that things were not good enough. However, she had to admit that overall they seemed to bring real concerns and use the supervision effectively. She decided to review the group systematically, to see why she felt they were doing less well than in fact they were.

Notes before review

M Surprisingly skilled in the group. Although no professional work with people before the course, must be a delightful mother and has obviously worked in teams. A gift for defusing tension which seems to spring from wanting to get on rather than from anxiety at conflict. Simple with a light, dry humour. Takes the role of beginner, and is very anxious about formal counselling. The others are quite gentle and helpful with her – K being motherly but not inappropriate. Presents rather breathlessly – not yet clear what she wants. Appears to connect easily with both her clients (one quite prickly) and respect them. Worries about what 'to do' with them.

Any anxieties about her? No. She will be a natural, but she starts a long way back. Must stop mixing her 'hurry up' with mine. It is clearly better for her to be in a group than one-to-one – she is learning a lot and quickly from the others – mainly about professional role. As co-supervisor, her simplicity is a boon.

S He has had two no-shows. (Wasn't it him who wondered what would happen if that happened?) That is not unusual for this agency, so I must not jump to conclusions. His manner is a bit – cool? buttoned up? nice young man? He has an easy confidence and I do not know how he comes across to clients. Perhaps a little removed. In the group he relates easily. As the only man he has a special place, but I think of him as the older son. He chose not to use the time when his clients did not show. I think everyone was disappointed – like me, they probably want to know him better. He presents quite clearly, but tends to analyse rather than empathize with the clients – despite being on a person-centred course. But he has a healthy curiosity and interest in the other group members. His responses to their work are intelligent and sometimes 'spot on'. At those times, I think he must have been a good H.R. (human resources) man.

Anxieties? Yes. I do not have enough information about his practice. Again it's early days. I think perhaps I am picking up his need to do things very well and his fear that he won't. It will probably be hard for him to admit difficulty or anxiety. I wonder what he will say in the review. Wasn't it he who thought it wasn't necessary? If I had him one-to-one, I would have even less sense of him.

K I really like her. She is a sensible, intelligent woman with a respect and understanding of clients. She has a social worker mind-set, and knows it. The trouble is, at least one of her two clients could probably benefit from a good social worker. It feels a bit as if she is 'having to do counselling'. Must remember to ask her next time she brings her client whether she thinks counselling is useful for him, and if so how? Also must remember that although she is most experienced, she has the least counselling training – i.e. the agency course.

In the group, she is usually pretty authoritative. The group seem to like that now, but I think it will be hard for her to let others take the role. As for me, at present I am just taking care not to compete. I seldom speak straight after her. Mostly, I agree with what she says. If I disagree, I usually ask other people what they think. I think I am beginning to pussy-foot around her a bit. Am I afraid for me or for her? Partly, I don't want her to lose face in the group. Partly, I think her jury is still out on whether I am a good enough supervisor. I suppose that is a real pressure. If I did openly disagree, what would happen between the two of us, and what effect would it have on the group?

Anxieties? As above. None about her ability to develop as a good counsellor.

F Of all the group, F is 'best behaved'. Her course offered three supervision prep. workshops, which she really liked. She presents well — lively, says what she wants, owns to difficulties. I think her course must be really good on groups. She knows all about feedback and gives it excellently. She speaks confidently, if a little bit didactically — cultural? school teachery? There is a compliance which I sometimes feel irritated by. Again, I wonder if this is cultural — indeed cross-cultural. We are the only two people not of British origin in the group. I know I can react against women from cultures where women have been (are) oppressed. I suppose I also wonder if, deep down, she trusts me as a black woman. Perhaps a 'proper' supervisor should be white for her. My projection? prejudice?

Anxieties? A great start. Waiting to see if she has empathic understanding beyond the start of the counselling. She is good vibes for the group at the moment — let's see how she and they develop.

So — **the group**. If I look at what I have written, they are making a good start. They are not unduly competitive, but seem to have fallen into a kind of hierarchy of competence which suits them all for the time being. They are not afraid to challenge me, or grumble at me, but as yet no real storming. Thank God. I suppose I am not ready or confident enough for it yet, and perhaps they sense that. Maybe they are protecting me — young, black, a woman. Oh well. But I do need to take time and space to explore difference — one young man, one woman in her mid-fifties, two in their forties, one Afro-Caribbean, one Pakistani; not to mention the different counselling courses they are on. I knew all that from the beginning, but there was too much and it was too soon. I will not raise it at this review. There is already too much. If it is raised by them when we look at the ground rules, I'll put a marker on it for the future.

How do I rate **myself**? They seem enough at ease with each other to get on and work — I think the first two meetings really helped. They have a good understanding of what is expected. I think I have held the balance between being too bossy, and engaging them in sharing responsibility. I don't encourage argument or drifting. I don't know about them, but I know that what *I* want is for us to get a bit more satisfying supervision and group life under our belt before I loosen up. I want to be sure, and I want them to be sure, that I can hold it if there are disagreements and irritations.

At the review Carmel sent them into pairs for ten minutes to share their conclusions from their homework. Back in the group, she asked them in turn to summarize their strengths and needed learning as supervisee and trainee. In each case, she asked the partner with whom they had paired to add one strength that the presenter had not mentioned.

She told them one thing, as supervisor and facilitator, she thought she did well, and one she wanted to work on. She asked them to tell her one thing they appreciated in her supervision and one thing they would like more or less of – very briefly.

Appreciations were:

- warmth
- humour
- briskness
- concern

The '*more-or-less-ofs*' were:

- work less hard
- say more about what you think and ask us a bit less
- more tips about counselling
- a bit less respectful/protective of us

In the last five minutes she asked them to comment on the arrangements and ground rules. The arrangements suited them all, more or less. The ground rules they said they had only just taken in. It was helpful reading them again and they now meant much more. Although a bit over-whelming, they acted as reminders of their responsibilities to themselves and each other.

In summary

The working alliance is not just words. It means that people ally themselves to work together for a common purpose. To do that, the allies have to have a shared idea of purpose and how it will be pursued. In group supervision, leadership is with the supervisor. She will probably know what the work entails better than the counsellors in the group who are in role of supervisees. They need information and help in developing skill as supervisees in the service of good counselling and also as co-supervisors. The skill and understanding that they already have needs to be recognized and valued, so that they can value themselves and each other. They need permission to trust that they are valued allies in their own development.

The supervisor's craft is grounded in transferable skills and ideas which are summarized in Figure 5.3. Like counselling, group supervising requires the temporary jettisoning of some previously automatic thinking and responses. It also requires the development of new ways of thinking – most importantly 'think-ing group' as opposed to 'thinking individual'. It demands flex-ibility in taking roles which call for active leadership, assertive

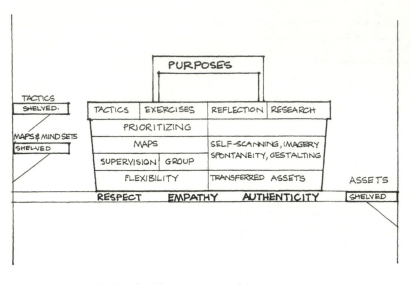

Figure 5.3   *Tool kit for flexible group supervision*

engagement and responsive following. All roles can be taken within a climate of empathy, respect, authenticity and straightforwardness about task and process. Working on communication microskills is desirable but probably not in itself sufficient to enable such a climate. 'Being centred means having the ability to recover one's balance even in the midst of action . . . . Being grounded means being down-to-earth, having gravity or weight . . . . The centred and grounded leader has stability and a sense of self' (Heider 1986).

Prioritizing immediate goals among a welter of worthwhile aims requires the ability for formation of successive 'gestalts'. These occur against mental frameworks for the processes of supervision and of participative group work. Rapid self-scanning aids instant response. Consistent reflection helps distinguish spontaneity from impulse and allows for verifying the trustworthiness of 'instinctive' responses. Informal research, including feedback from the group, generates new hypotheses for better practice.

6 Strategic priorities

What is happening and what needs to happen?

Supervising a group calls for expertise in pursuing long- and short-term supervision goals and in prioritizing what is most important to attend to at any time. The last chapter looked at skills and abilities for facilitating a group to use supervision well and participate in supervision work. One of those abilities was having clear mental frameworks to call on to act as a reminder of strategic aims. So what frameworks outline, in some useful way, the complexities of group life? How can strategies for developing a participative group be laid down? What is happening at the moment and what might that be signalling? What is the positive intention behind some apparently meaningless comment? What tactically needs to happen in the group at any one time in the interests of good supervision – the task?

The strategic maps that I had access to in my early group-working career have stood me in good stead, with some amendments. As Figure 6.1 shows, they fall into three categories.

1   The *two tasks* that the group supervisor/leader needs to bear in mind, minute-by-minute and over time.

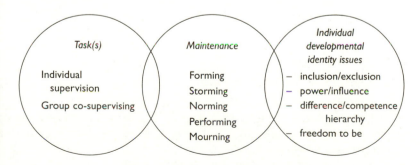

Figure 6.1   *Frameworks for group management*

2   The process which the *group as a self-regulating system* is likely to engage in with the leader as it is born, discovers its own strength and ability and comes of age. I have imposed the frameworks of Tuckman (1965) and Schulz (1989) on to the basic framework of TMI (Adair 1987).

3   The needs and preoccupations of *individuals* as they test the territory of an unknown task group as it forms and develops.

I suggest them here as examples of 'useful' frameworks – useful because they can help to choose how to plan with and for a group. They also help determine what to do, say or not say when there is a need to make a conscious choice as a particular highlight emerges. In retrospect, they can help in making sense of puzzling incidents. Supervisors need to discover alternative hypotheses of group development and interaction, and invent their own. Maps of pathology – what may be happening when the group does *not* seem to be getting on with the work of supervision, or of becoming a coherently working group – can also be useful. However, on their own they are diagnostic rather than facilitative. If the group-as-system (1) is understood to be seeking differing psychological climates at different stages of development (like an individual 'person system'), and each member is doing the same for himself or herself, the supervisor, by being sensitive to this in good time, can often prevent the worst possibilities of group dysfunction. First, trust the group and wonder 'What is it struggling to communicate to itself and to me about the climate it needs if it is to develop into a well-working group?'

Task, maintenance and individual

The first framework was mentioned in Chapter 3 when we considered the shift from supervision *in* a group to supervision *with* or *by* a group. This map suggests that there are three central foci, which the supervisor may need to have regard for, and, if necessary, draw the group's attention to:

- the supervision *task*, i.e. doing good supervision of each individual's work and helping participants co-supervise effectively;
- the formation, *maintenance*, and when necessary repair of the group as a whole;
- the concern for *individuals* and their professional and personal development.

Since this book focuses on group supervision, little has been said about models of the supervision *task*. However, having clarity about tasks, roles and priorities of the work of supervision must underpin everything that is done with a supervision group. If a group supervisor has his or her own supervision aims and values unselfconsciously in place for most of the time, some strategic priorities are predetermined.

Since the role of supervisor implies responsibilities for the skill and development of all individual supervisees with their client(s), concern for the individual can never disappear. It may temporarily cede precedence when task, or group maintenance, takes priority. Similarly, since the task is undertaken in, with, or by a group, the task will not be done, nor individuals be well taken care of, if the group is in disarray.

Prioritizing requires that, from minute to minute, the supervisor (and maybe, eventually, the group) will need to make rapid decisions as to which focus is the most relevant at any one time. When Carmel decided to do some initial 'getting to know you' exercises, she made a conscious decision. She judged that doing good work would be best served by taking time to break the ice. Despite the fact that some of the group were anxiously impatient to 'get on with the work', *group* formation was given priority over premature *task* focus. She did not disregard task, nor individual anxiety. She left time for doing supervision work before the first group meeting ended. In addition to group formation, she believed that the exercises would help *individual* participants get the lie of the new country they were entering. This simple framework of distinction – task, group maintenance, individual – offers an extremely useful 'quick sort' procedure.

Individual preoccupations

It can be easy to assume that when counsellors – either trainees or established practitioners – come together to share their supervision, working together will be relatively straightforward. The exploration of supervisee skills in the previous chapter suggests that this is unlikely to be the case. Coming into a new group, with perhaps an unknown supervisor, not only reawakens old authority relationships, but also old peer and sibling group experiences. Transferences, counter-transferences, self-protections and unaware interpersonal management strategies spring into play. Untested and unconscious expectations can subvert the potential for working well together. Indeed some supervisors assume this will be the case – the group will be at the *mercy* of interpersonal unconscious processes. Perhaps I should reiterate that the view, given here, of the task and process of group supervision is rooted in the assumptions spelt out in Chapter 2, and all the maps I find useful are also based on those assumptions.

A group leader/supervisor needs working hypotheses that help him tune into the preoccupations of wary or eager new group supervisees. If he recognizes the identity needs that individuals typically seek to satisfy when they are in a group he can speed their development as co-supervisors. An amended version of Schulz's (1989) framework is given here. Supervisees in individual supervision also have identity needs, but this framework focuses on the individual as he is orienting himself in the specific context of a group. It suggests identity issues that necessarily preoccupy members at different stages of group life.

In or out?

In brief, Schulz suggests that, on joining a group, each person will have decisions to make about *inclusion and belonging*. They will be asking themselves, 'Do I belong?' 'Will I be accepted?' 'What do I need to do to be included?' They may also be asking, ' Do I want to belong here?' 'If I want to sit on the sidelines, will that be allowed?' As the group life takes shape, they may be seeking to answer: 'Who are the included here, and who might I want to exclude?' 'Is the supervisor fair and even-handed?' 'Are there favourites?' 'Where do I stand?'

Who rules which roost?

Overlapping that preoccupation, and becoming foreground when the question of belonging is at least temporarily laid to rest, is the issue of *power and influence*. 'Who is powerful here – who calls the shots?' 'I really liked him at first, but now he is throwing his weight around and getting on my nerves.' 'Can I make myself heard/felt when I want to?' 'How much power and influence does the supervisor have/do I want him to have?' 'Will I be discounted if I am quiet?' 'I thought she was a mouse, but she spoke out strongly just now. I shall look at her in a new light.'

Where do I stand?

There are other preoccupations which overlap with the power and influence issue. Those are issues of *difference, competency,* and *hierarchy.* A group may have failed at the outset to include sufficiently members who are visibly or audibly different from what seems to be the group norm. Those members may also at some level have counted themselves out as fully fledged members. At this stage, that unfinished business will surface again. Even when people have felt they belonged, they will feel the need to assert their individual or cultural identity. Any 'pseudo inclusion' ('we're all alike really') will not be good enough. At the same time, members who have been seen as the 'in-group', and used that as a refuge, will feel powerful enough to assert their individuality – or if they do not, they may be summoned out of hiding by those who may be impatient to know their metal.

In addition, in the Western tradition of highly competitive education, there will be the compulsion to affirm or discount one's competency. I have seldom met anyone who does not admit to measuring themselves against others. They may have found elegant ways to deal with what they discover from the comparison, but they do it nevertheless. In a group of counsellors, members will be measuring themselves favourably or unfavourably (according to their habit) against other workers. At her first review, Carmel noted that the group had found its way to a tacitly agreed 'hierarchy of competence'. This unconscious agreement (sometimes rather judgementally called 'collusion') allowed them to get on and work. Later, that hierarchy, and the individual identity presumptions on which it was based, would almost certainly be challenged.

As group members become freer to be more powerfully themselves in the group, their work and thinking is more visible. They will be freer in offering supervisory comments. There is usually a stage in group life when competitive supervising is to the fore, and disclosure of counselling work is correspondingly inhibited. Observing this, Janet Mattinson (1977) hypothesized that the way in which a group reacts to a presentation often mirrors the issue with the client that the counsellor is not publicly (or consciously) presenting – a phenomenon she named parallel process (this will be explored elsewhere, in relation to group life and supervision work).

Free to be me

Collective energy is released when supervisees, with the help of a facilitative supervisor, can sufficiently acknowledge and respect their own, and other group members', needs for identity. By experiencing themselves as included and including; sufficiently influential and acknowledged; clear where they stand; acceptant of differences and of strengths and shortcomings, members can work freely, purposefully and creatively – at least from time to time.

Individuals may be aware of these preoccupations as they arise. Often, the identity issues will be worked out subconsciously, becoming available when focused or reflected on. For some, they will remain a hypothesis on the part of the supervisor. He may surmise from indicative behaviour that an individual is working on an issue of identity in the group, and act with appropriate empathy and respect .

The framework *can* be an insight tool for members but it is most useful for reminding facilitators that if they do not have regard to the nature of identity needs, participants will have less energy available to do the work. At some level, they will be engaged with their current preoccupation.

The framework also helps me remember that even the most irritating of participants is doing the best they know how for themselves in this new context. It is up to me, as facilitator, to appreciate what they are striving for and to model how to respect their own and each other's identity anxieties. I may sometimes need to take the lead in creating an atmosphere and even structures which can openly address their preoccupations and help them take responsibility for becoming aware of what they need from me and each other in order to work well. The primary object will not be to increase their personal and group awareness, though those will be outcomes. It will be to help them learn how to signal or speak about their discomforts rather than enact them, so that they have more attention for supervision.

The group as a developing system

A group is not only a collection of unique individuals – it is also a self-sustaining and self-regulating system (1). When each member speaks for herself she will be contributing to the task of super-vision and she may also, if Schulz is right, be marking out her own identity within the group. In addition, she may be voicing something which the group, as a system, wants voiced – or is seeking to keep under wraps.

If, for instance, she expresses herself as moved by a client's story, the group may give attention to her more than to someone who is intellectually interested – or vice versa. The group is establishing its own norms and she is the spokesperson for a particular set of values. If a member challenges the supervisor forcefully, she may be 'doing her thing'. At the same time she is also likely to be signalling a group impatience. How she is responded to by group and supervisor will determine whether the group is now safe enough to be able to engage forcefully with each other and the supervisor.

Healthy group development

Hypotheses of the stages of healthy group development help clarify these usually unconscious group processes and dynamics. 'Healthy' can be a rather depressing word, intimating a blandly conformist, characterless, group. Here the word is used as in 'healthy child development' – that is, involving stages and pro-cesses that are hypothesized as having happened wherever a child (or group) ends up functioning well enough. A co-operative supervision group that is working well enough will usually be characterful, productive, spontaneous and self-disciplined. It will have members who have an ability to be appropriately independ-ent, interdependent and dependent. (This is a rather arbitrary list of characteristics – many others could be identified.) Such a group will usually have lived and worked through some identifiable developmental stages.

I notice that I have some hesitation in giving a particular formulation of stages that is well-known and long-standing in the annals of group work (Tuckman 1965). However, I know none that stands me in better stead. *Forming, storming, norming* and *perform-ing* (with the addition of *mourning* expected demise) equate to infancy, adolescence, young adulthood, achieving (and dying) in the life of an individual.

These are not 'phases to be got out of the way before achiev-ing . . .'. A lot of excellent achievement happens from the earliest days of a group. At first, the quality of the achievement will be experimental and happen through 'follow my leader'. Individual preoccupations, as suggested by Schulz, will be about getting or keeping 'in' or marking oneself as 'out'. The group-as-system will be seeking to become a group, and to the extent it achieves some shared aims it will experience *forming* and relax as a system.

In the stage of *storming*, the-group-as-system will become restive with dependency, at the same time as individuals are actively working to identify the extent of their power and influence in the group. Attention will turn to the leader. If the quality of safety in the group is good enough, and the supervisor is grounded enough in her own realistic power and powerlessness, the group can cut its adult teeth in safety – between each other or in relation to the leader. In the process of doing this, the unique climate which will characterize this group of people will be emerging.

Case study 2 – Carmel

Carmel had intentionally managed some key developments in the group. As we saw in the account of her preparation for the first review, she became aware that she wanted the group to keep anger, frustration or competition under wraps for the time being. She felt vulnerable and sensed that several members of the group were also vulnerable in different ways. She was not ready for them to storm their way through adolescence as a group until they had the reassurance of doing good work together. However, she also knew that individuals should not be discouraged from exploring their differences when they felt ready. They might need to do that before, as a group system, they could begin to experiment with their strength.

She began to set up semi-structured supervision work which would encourage them to take risks with 'being themselves'. [One of these exercises is described in Chapter 9.] Soon after this, the group members became more lively and began to be competitive in supervising. Carmel disciplined herself not to intervene in several minor altercations. She still stuck to this intention on an occasion when Farah told Stephen that she resented him describing his client as 'an Asian girl'. Kate made some move to 'excuse' Stephen and Farah told her she should know better. Stephen asked to be told what was the right terminology and Farah told him he should discover that for himself and not rely on her to educate him. Carmel felt this remark was a sideways message to her, but decided to shelve a response. She thought that she would have been diverting Farah's challenge and protecting Stephen at a point where he was sufficiently 'in' the group and had the potential to find creative ways to meet the challenge.

At the check-in during the following session, Mary said that she had left feeling very uncomfortable the previous week. She wondered why Carmel had not helped Farah and Stephen out. Carmel said that since the review she had been acting on the feedback that she should be less protective. She thought both Farah and Stephen were experienced enough to be able to take care of themselves and discover something useful about their values and understanding. Kate retorted that she thought that a bit of a cop out. She expected Carmel, as an Afro-Caribbean supervisor, to have some easy understanding of racist situations, and have the courage to address them in the group. Carmel said 'Ouch'. Farah angrily interjected, but Carmel said, 'No, hang on a minute, Farah. Thanks for the support, but I need to give this some thought. Are you saying, Kate, that you want me to adjudicate on what is politically correct?' Kate said she supposed not always, but she thought that people would need to know what Carmel thought under the circumstances. Carmel replied that Kate could ask her if she wanted to know, but no one had at the time.

There was an uncomfortable silence, until Mary asked Carmel whether she thought it was racist of Stephen to say 'Asian girl'. Carmel said she thought that 'young woman' was a more respectful description of a 17-year-old. As to Asian, she thought Farah's challenge would be useful to Stephen in becoming more educated about the variety of cultural and ethnic backgrounds from which their clients came. She could identify with Farah's irritation at having to act as 'political arbitrator'. Perhaps they should all, including her, make a point of sharing that role in the group, and educating themselves as to what can be experienced as offensive.

Carmel thought she could almost 'see' Kate giving an inner smile of approval. It irritated her that she should have, at some level, acted to get that, but she admitted to herself that the sense of 'being tested' had helped her to have the courage to act authentically, as well as, hopefully, showing respect and empathy.

The term storming (sometimes even called 'kill the leader') seems to find its way into every group facilitator's vocabulary, and stay there. The experience generally hurts – the supervisor will feel knocked in confidence, and may lash out or protect himself in ways that encourage the testing to go on. This group began to go into a Drama Triangle – a very familiar pattern during the storming period (for further description of this, refer to the next chapter).

At points where members are challenging each other and the supervisor, the balance of power is being tested. Re-balancing cannot happen smoothly. If the facilitator is to let individuals test their personal power and the group as a system to grow up, he has to allow that kind of interaction. He needs to test if the group can sustain disagreement without Mummy or Daddy keeping the peace. That is always a risk, and, as with Carmel, prior calculation can be useful.

That group episode illustrates that tussling was not a troublesome interlude to be got through somehow. It was the means of challenging each member to bring him or herself as a potent person to the task of supervision. It gave everyone in the group vital information. Carmel would not easily be damaged – but she could hurt and they could hurt her. They could no longer rely on her to 'make things nice' – they had to begin to take responsibility for self-protection and risk-taking, as in the world outside. Farah could show her claws. Kate – well, what about Kate? Stephen was challengeable. He played fairly straight and did not attack, sulk or run for cover (important information for women to know about the only man in the group). Mary, the counselling baby, took leadership in 'grasping the nettle', and pursued it with Kate's backing.

The storming process, according to this framework, will lead into the *norming* process – what for this group is not too hot, not too cold, but just right. *This* is how *this* group works well and takes initiatives and relates with each other and the supervisor. The group has an identity, sufficiently shared values and ways of working and could give itself a name. Its supervision work in the storming stage will have been a little ragged. The supervisor will either have given the group its head and allowed some bumpy passages or will have striven to hold the reins, inhibiting potential and probably getting kicked for it. In the *performing* stage the supervision work will, at least from time to time, be reflecting the full potential of members' skill and experience.

Some groups will always have an end in sight. Trainees will have one or two years together. In most groups, members leave and new people join. At finishing and at each leaving, the group will have relinquishing and *mourning* to do. That may be straightforward, but if a member is leaving in discomfort, frustration or anger, the group system will need to spend time in repairing itself. Each time a new member joins, the group is new. Forming and norming need to be readdressed and some storming may ensue.

Fostering the group

Forming

If stages are necessary processes in a group's coming of age, then they need to be fostered – first by the supervisor and increasingly by all participants. The process of clarifying the overall contract and negotiating the working agreement is one major aid in creating sufficient shared purpose. The group can cast off the anchor and get underway. At the same time, structures for meeting and making quick initial contact with each other can acknowledge and often dispel anxiety and satisfy curiosity. Paying attention to the comfort and convenience of the environment (however unattractive) signals the supervisor's intention to 'care take'.

Initial impressions die hard. Equal attention to all members is important when individuals are preoccupied with inclusion issues. Managing the need for rules and contracts without being rigid or authoritarian is difficult but necessary. Christine's solution is a good example of offering only what is necessary for immediate group safety and trust.

In the case studies, Martin is the only supervisor who did not take time to create a clear working agreement. Neither did he appreciate the degree of anxiety of his experienced group. Felicity, the initiator of that group, was wondering if the members were too diverse, even before they met. Martin thought that it would be patronizing to set up getting-to-know-you exercises for such established counsellors. Apparently he found no alternative way to encourage members to meet each other across their interpersonal differences and fantasies. After setting up the group, he did make clear the rather laid-back role he intended to play. He did not clarify members' roles and responsibilities, nor negotiate his own.

Storming

The effect of paying insufficient attention to the forming process can be to precipitate the group into normlessness. Individuals become uncomfortably aware of their many differences. Not having acknowledged their own childhood together, they move straight into storming. Had Martin not taken care to institute a review, he might have had a permanently dysfunctional group on his hands. Luckily, he was open to feedback. He felt it as hostile, but chose not to interpret it as 'mere storming'. Taking it at face value, he renegotiated his role, while asserting his wish for the group to grow into a fully co-operative, Type 3 group. He took time to ask participants to reflect on their experience to date and offered an exercise that underlined joint responsibility for their own and each other's reflective space (see the following chapter).

It could be said that his group had 'won'. Another way of looking at it is that they had succeeded in conveying to him the conditions they needed in order to work better. Some members may have been able to convey this in a straightforward manner. Mostly, they probably enacted their dissatisfaction in attacking ways.

A newly negotiated working agreement might enable them to address such issues more straightforwardly at later reviews. Martin could challenge them on the grounds that they were working to a new pattern of responsibilities with informed consent. They would have the right and responsibility to challenge him if he was not working to their agreed responsibilities. They might still have impulses to 'kill the leader' but if they acted with hostility they could be 'called' on whether they were acting with respect and taking shared responsibility for the task and each other's learning. This second agreement, since it was made at a time when the group had experience of the supervisor and each other, was a norming procedure. The stage of group life ensured that it was different from a 'forming' agreement. Nevertheless, Martin and the group would need to revisit it after they had experienced doing more effective supervision.

In the storming stage it is important to take criticism seriously, without collapsing under it or becoming defensive. The balancing act is between being open and flexible, and standing firm by strategic priorities – 'We will renegotiate, and I want you to take increasing responsibility.' If the phase is anticipated, the supervisor can manage anxiety or fear realistically, and not be at the mercy of bullying behaviour by aggressive members. Such behaviour is usually expressing something for all the group – however inelegantly. Labelling and scapegoating is unhelpful and allows other group members to hide behind those who are more vocal.

Norming

Since this process is about developing a sufficiently shared culture and values, the facilitator has the responsibility of encouraging people to identify the attitudes and behaviour which are person-ally helpful to them. He also has to provide licensed opportunities for that to be spoken about safely and openly. In addition to scheduled reviews, taking time to deal with specific issues can be booked at the start of the session. He needs to make clear his own values about 'good manners' and good supervision and counsel-ling practice, and indicate when he considers a professional or ethical issue is at stake.

Performing

When a group moves successfully into working as an engaged group, it is harvest time. Participative and co-operative groups will have a different climate from a Type 1 group, but if set up in a way that sufficiently fosters group members, that, too, reaps a harvest.

Case study 1 – Ruth

Acknowledging difference and natural progression

By the third term, the supervisees began to argue among themselves and sometimes disagreed with Ruth, giving her some feedback that bordered on criticism. To her supervision consultant she remarked wryly that the group were into fight and flight. She found she was able to encourage this as a sign of enthusiasm, engagement and growing professional autonomy.

As her knowledge and respect of the trainees grew, Ruth noticed that she felt less need to direct their learning about the psychodynamic tradition. Members varied in the extent to which they appreciated it and wanted to work psychodynamically. Two were already sure they wanted to do a psychodynamic psychotherapy training, while two others found themselves more drawn to working in the immediacy of the here-and-now relationship. Ruth found that she was able to respect their work, while challenging them to be aware of the alternative perspective of transference relationships.

Without knowing about Type 1, 2 and 3 groups, Ruth had, in effect, facilitated a participative group. While remaining authoritative, she was negotiating about order of presentation and asked for 'bids' rather than sticking rigidly to equality of time. She consulted with the group while she was supervising and sometimes experimented with orchestrating them to offer differing perspectives on the case. However, a fly on the wall would not have had any doubt who was in charge. The trainees found that their sessions in the pub after the group had a slightly manic out-of-school atmosphere. Ruth believed that supervision in the group was the necessary starting point for trainees. She considered that she had been lucky to have participants who were able to move into shared supervision and attributed that to their natural abilities, rather than to her conduct of the group.

And who is to know if she was right?

Mourning

If the group has done good work together it will have become a significant life experience for supervisees. Disruptions and endings can cause grief or anxiety which seem out of proportion for a 'task group'. The supervisor, who may already be gearing up for the next 'intake', should take time to appreciate the ending (or change) of this human system. Coming changes or group demise should be signalled well ahead and suitable leave-taking rituals co-operatively planned. Reflecting on learning – from supervision, from each other and from group membership – yields professional and personal fruit.

In summary

These three frameworks help me make rapid decisions about what may be the most effective and economical intervention (or non-intervention) at any one time – to plough on with task, to focus on individual identity issues, or to work with the group-as-a-system. They also help me when reviewing the developmental stage of the group (2, 3) and the individuals within it, and perhaps in planning to work directly on some developmental issue. They are elderly frameworks – group supervisors need to be updating them and finding or inventing alternatives which stand them in good stead.

Complications and systems dynamics

When members of the group have other role relationships with each other, Tuckman's (1965) and Schulz's (1989) frameworks are less helpful. If trainees are on an exciting or a troubled training course, the group supervision will be performing some function for them in relation to the dominant system of which it is a sub-system. Likewise, when members belong to an on-going team, the existing interpersonal dynamics and organizational processes will make it difficult for the supervisor to hold a clear space for the formation of a supervision group.

Case study 3 – Christine

Christine followed her plan to take half an hour at the start of each supervision session for building up the working agreement. On the second week, she checked that the interim agreement they had made was suffi-cient, and then focused on the overall contract with the organization.

She used a set of Russian dolls to introduce the idea of different levels of agreement. She invited the team to talk in pairs about what the Big Doll signified for this group. She herself paired with Maria, the service manager. She clarified her supervision contract with the agency and asked Maria about their respective responsibilities. The two pairs of counsellors, when they returned, asked and received clarification about roles and responsibilities in the case-discussion group and in this group.

Christine made clear that she had no responsibility for appraisal. She raised the thorny issue of what her course of action should be if she had reservations about the safe practice of any of the team. It was uneasily agreed, after discussion, that she should raise it privately with Maria. Furthermore, in addition to a group review, Christine intended to have her management review with Maria about the efficacy of the super-vision group and whether both parties wished to renew the contract. She again reiterated that she would like to take the opportunity to clarify agency policies with Maria, in the group, when confusions arose. Maria did not feel very comfortable about this, but realized that it could hardly be otherwise.

Maria undertook to get the organizational contract written up and given to Christine and the group members. Christine said that the following week they would focus on the arrangements for managing the session work, and, after that, formulate a more permanent working agreement for the group.

In these ways, Christine hoped to help Maria and the team understand the tensions in the current arrangements and hopefully take some responsibility for not letting them interfere with the supervision work. During the following weeks she sometimes wished that she had been firmer at the outset, and had refused to have a manager in the group.

However, she was learning a great deal about the working realities of the team. The amount of unspoken tension that would suddenly flow through the group was a strain. Christine felt that she was considered a safe holder of the task of supervision, but that there was also an urgent current propelling her to be the catalyst for some sort of showdown.

She continued to resist this pressure, concentrating, with difficulty, on keeping safe enough supervision space. When counsellors were presenting their work, she would clarify the agency policy with Maria if that was the sub-plot of the piece of work. She was careful not to be too protective of anyone in the group or to take sides. The supervision work went well (see the extract in the following chapter), but she noticed that she was exhausted after the sessions. The informal feedback that she received was highly appreciative.

The sixth session was the last one of the initial contract. Maria asked to take some time during the check-in period. She said that she had been thinking about the review and that she had decided she would not continue in the supervision group. Because she had so enjoyed the work, she felt deprived and sad. However, it had become clear to her that the tension of the dual role was tiring for her. She could not relax and use the supervision as a counsellor. She felt responsible for policy, and that could not be good for the team members. She knew now that she could trust Christine to recognize the difficulties that they all worked under, and to respect the boundaries of agency practice.

Christine was taken by surprise. She had expected that kind of information to be given to her during their private review. She admired Maria's courage and dignity and was amused to see that the team were thrown off balance. It became clear how much covert storming had gone on which belonged with the team rather than the group. They were hard put to respond to Maria in any convincingly honest way.

In the private review, she said that she admired and respected Maria's decision, and the way she had conveyed it. Maria wondered wistfully if Christine would supervise her individually, but clearly expected Christine to say no. Instead, Christine suggested someone she could recommend to supervise her as manager in this kind of service. She told Maria that if she should use this colleague of hers, she (Christine) would not discuss the service or any of its members with him for any reason. Maria wondered if a tripartite meeting might be useful at some stage. Christine said she presumed Maria was wanting her to continue to be the group supervisor. Maria said that the supervision seemed to be improving the morale and communication in the team and was clearly appreciated by members. Christine agreed to continue and reminded Maria that they would be meeting for six-monthly reviews. She pointed out that they must both take responsibility for not talking about team members individually unless one or other of them had ethical anxieties.

From then on, the group was much less exhausting. However, Christine would often feel that she was being invited to side with the team against Maria. Although she sometimes felt that their frustrations with Maria's inconsistencies were justified, she almost always threw the communication back where it belonged – 'What are you going to do about it?' 'Have you told Maria?' 'Have you talked with each other about it?' 'How does it affect you working with this particular client?' It was encouraging that there was almost always one member or another who would insist on the group not getting side-tracked, but giving full attention to their clients. This responsibility would be taken in a hearteningly random way.

The Schulz framework (1989) is clearly less useful when group members have already 'done' their identity issues elsewhere – in this case as working colleagues in a team which predated the group. The dynamics of any already existing system will take precedence over one of its sub-systems. The most that a supervisor can do is to be scrupulous in continuing to clarify the supervision agreement, and reminding members of their shared responsibility to their clients and their own development as counsellors. If that is well enough done, the team can look forward to the supervision as a time and space relatively free from team and organizational dynamics.

7 Hot issues of group life

Strategic maps are essential for pursuing long-term aims. They may not be sufficiently detailed to help in the everyday story of group life. Competent group supervisors need frameworks which make sense of personal interactions and session moods. Equally, the supervisor skills and abilities in Chapter 5 (pp. 76–7) outline the *possibilities* of 'how to be'. They do not help with knowing exactly what to do or say. This requires the development of a ready repertoire of skills for communicating clearly and with intention.

New group supervisors may have frameworks and skills already in place, to be adapted to the new context. However, a group is not only a different context – it is a complex one. Anything said and any decisions taken have different effects on each group member. There is less leeway to 'tweak' communications. Things have to be said more cleanly and more clearly than in a one-to-one setting.

Some of the 'how tos' which perplex new group supervisors are:

- how to bring a group 'back on course' when disharmony is interfering with work;
- how to decide which is paramount when the chips are down – empathy, respect or authenticity;
- how to make sense of puzzling interactions;
- how to interrupt Drama Triangles and convert them into positive interactions;
- how to manage diversity when it is destructive to the task;
- how to address 'hot' issues of anger, fear and shame;
- what to do if someone is not practising well enough, or unsafely;
- when to admit that a group member wants to go, or that you want him to leave.

This is a selective list of the problematic in group life. It suggests some of the predictable and unexpected emotions which groups can trigger. Failing to recognize these, or to acknowledge them with respect, empathy, or at least honesty, can lead to a destructive cycle. The group becomes dysfunctional.

The Group Supervision Alliance Model assumes that if certain ground rules and agreements are skilfully negotiated, clarified and maintained, dysfunction does not usually occur. If these are not well in place initially, the group may be an unsafe forum for sharing counselling work freely. However, people, groups, organizations and professions are never, thank goodness, predictable. Like a parent, a group supervisor can only do the best he or she can at the time. Groups, like children, can grow up wilful. It does not necessarily mean that the parent was not 'good enough'. If the supervisor is 'good enough' and the group is not functioning well enough, there are remedial actions which can be taken. This chapter offers some thinking about remedial action, and also suggests frameworks and skills for preventing routine 'hot issues' becoming causes of group dysfunction.

Maps of dysfunction

Table 7.1 compares the Bion (1961) framework with Tuckman's (1965) framework. Both authors recognized a similar group development map – one framework describes the phases as necessary to healthy development, and the other describes the equivalent pathological phases. The Bion map does not offer help in knowing what to do. It can be useful diagnostically. If a supervisor, or group members, are caught in feelings which are so strong that they interrupt basic trust, and the supervision work, something drastic needs to be done. The group is dysfunctional and a pathological frame may serve to alert the supervisor to that need.

Table 7.1   *Functional and dysfunctional group phases*

Tuckman	Bion
Stages of Group Development	Basic Assumptions
Forming	Dependency (on leader)
Storming Norming	Fight or flight (leader and members)
Performing	Pairing (leader and member or two members 'do it' for the group)
Mourning	

Case study 4 – Martin

During the first review of his group Martin felt quite pleased with himself. He survived a concerted attack on his way of leading and supervising. He listened with what felt like respect and refrained from blaming his 'attackers' or justifying his style. His experience as a trainer stood him in good stead – he did not automatically go on the defensive. He could not empathize with individuals – it seemed to take all his skill to stay open and hold his ground. He noticed an edge of irritation with Felicity, who, while not attacking him, made no effort to support him. He also noticed himself bending over backwards not to criticize her friend, Peter, who was particularly vocal. He felt grateful to his own supervisee, who took the role of 'cleaner up of communications'. (Probably her marital training surfacing in a crisis, he thought.) She did not defend him, but she clarified some of the more muddled messages.

In the night he had a vivid dream and woke up sweating, with his heart thumping. He thought back to the group and felt quite tearful. He found himself hating Peter and Felicity and wondering if he could ever have good-will for them again. He then felt despairing with himself – would he never grow up? He had imagined that he had finally reached equanimity. His training work went so well now and he thought he had learnt all the tricks of the trade. Why had he ever taken on this wretched group? And why had he become so disempowered that instead of being facilitative he had been helpless? Even while cogitating in this manner, his less primitive coping strategies were taking over. He allowed the emotion to flood through him, and by breathing appropriately he began to calm down. Through the day vengeful fantasies ran themselves uninvited, but by the next day he was able to view the group with some composure.

Even before his consultation session (which he was not looking forward to) he began to imagine what had been going on for some, at least, of the group members. There must have been more emotional distress in the group than he had realized. Since he felt some shame at having to tell his consultant about the review, he wondered if this mirrored shame in the group. And if *he* had felt helpless, when he had the designated power as leader, how must they have been feeling?

His consultant did more than empathize – he identified with Martin quite strongly which did Martin a power of good. Together they devised some alternative plans for the next meeting. This allowed for flexibility and preparedness. He did not know what group members might come with. His intention was to discover if there was sufficient 'shared desire' (Randall and Southgate 1980) for the group to continue together; and then to establish if there was sufficient good-will. If so, they would together devise a new set of ground rules, arising from their experience together.

He led by saying that he had thought a great deal about the group and had taken their feedback seriously. He wanted to renegotiate their agreement together in the light of their dissatisfactions, and he would like to take an hour of group time to do that. Everyone spoke in response, the gist mainly being that perhaps they had been too critical. Martin said that he, too, had often felt frustrated and wanted a change of contract, so that he felt empowered to take the lead in doing better supervision together.

The tone of the gathering felt so different that he decided to bring out the plasticene modelling material he had brought with him. He reminded them that respecting the 'transpersonal' had been the shared interest of group members. Would they model a form which expressed what they wanted for their clients? They spoke about their models and then Martin asked them each to say first how the group could help them facilitate clients in the way they wished, and then how it had been hindering. They divided into pairs to reflect on the exercise and each pair returned with two suggested ground rules. Martin asked for a volunteer to write them up. In the group, they worked through the list, eliminating overlap and adding some obvious basics such as confidentiality.

Martin then suggested one round of 'devil's advocacy' – what *should* be on the list but was absent or skirted around. He put an empty chair in the middle to be the butt of those remarks. There was some laughter and strong statements emerged. 'Don't dare interrupt me when I'm reflecting for myself.' 'Don't analyse my clients, be on their side.' 'I'm a person too – trust I'm working the best I can.' 'Stop blaming and take responsibility.' 'I want to like coming – let's be nicer to each other.' 'Think clients' (that one from Martin). He reminded them of the Gestalt assumption that what we want from others is a projection of our agenda for ourselves. For instance, he most needed to remember to 'think client'. If he did, it would empower him to take the lead when he wanted to.

There was some general chat – it seemed to ease the rather tense self-consciousness which followed the devil's advocacy exercise. Someone asked for a break before they moved into supervision. Martin agreed, after saying that the following week he wanted to fix a date to do some work on the differences in theoretical orientation and assumptions. He would like people to think about what they valued in their own way of working, and share it. 'It might help us appreciate and engage with our differences rather than enact them.'

The intensity of his emotion alerted Martin to the extent of the group's dysfunction. Although members distanced themselves from their previous dissatisfactions, they would probably not have done so if they thought they had not 'got through to him'. They had, and he let them know that. He had genuinely wondered if there was sufficient 'shared desire' – he did not want to work with a group if there was not.

By having clear aims, and communicating those clearly, he helped the group take responsibility for expressing their own 'professional' needs in the group. He focused on the task, rather than on issues of individuals. Being pathologized by the supervisor is one of the most frequently mentioned hatreds of group members. Internally, members were probably coping with discomfort – feeling guilty, defiant or ashamed, or relieved and optimistic, or so on. By focusing on task, while acknowledging emotion, Martin invited the Adult and Parent of the supervisees, while engaging the playful Child. Had bad feeling gone too far, he might have disbanded the group or one or more members might have left. He would certainly not have invited them to play seriously at modelling. For that, he had to judge that there was sufficient mutual trust.

Maps of interaction

The earlier review session illustrates the 'feel' of a session in which members are moved to fight or flight, with a barely hidden longing for dependency. If Martin had been less experienced, he might have attributed his subsequent feelings entirely to his own inadequacy or to the bloody-mindedness of group members. He did not discount those possibilities. In also recognizing that he might be 'picking up' some unexpressed emotions from the group and its members, he was using a different map to help himself make sense of the unexpected. The Bion map made sense of the intensity of feeling. Maps of *interaction* explain the transfer of emotions.

When group supervisors are inexperienced they often seem to forget about interaction. They fall back on individual modes of explanation – me *or* them, rather than me *and* them. Every theoretical orientation has maps of interaction and each supervisor will have their own favourites – transference, counter-transference and projective identification; projection, introjection, retroflection; transactions and games, to name a few. Three that I find most useful (though not necessarily in that order) in understanding and facilitating group life are:

- an extended version of the Parallel Process framework of Janet Mattinson (1977) (1);
- the interactional effect of Rogers' core conditions (1961);
- the Drama Triangle (Karpman's 1968 description of the basis of psychological games in Transactional Analysis).

Parallel process

The most common use of this framework is in understanding interactions in the supervision *group* as reflections of interactions in the *counselling relationship*. If the group is acting in an unusual manner, it can be useful to hypothesize that, collectively, they are picking up from the presenting counsellor what is not being recognized in the counselling session and relationship. This, presumably, happens because we are far better at subconsciously receiving and transmitting what is experienced than we realize. Paralleling may happen all the time, but if not focused on, it is unrecognized. I have written elsewhere about the uses and the possible misuse of this framework in doing supervision work (Inskipp and Proctor 1995: 154–6). There are two extensions that I think are particularly useful for groups. One is looking at reverse paralleling; that is, how creative or destructive group interactions can be carried back into creative or destructive client work, over and above the conscious learning from the supervision. The other is noticing and learning from parallels in other interconnected systems – an organization, agency, or the internal processes of supervisor or supervisee. In the previous chapter there is an example of parallel process between group and organization. Maria gave feedback that Christine's group had improved the everyday working of the counselling team – consciously, but probably also unconsciously, paralleling the working spirit of the supervision.

In Martin's case, the reverse parallel process emerged through his 'dreamer'. In his sleep, he picked up the strength of the emotions which were not expressed openly during the review. By recognizing this, he could 'come back to himself'. He knew that, since he was the mediator of this experience, he was a ready receiving set and there were messages in the experience for his own life. However, the immediate messages sprung from the life of the group. In distinguishing the two, he was able to return to the group and transmute the potentially destructive energy. This served not only to do repair work, but also to facilitate the group in moving into a new developmental stage – norming. (We do not know what happened internally to group members in that fortnight though we could speculate from the 'sheepishness' that they too may have experienced a parallel backlash.)

Traditionally, parallel process is picked up through discussion.

Case study 1 – Ruth

Parallel process

Halfway through the second term the group was going well. Members took supervision seriously and seemed both supportive and quite challenging to each other. Ruth began to engage them more actively in the actual supervision. She drew attention to occasions when the responses from members were different in tone than usual, and invited the presenter to consider if the group might be reflecting something unacknowledged in the counselling relationship.

The group began to notice how thoughts, feelings and behaviour within the group mirrored some of the unconscious processes taking place in the counselling relationship being supervised. On one occasion, the presenting counsellor, Federica, felt attacked and responded to her colleagues angrily, defending her perception of the client against theirs. However gentle they tried to be, she felt they were pushing her to deny her own truth of the situation. Ruth interrupted the process, suggesting that the members give Federica some space. She then quietly asked Federica if she imagined that her client ever felt like that? Taking a deep breath, Federica looked around and, to her colleagues amazement, started to laugh.

She said that her client could not bear the slightest interpretation, and that she often felt she was afraid to speak – or even breathe – for fear of giving offence. She had not realized that she was afraid of her client becoming angry and rejecting of her, as he was of most of his friends and family. She genuinely wished to communicate to him that it was his perceptions that were important, but she felt helpless to do that. Ruth asked the others in the group to share their ways of understanding the client's behaviour. She also canvassed ideas for how Federica could best proceed when next she met the client.

The phenomenon of parallel process can only happen if a group has reached the stage when individuals feel free to assert their difference. If this kind of exchange happened all the time, the group could be thought of as stuck in preoccupations of competition and power – 'I'm right – you are wrong.' Because the amount of altercation was unusual, Ruth was alerted to make a tentative interpretation that the responses were paralleling the relationship between counsellor and client. Parallel process can also show in supervision 'exercises' in a very forthright way. There are illustrations of that elsewhere.

Debriefing

In terms of group life and interaction, parallel process is an important concept because, even when recognized, it can cause a knock-on effect in the group. Since individual members mediate emotions or behaviour, parallel process will amplify what is already there. If someone pushes Federica particularly hard, it will be because that person can easily become pushy. Events that reflect an event 'out there', actually happen 'in here'. When a reflection is recognized, it is crucial, for the sake of the group relationship, to process it there and then. Unrecognized it can be destructive. For instance, supervisor and group members can get caught in 'trying to find answers', paralleling the interaction of 'yes . . . but' between stubborn client and relentlessly persevering counsellor. The supervisor may allow the group to go over the allotted time for that bit of work. That transgression is real. The presenting counsellor may feel persecuted and unprotected. The counsellor who loses supervision time as a result will harbour resentment if she does not express her frustration or have it recognized. By repeating the parallel process, the members have unawarely 'taken roles', and debriefing and processing are as important as in intentional role-play.

Empathy, respect or authenticity?

Like love, the core conditions do not always flow to will. However rooted and grounded in respect, empathy and authenticity a group facilitator may be, there will be times when one, or more, do not seem accessible. On those occasions it can be helpful to decide, consciously, which one is the most readily available. Interactions that lack any of those conditions are seldom facilitative. Martin, during the review, found that he could not feel empathic with his supervisees when they were criticizing him. His intention to hold his ground was authentic, but did not communicate his sense of batteredness – it seemed of paramount importance to him at that moment to 'act cool'. He was able, just, to hold to a sense of respect – at least for their wish and right to criticize – and to his trust in their basic good-will. By the start of the next group meeting, he was able to be both respectful and authentic – his empathy probably took a little longer to surface.

In other circumstances, the right choice might seem to be empathy. An internal conversation might go like this: 'I can't understand a word she is saying and I feel incredibly irritated. I think she is being thick. It does not seem right to say any of that at this time in this group. What I can do is try and understand what she *is* saying.' It is amazing how if, at that point, one can make the shift into curiosity, and either reflect back or paraphrase the content of the message, all becomes clear. Respect tends to flow again, and the curiosity and interest has become authentic. Better still, invite the group to do it – they are probably just as confused and irritated and one or two of them may be able to make the same switch, and, in that way, do it for the group.

The same event at a different point of group life might call for authenticity. 'Federica, I can't understand that. Can you put it more simply?' The remark comes from the same sense of frustration and lack of empathy but it is authentic and respects Federica's potential to accept challenge.

The Drama Triangle

Figure 7.1 gives an amended version of the Karpman Triangle (1968). It illustrates how difficult issues can be avoided by people taking up one of three familiar and stereotypical roles – Victim, Rescuer or Persecutor. (These 'taken roles' are not to be confused with the straightforward experience of being a victim, protecting real victims or persecuting others.) Karpman suggests that we all know well, when our attention is drawn to it, which are our favoured roles on such occasions. For instance, refer back to Carmel's group. The event which was used to illustrate the process of storming also includes the ingredients for the enactment of a Drama Triangle.

Farah was hurt and angered by Stephen's reference to 'an Asian girl'. It seemed to her to signal a disrespectful attitude in which, as

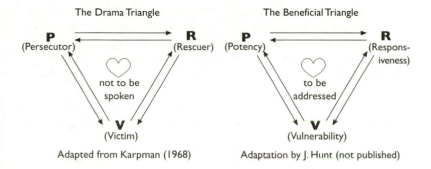

Figure 7.1   *The Drama Triangle and the Beneficial Triangle*

a Pakistani woman, she felt herself involved. The best thing she knew how to do at that moment was to rebuke him. Kate reacted to this by intervening on Stephen's behalf. That was undoubtedly supportive. However, she had not been asked for support and she spoke before Stephen had the chance to reply for himself. On both counts the intervention could be thought of as Rescuing. Farah experienced it as such – and probably felt attacked by it. She turned on her sharply: 'You should know better.'

When Stephen asked what he should have said – on the face of it a request for information – Farah neither gave him her opinion nor said she did not want to. Instead she 'played Victim' – she 'should not be expected to educate him' about his disrespect. We subsequently learn that Mary had looked to Carmel to rescue the situation, but that Carmel had felt it would have been a Rescue – lacking in respect for Stephen's ability to speak for himself. We may conjecture that she also did not want to be perceived as persecutory to Farah. No one asked for her help or asked her what she thought.

The group had formed satisfactorily enough to start working well together. However, it transpired that diversity was a 'hot issue'. The supervisor was aware of being young, black and a woman. Group members, too, were aware and must have had varying thoughts and attitudes. These facts of life had not been spoken about, and they complicated the interaction about 'the Asian girl'.

The following week, when Mary returned to the issue, Carmel was aware of the heat. Kate took her cue from Mary and prodded at what for *her* was the 'heart of the matter' – 'That's a bit of a cop out. As a black woman, you must. . . .' Carmel felt the remark as a blow – 'Ouch!' Farah moved to support (or Rescue?) her. Carmel thanked her and indicated that she wanted to speak for herself. She moved into somewhat Persecutory mode. 'You mean, Kate. . . .' By the time she had finished paraphrasing what she thought Kate was saying, she had understood something important in it – instead of a Persecute, it became a message she could hear and feel respect for, though not go along with whole-heartedly. 'Perhaps we should *all* make a point of sharing that role and educate ourselves and each other about what can be experienced as offensive.'

Since the Drama Triangle on its own is a 'map of dysfunction' it can be used to diagnose pathology. Group facilitators have been known to use it as an aid to negative, rather than positive, intentions. 'I must not Persecute.' 'Oh, dear, I am Rescuing again.' 'Will I never stop playing Victim?' Worse, it can be used as a basis of negative injunctions to group members – 'Don't Rescue', or 'You're playing Victim again.' It is a brilliantly illuminating map of potentially destructive interactions. When viewed in conjunction with the second triangle, the Beneficial Triangle, its creative counterpart, it is enabling.

The Beneficial Triangle emphasizes the potential that we all have for addressing hot issues. Playing Victim is replaced by vulnerability, Persecuting by acknowledging potency, Rescuing by responsiveness. Instead of roles taken, it offers realities to be addressed. Issues are hot *because* participants in the Drama recognize vulnerability – their own, someone else's, or both. Issues will also be hot to the extent participants are potentially responsive – to self and to others. In addition, when issues cannot be addressed there is a wariness about destructive power – again in self and others. Potency will be around, available for creative use.

If, as facilitator, I should not easily fall into playing Victim, Persecuting or Rescuing, what is it I *must* do? I need

- to recognize my vulnerability and be responsible for protecting myself appropriately;
- to recognize the vulnerability of group supervisees, including
  personal vulnerability
  role vulnerability within the group
  vulnerability in the wider culture;
- to remember their right to self-protection;
- to remember that I have
  well developed *personal power*
  the *power* transferred to a *designated* group leader

systematic power in relation to trainees, counsellor accreditation, references;
- to remember that they have
  personal power – well developed or to be developed
  the *power* of the *learner/receiver* role
  systematic power to complain about me;
- to be clear about my role responsibilities – extent and boundaries;
- to have identified my human responsibilities which may supersede role;
- to be clear about the responsibilities of others – extent and boundaries;
- to check that they and I have mutual understanding about our responsibilities.

Routine persecutory behaviour

There are some supervisor behaviours in groups which are routinely experienced as persecutory by group members. They will, therefore, routinely trigger Drama Triangles since they are likely to be hot for supervisees to handle. These often flow from 'thinking individual' rather than group. They fail to take into account the vulnerability of group supervisees.

'Take it to counselling' is a confusing message. If it follows from a supervisee taking up too much time or being 'too emotional', it is more honest to find a way of marking a firm boundary at the time. The responsibility for sharing time fairly is clear. It is a hot issue to insist on it when someone is upset, but it is a reality. To spend a few minutes asking where she will get support if she is still distressed may result in the supervisee mentioning her counselling as a resource. That is more useful than the supervisor publicly suggesting counselling, which has a variety of implications. If a supervisor wants a supervisee to become a more skilled group member, or a more empathic counsellor, suggesting counselling is misleading. For a start, counselling and therapy are not there to 'cure' wrong thinking or feeling and it is bad modelling to suggest, especially to trainee counsellors, that that is the case. Second, the person may not be aware of why and how she is meant to change.

The supervisor is well advised to discuss with a supervision consultant before publicly suggesting counselling as a behaviour limiting strategy. He can identify what he is thinking, feeling and reacting to, and why that is the message he wants to deliver. What is he wanting for that person, her clients, the group or himself? Does the supervisee know that? How could he communicate that in an authentic way? Is he avoiding a hot issue that would be better addressed openly in the group? What would be the consequences of doing that for the group and for the particular supervisee? Does he have a contract to talk privately with group members? Does he have an appraisal role and when is the next review? Having taken stock, he can then consider if counselling or psychotherapy would be a potentially useful resource for the supervisee, and how he could suggest that in an empathic, respectful and authentic way, with clear purpose. Ruth, however, in an example in Chapter 10, found a respectful and authentic way of publicly pointing a supervisee towards counselling.

Role circulation

Another process which results in supervisees feeling shamed and angry is covert 'therapy' in the group. Ruth's delinquent supervisee made a point of thanking her for not 'publicly analysing' him because of his shortcomings. Ruth had been tempted to 'explore' his 'failure' in the group. Instead, she consciously decided to put down a firm boundary marker. In doing so, she probably acted as a catalyst for him to take his 'deadline' issue to his counsellor. If the group is experiencing difficulties, the easy way out can be to allow or trigger someone into being 'client'. Unless this is done with full consent and open intention on the part of the supervisor, it amounts to scapegoating. It will be perceived as persecutory by the 'client' or some other group member/s and trigger a triangle.

Informal group roles

Individuals in a group will often appear to be taking stereotypical roles. The 'thinking group' view of persistent taking of a role – feeler, theorizer, agitator, competitor, client (2) – is to understand it as a group representation. Members of the group, instead of isolating the role-taker, can be encouraged to act as devil's advocate and say what they identify with in what is being said, or how. 'I felt a bit upset when. . . .' 'I must admit I was feeling frustrated too, but. . . .' 'I was sorry for J but I wasn't going to stick my neck out – I was chicken in that atmosphere.' The relief for the identified client – or other scapegoated member – when these identifications emerge is palpable. As a result, the group can be encouraged to take their less usual roles from then on, to give the usual occupants a chance to develop flexibility. Christine had this in mind when she suggested to Maria that if she intended to stop carrying the role of agency advocate in the group, the others would first have to be prepared to take it instead.

Groups need members to carry a diversity of roles at different stages of the group's life. What may be appreciated at the outset – Kate taking the role of wise woman in Carmel's group, for instance – may pall when others are becoming more experienced. Peter was used as the leader of the opposition in Martin's group review, but could expect short shrift if he continued to take that role when the group had fallen in behind Martin's new leadership style. Who would take the brunt of the group's disguised irritation once Maria had left Christine's group? Drama Triangles develop around all such issues if the supervisor and the group together do not take seriously their responsibility of self-and-other protection or self-and-other autonomy.

Difference as a fact of life

If the supervisor acts in ways that recognize those realities, and helps the group become increasingly able to do so, that will go a long way towards easing the group into addressing hot issues. That does not necessarily mean the issues go away. Difference stays difference. Race, gender, power and oppression carry too many parallels from the wider world to become easy facts of life in a group (3). A trainee who is not working well enough cannot be 'eased away'. Y may not like the way Z works. Z may so dislike or feel persecuted by Y that she decides to leave the group.

Inherent stresses

If members of the group are visible or acknowledged members of a minority, they bring with them an added social stress. They will have had to work hard in the world to be accepted for who they are, maybe to accept themselves. If this is true of the facilitator, it offers group members and supervisor a particularly challenging opportunity to break through stereotypical ways of thinking and being. Members of the corresponding majority – straight to gay;

female to male (in the counselling culture, at any rate); white to people of colour – will have developed their own way of dealing with their majority status (3, 4). Sometimes this amounts to ignorance and subtle persecution; sometimes to fierce championing of minority members.

Case study 2 – Carmel

When discussing her group with her consultant, Carmel realized that most members of the group had some social vulnerability that came with them to the group. She had the stress of being black in a white culture – as well as the stress of being in a role more usually occupied by someone of a majority ethnic group. Kate brought the stress of being older than most people in her job, and than the others in this group, including Carmel. She was also less familiar with counselling culture. Stephen was the only man and was the member of a very small minority on his course and among the agency volunteers. Farah was Pakistani and Muslim. Only Mary seemed to belong to no identifiable minority. In the group, of course, she was the only person who had not worked professionally with people. Carmel joked that she would not like to put a weighting on the different social stresses, and realized that, in saying this, she was acknowledging to herself and her consultant that it was a hot issue for her.

She decided that the time had come to help herself and, if possible, the group to acknowledge their differences with less anxiety and embarrassment. Apart from the loss of the potential which enjoyable diversity can offer to a working group, it was a resource for professional development. Stephen was already more guarded in what he said about his young woman client, and the same might be true for the others if they had clients with identifiable social differences from themselves.

A week or two after the session (above) she used the check-in to say that she would like to take time in the following session to explore diversity in the group, with a view to 'helping us all acknowledge differences and hopefully come to value them in ourselves, each other and our clients'. In the interim, she wrote out several pieces in preparation – about diversity, difference, minorities, oppression – and tore them all up in succession. Each time it felt that she was trying to determine the agenda in a way which would keep the reins in her hands. While she had every intention of holding a safe space, she found she did not know where individuals in the group were starting from. So, in the end, she went without handouts and without having set them homework.

She asked for half an hour of time, and everyone in the group said they would like that to be the first item of work. She asked them to talk in twos about what they were hoping and fearing from the session, and then, from that, to come back and say what they wanted. There were fears about saying the wrong thing, about dishonesty, about hurting each other and losing the warmth of the group. Carmel's fear was that she would be too controlling of them. The hopes were that there would be an increase in appreciating how different everyone was; a discovery of what they shared; a lessening of apprehension about acknowledging ignorance; a greater awareness of the experience of clients. Carmel's was that she could become less protective of herself and others.

She then asked them to say, in turn, one way they were different from everyone else in the group and what importance that had for them. Then something they had in common and the importance of that. They processed that in pairs and came back into the group to say what had been useful/significant for them. Mary said that she would like to continue to be a bit more adventurous about differences. Could they regularly do a round? Everyone nodded vigorously, and it was decided that one person each week, during the check-in, would say briefly one way they thought they were different and the importance of that for them. Stephen said he thought they ought to book their order of 'going' now, so that they did not waste time each week. So they did. Carmel suggested that they review the process after two 'gos' each.

Strategically, the group was moving from storming into norming. Since the review, the ground rules had become real for them. They had developed courage in, however gently, handling hot issues. Carmel had taken the lead in this, but discovered that there was a fine line between taking the lead and seeking to control. She felt the need for self-protection and took responsibility for her own protection as well as that of the group. However, by joining in as a participant in the exercise, she exposed herself to any risk she was asking of them. The reward for her courage in not controlling the agenda was that Mary took the lead in suggesting the next move and that the group members were trusting enough of each other to follow that lead – as was Carmel. Something had happened in the balance of power. However, unlike the storming phase, no one felt in danger of being disempowered.

Bad counselling

I imagine that any one-to-one supervisor dislikes finding that a supervisee is not practising well enough (5). The reality can gradually emerge that this is not just slow learning (for a trainee) or a result of the supervisor's different orientation (with an experienced counsellor) but ineffective or dangerous practice. In a group, there are two added discomforts.

A group can be such an inhibitor for some shy or inarticulate practitioners that it takes longer to ascertain how much is role-inadequacy as supervisee or group member, or how much is counselling inadequacy. Secondly, supervisor, supervisee and group members have the embarrassment of dealing with this hot issue publicly. As suspicion begins to dawn, there is fertile mulch to nourish Drama Triangles. Some supervisors will be protective beyond the point of honesty, leaving members to pretend or challenge – and risk being seen as Persecutors. Others will challenge soon and consistently, almost certainly triggering Victim and Rescuing behaviour from supervisee and group members.

Course and agency procedures and criteria

Preventative measures lie in an adequate contract and working agreement. In the case of training supervision, the contract with course or agency must include provision for some on-going appraisal (5, 6, 7). This is also the case where trained counsellors are employed by, or volunteers with, an agency or organization. The contract should be clear as to any reports, public or private appraisal sessions, or responsibility for assessment which belongs with the group supervisor. This should be clarified as the group reaches appraisal points. Having some systematic self-appraisal sheet from course or agency which requires supervisor and peer feedback helps 'cool' the process and keep it functional. If 'use of supervision' is an item, it can be clear which feedback belongs with supervisee behaviour (6, 8) and which with the fantasies about the counsellor's work with the client. I say 'fantasy' not because I do not trust the judgement of groups and supervisors, but to remind myself and others that we never really know what is helpful to *clients* and we only know what a counsellor is doing if we see live work or hear a tape. The best we can do is identify criteria and levels of achievement and do our best to ascertain the extent to which the counsellor's practice meets them (7, 9).

If this systematic appraisal is carried out in a functional manner, the failing practitioner has an opportunity to prepare herself for failure or referral or to make her own decision whether or not to proceed. Her vulnerability has been acknowledged, she has been through the same fair procedures as others, and if she should 'play Victim' because that is the best she knows how to do, at least the supervisor and group are somewhat protected from falling into Rescuing or Persecuting.

Freelance counsellors

If the supervisee is a practising counsellor in a freelance group, the supervisor, in making the working agreement, must make clear his professional responsibility. He is undertaking to be the person to whom supervisees are professionally accountable and has the responsibility of challenging practice which is unwise or unethical. In a Type 3 group, he will have asked members to share this responsibility with him, though he is ultimately accountable.

If this responsibility is taken seriously, regular reviews are crucial. Some device, such as devil's advocacy, can help to encourage peers to give each other challenging feedback at reviews. 'If there were something I would like more or less of in your work, it would be. . . .' As groups become more established, the ground rules can be amended to support risk-taking and challenging feedback in the group.

This having been done, the supervisor has to allow those challenges, and not be over-protective. He also has to use his potency to challenge wisely and fairly and not to become the sole challenger in the group. He needs to be clear for himself and with the group if private meetings with group members, for systematic or occasional appraisal, are part of the professional contract. Ultimately, his responsibility is to clients, and he needs to grasp the nettle – publicly or privately.

In summary

As in life and families, so in groups: some issues are hard to handle and may interfere with the responsibility supervisor and supervisee have to the client. When a group is not carrying out good enough supervision because of strong interpersonal emotions or withdrawal, the supervisor has a responsibility to group and clients to take reparative measures. These most usually consist of revisiting and reviewing the contract and working agreement. Ground rules may need to be amended, or the group constituted within a different set of responsibilities. Members may choose to leave, or even be asked to leave if they do not share a commitment to the ground rules.

Preventative measures rely on the supervisor developing clean, unambiguous and purposeful communication, and some ready ideas for why there may be tension in the group. These ideas are drawn from frameworks for making sense of interactions rather than from maps of individual behaviour. They include recognizing stereotypical and necessary group roles. If recognized, stereotypical roles can be interrupted creatively and the group encouraged to become more flexible and functional in the roles they take.

Some supervisor behaviours dependably trigger enactments of the Drama Triangle. Others dependably interrupt those enactments and can transform them into creative interactions. While each group member should be treated equally, they are, in fact, never equal. They differ along many dimensions and this allows the group to benefit from diversity when members are free to be themselves. Some members come into a group with a weighting of social vulnerability which the supervisor has responsibility for recognizing. One of the differences is in counselling competency. Since the developing and monitoring of the ability to work well with clients is the basic professional contract, practice that may be ineffective or harmful has to be addressed. Doing that in a group context calls for systematic arrangements and agreements as well as the exercise of the core conditions.

The case studies have all featured participants who had basic good-will and at least the potential to develop 'good group manners' and counselling competency. Group supervision examples 1–6 (vignettes devised by Michael Carroll) recount awkward situations, for supervisors and groups, which were interfering with the group's ability to work well. Would any of the summarized frameworks be helpful in identifying strategies and tactics for addressing them?

Example 1

You are supervising a group of trainee counsellors (Jack, Jill and Joanna) all from the same training course. To date you have had about eight meetings. While they are still young counsellors, Jack and Jill have taken to supervision well and use it effectively to learn and reflect on their client work. Joanna, on the other hand, seems to drain the group's energy. At every opportunity she talks about herself, her past, the difficult times at home. She relates this to almost all the cases brought by the others and her own cases are related in a similar ego-centred way. Towards the end of the last session Jill exploded when Joanna was in one of her 'victim' talks and said that Joanna should take this to personal counselling instead of dumping it on the group. You had to end the session but promised to look at the group interaction in the next supervision.

Example 2

You are supervising a team of counsellors (four in all, the team leader and three full-time counsellors) who work in a college setting. After the last supervision session one of the counsellors asked to speak to you and said that the team leader had been using information from the supervision sessions to criticize counsellors or challenge them. On several occasions he had spoken to different individuals and the previous day had spoken to the counsellor who has approached you. He (the team leader) had asked to see her and expressed surprise that she had handled the case she brought up in supervision so badly. He said that he expected more from an experienced counsellor like herself. She wants you to discuss the situation in supervision.

Example 3

John is one of your supervisees in a small group of four. He finds it difficult to take on the supervisee role and is constantly edging towards being the co-leader with you in the group. He is always polite and grateful but you sense that he doesn't really think he needs supervision and that he feels he is far more experienced and able than the other members of the supervision group. You sense also that he is overtly working with you but covertly there is a lot of competition in his relationship with you. Because he has specialized in Object Relations Theory he is constantly reminding you, who do not know too much about it, how valuable it is and how applicable to the cases brought to supervision. You feel de-skilled and somewhat put down, especially since the previous week he expressed surprise that you had not read a current book in counselling. Should you take any action?

Example 4

You see five counsellors, who work in a team, for supervision paid for by their organization. The work has been going well and on a number of occasions they have talked about their organization and the management structure, with which they are not very enamoured. One of the group asked to see you after the last meeting and showed you a private letter from their direct manager in which she asked your supervisee to keep an ear open for criticism of the organization, poor practice and any troublemakers and report back to her. The supervisee wants to know what to do?

Example 5

You have been seeing two counsellors who work in a doctor's surgery, for group supervision. They are both psychodynamically trained (you are humanistic) and in your view they are finding it very difficult to think and work in brief therapy with the clients sent them by the doctors. The surgery has agreed a maximum of six sessions per client. Your supervisees are continually complaining they cannot work within this restriction and indeed their whole way of assessing and intervening makes it very difficult.

Example 6

You are the supervisor in a small group of four supervisees, all from the same training course. One of the supervisees has written you a letter saying that she and one of the male trainees, also in the supervision group, are having a relationship and intend to 'move in together' within the next few weeks. She wants to know if this will affect their being in the same supervision group – they find it very helpful and desperately want to remain in it. If it is all right to remain in the group what are their responsibilities to the other members of the supervision group and of the training course?

Type 1, through 2 and 3 to 4

The skills of determining strategic priorities and addressing awkward group situations effectively and economically are of greater importance to supervisors in participative and co-operative groups. They have undertaken to act as teacher, trainer and facilitator of co-supervisors. Work has to leave space to allow for that development – room for members to try out new behaviour and roles, or maybe just to behave badly and let the group find how to cope. Interaction is not only encouraged but required. However, the supervisor carries ultimate responsibility for the 'well-enough-being' of group members and for the quality of supervision work. In a peer group – Type 4 – no one group member carries that overall responsibility. That, too, is taken co-operatively. The power given to, or taken by, a designated leader, is never so apparent as in its absence.

8 Sharing responsibility – peer groups

Designated authority

> We are a very experienced group of psychotherapists, led by a friendly and open supervisor. The sessions are lively and spontaneous and have a collegial feel to them. Our supervisor is authoritative but never authoritarian – our working agreement is somewhere between a participative and a co-operative group. The other day, the supervisor had to leave early and we finished the session as a peer group. As soon as she went, the whole atmosphere changed – we broke for a cup of tea, and chattered animatedly. It was exactly as if we were back in school and teacher had left us on our own. We soon got back to work and had a good and disciplined session. But somehow, it was different from our usual meetings.

This was said to me recently and I recognized it from similar experiences of my own. It reminded me of the mystery of designated leadership. The supervisor of this group is known to me as a person who easily takes her place, as supervisee, in a group led by another counsellor/psychotherapist. Indeed, she would have given my informant that designated authority, had she not already been her supervisor. If my informant could offer specialist knowledge, could they, I wonder, have switched roles – supervisor one week, supervisee another? And could they have worked as peers in a group with no supervisor?

A group with a designated supervisor may, as we have seen, benefit from several levels of expertise. It may have an excellent supervisor who has more experience, skill, and understanding as a counsellor than the members themselves. He may help them work skilfully together, in a way that is economic of time and expertise. Members have a right to expect that they will be suitably protected from dysfunctional group interaction, with its potential for wasted time and personal discomfort or distress. For the duration of the group they can relinquish overall responsibility for giving and getting their reflective space, and be assured that their development will be taken seriously. Even if their supervisor does not have expertise that is greater than their own in all areas, the chance of being 'looked after' for an hour or two is restorative. In the working life of counsellors, personal responsibility to (and even for) others predominates. Who cares for the carer?

A well-working peer (Type 4) supervision group has other refreshing qualities.

> The level of trust that we have is extraordinary. As soon as we meet we know that we can drop our guard and talk freely. That does not mean that we collude with each other – although of course we probably do, without realizing it. We are quite challenging – we can afford to be with that degree of trust. I think we must be more challenging to each other personally than most led groups. We know each others' patterns well by now. As we are all busy people with a full and varied working life and other responsibilities, we tend towards mild but chronic workaholism. We make regular audits of our workload, and have a mutual contract that if we fancy taking on some new challenge (which three of us often do) we will first relinquish an existing responsibility. The other two tend to prefer staying with what they know, and they have been challenged to be more adventurous – with good results. Our areas of specialist skill and knowledge are very varied. Each person contributes expertise as well as their own special personal qualities. We have been together for three years with two successful changes. We all have an individual supervisor – for me that is an hour and a half a month. I would not be without that, but if I could not find a good supervisor, I would consider that my group fulfilled my supervision needs and professional requirements.

Anecdotal evidence suggests that not all peer group experiences are similar (1) – just as it suggests that not all 'led' groups find the advantages outlined above. Referring back to Figure 5.1 (p. 81), the abilities for leading, following and asserting need to be more in balance for members of a group that is truly 'peer' than for the supervisor of a Type 3 co-operative group. 'The peer group needs to be leaderful rather than leaderless' (G. Houston, spoken comment). All the skills of supervisee and supervisor need to be developed by each group member. In addition, there will be times when, even if designated leadership is given to individuals in rotation, authoritative challenges or even confrontation may have to be made without the role protection of the 'expert supervisor'.

Peer group realities

Already trusting

In talking with numbers of counsellors – mainly quite experienced – who have been in peer groups, certain patterns emerge. The majority of groups are formed from people who have known and often worked with each other prior to becoming a supervision group. Frequently they have met on a training course, and remain together as a peer supervision group. Usually, individuals like and respect each other's work (and each other). Often, they want the chance to talk about work with like-minded people, who share their theoretical orientation. If the training has been significant to them, ties are special and established trust is precious as they start work as fledged practitioners. Sometimes, the group may stay together because of geographical proximity or because of special-ist interests – student counsellors, primary care counsellors or a shared philosophy or faith.

Already known

Other groups (such as the group that Christine – case study 3 – supervised) work as a team and alternate between a led group and a peer group. This is economic for agencies and organizations and, where it works well, is greatly appreciated by team members. Less frequently (in my experience) members have deliberately sought out other counsellors to join a peer group (rather as Felicity did, but without 'employing' a supervisor). Sometimes, this is through a network of practitioners previously known to each other. One group I know met on their return journey from a training course anniversary which they all attended. They had been on different years and had not known each other before then, but their shared philosophy led them to initiate regular peer supervision which has lasted for ten years, with a few changes.

When I inquired about another group I knew of, I heard that it was still going successfully after five years. That had its early difficulties – as in all geographical areas where counsellors are fairly thin on the ground, the members had mostly been trainers or trainees, supervisors or supervisees, of each other.

> We got over that problem after I had discussed it with you. I went back and told them about my frustration at being assumed to be leader. We made a new working agreement, and people have been much more

willing to share responsibility. Recently we have had two new members. Of course, we use the Durham model [see Figure 8.1, p. 142], although we have modified it a bit. The first hour we spend in pairs – half an hour supervising one person, and half an hour being supervised by a different person. We change 'partners' twice a year or so. The second hour we mainly discuss issues that people bring – sometimes to do with a particular client but more often general professional concerns. Since the new people come from totally different settings, it has widened the group's perspectives. It works excellently, but it means we never use creative group methods. That is a loss – I think I will initiate a new group with that as its focus. I know several people who would be interested.

Well, why not?

Potentially ground-breaking

Writing about peer groups, I notice in myself a parallel process to the experience spoken of in the first paragraph of the chapter – being let off the leash. It is a relief to appreciate what 'is', and I am reluctant to start prescribing. I want to honour the freedom from a fixed authority figure. Once designated, an authority figure so easily elicits the habit of uncritical respect or disrespectful criticism from those who subscribe, by choice or seeming necessity, to that authority. Whole institutes and most group theory are based on the dynamics that are generated in response to leadership and authority – our human longing for the perfect leader and our human will to control our own lives. In joining a peer group, counsellors are inevitably 'dealing' with this problem. I have heard peer groups spoken of as 'avoidant' and 'collusive' (2). They may be – just as led groups may be avoidant and collusive of other facts of life.

I prefer to think of them as potentially ground-breaking. As a profession, a culture, and a species, I believe we need to learn how to give authority to designated suitable others when and as appropriate, and then gracefully withdraw that licence. Equally, we need to learn how to take authority gracefully, knowing we only hold it by licence, and with clarity about its limits, and respect for the responsibilities that go with it. Peer groups have a clearer start at this enterprise. They are likely to be less cluttered by the primal transferences, counter-transferences and projections that hang around authority figures. They have problematic sibling dynamics, but they are the dynamics of co-operation, and that makes a change.

Intermediate technology for shared responsibility

My colleague, Thom Osborn, speaks about 'intermediate technology' for social change. Most of us have been brought up in a competitive environment, and skilfully educated in competitive and hierarchical ways. We have little experience of leaderless situations, or truly responsible co-operation. We sensibly seek, less than consciously, to re-create the known. We have learned ways of coping with the known. The unknown can be unattractive and perilous. The concept of intermediate technology assumes that our social and political arrangements are still in an early stage of development, and that there is a socially and personally responsible social order that we are, or could be, moving towards. I would hazard that most members of successful peer groups have been offered some intermediate technology to help them – usually before joining the group, but possibly within the group.

Many counselling courses now have pockets of shared responsibility – skills practice, self- and peer-assessment, group decision-making. In these pockets, trainees take on temporary roles of leadership and authority and have real and clear, if limited, responsibilities. Course leaders may specify, and coach trainees in, the skills of feedback, evaluation, assessment. They may offer clear working agreements for that task. They may suggest creative structures for group decision-making. By helping groups to make ground rules for their work together, they will be facilitating their development of good group manners. All these are intermediate technology. They give people an experience of what co-operation means, and they offer some 'how-tos'. Other courses give space for trainees to 'discover' the how-tos, with more or less support. If they are lucky and the wider culture is a facilitative one, trainees re-discover how to co-operate without a designated leader. If unlucky, they may vow never again to work other than independently or with a leader. Some become addicted to the 'tyranny of leaderless groups'.

Self- and peer-accountability

The wise and experienced trainer and leader in the profession who said to me, 'I think peer-assessment is cruel and sadistic' must have had a bad experience. The trouble is that, in reality, we are all peers in many ways. Constantly designating monitors and assessors who are supposed to 'know better' takes care of some discomforts, but at the cost of a pretence which can be costly to innovation and the potential for self-determination. As I have said in an earlier chapter, existentially we are self-accountable – we cannot abrogate our responsibility for ourselves. We are also, both within our profession and in the wider world, accountable to our human peers. Peer groups address this tension in a way that is different from supervisor-led groups, and innovation is an essential component of their working together. They should not be hung about with doubts and fears of avoidance and collusion. They may welcome some suggested 'how-tos' and a reminder of their potential for self- and peer-responsibility within a wider professional system.

Intermediate technology for peer groups

Having indulged myself in polemic – briefly taking the 'helicopter position' to look at supervision groups – my return to earth is quite prosaic. Most of the aids to good supervision group practice outlined in earlier and later chapters are applicable to peer groups. The additional 'how-tos' are when and how to take and relinquish authority and leadership for shared responsibilities.

Aims and definitions

In the previous examples, all the groups associated around some 'shared desire' (Randall, Southgate and Tomlinson 1980) or known common task. However, people also take the initiative to start a peer group from a 'standing start'. There are some predictable difficulties in establishing such a group.

> I was feeling very isolated and I wanted to have contact with other freelance counsellors. I took local names from the BAC directory, and wrote a letter canvassing for people to join a peer supervision group. I got disappointingly few replies, but enough to have an initial meeting. Of the four people who came, one was, to say the least, peculiar and another had such definite ideas that I could not imagine being given my 'reflective space'! They all seemed to want support more than supervision, and probably I did too if I was honest. I had not laid out very clear aims for the meeting, so I didn't know who could say yes or no to whom, and how. So I suggested we all go away and think about it, and I quietly let the idea drop. When two people got back to me, I just said there were not enough takers. I don't know how I can have been so naive in the first place.

Table 8.1 outlines the steps which need to be taken if a peer group is to be well set up. At each stage, someone has to be prepared to

Table 8.1   *Steps in setting up a peer supervision group*

Assume initiator power (mobilizing for setting up the group)

Stages

1   Define the purpose of the group
2   Agree criteria for membership
3   Determine system for selecting members
4   Select
5   Agree an overall contract (extent and limits of co-supervisor responsibility)
6   Negotiate a working agreement (ground rules, way of working, administrative arrangements, learning agendas)
7   Manage the supervision work
8   Review and arrange for consultation

initiate. The first responsibility is defining the purpose of the group. This can be a sketch plan, at the outset, which subsequently gains definition and body. As the 'standing start' experience demonstrates, he who initiates has to take responsibility for defining what is to be initiated. Peer groups of counsellors can associate for a variety of purposes – exchange of ideas, pressure group activities, professional development, therapy or personal development, mutual support and, of course, supervision. 'Standing start' initiators will benefit from some careful prior thinking. What is a peer supervision group? Some possibilities are:

- *The sole arena for sharing counselling work.*   This entails members taking full, though shared, responsibility for being the colleagues to whom each is accountable for good enough and best practice.
- *One of two or more arenas.*   This entails identifying the extent and limits of co-responsibility and the nature of the interface with other supervision arenas.
- *A combination of supervision and support (or other purpose) group.* Again, this entails suggesting, and eventually negotiating, clear boundaries and responsibilities and identifying a sufficiently shared understanding of the two tasks.

These, or other possibilities, are the sketch plans which the initiator(s) could propose which will form the basis for canvassing.

Known criteria

The experience of Felicity and Martin (Case study 4) indicates some of the difficulties of setting up a group which could work well. Martin recognized that criteria were needed, in order to establish whether prospective members had sufficient shared values and practices, so that they could effectively support and challenge each other. He chose not to take his designated authority to thrash out some of the implications of membership with Felicity, the initiator; nor did either of them wish to use their initiator power (or privilege) to interview, or run a 'self-selection' meeting. In that case study, Martin had designated authority which he could draw on – or be reminded of – at the first review. That allowed him to assume responsibility for group-building and repair.

In setting up a peer group, failure to take initiator power will almost certainly result in abortive efforts, as in the previously described 'standing start' débâcle. The easy route is to use the old boy/girl networks, however uncomfortable that may feel. Only known and safe people are approached (as with Martin and Felicity). This may include, as in that case, actively seeking variety. The alternative is to canvas more widely, but within stated parameters such as:

- theoretical orientation
- working context
- x years of experience
- membership/accreditation with a professional body, etc.
- experience of working in participative/co-operative super-vision groups

Since my schooldays, I have noticed that, contrary to most people's expectations, groups that do *not* choose each other often work better than those that *do*. Many groups that stay together after training were 'thrown together' on the course and 'took', often to their surprise. There is no prescription for the best balance of apparent risk and apparent safety. It is sensible to be aware of the issues and thoughtfully intentional in taking initial steps.

Procedure for membership

Aye, there's the rub. Sufficient definition of the group's task and the criteria for membership may still throw up potential members who do not feel right for a peer group, or for *this* peer group. It is uncomfortable for me to write about this. For those who tend to inclusivity it is uncomfortable to be engaged in selection proced-ures, especially for a peer group. Equally, those who have little difficulty with exclusivity may unintentionally set up a group which turns out to be highly competitive or uncomfortably bland.

Awareness and courage in considering hot issues, laced with pragmatism, are helpful at this juncture. Good supervision and the preservation of reflective space are shared aims. Honest accountability to practitioners who are practitioner-peers (not just human being-peers) is the professional requirement. Sufficient variety allows this accountability to be more effective as 'client advocacy'. Adequate shared understanding allows for 'professional advocacy'.

The initiator(s) may need to take the power of final decision-making. He/she/they will need to make clear ground rules for how decisions are made at this stage.

> X and I wish to form a peer supervision group which will be our main supervision forum. We are inviting you (or humanistic/psychody-namic/cognitive-behavioural/neurolinguistic programming/person-centred/primary care/freelance, etc. etc. counsellors/psychotherapists) to a meeting at my house. X and I will introduce our ideas and talk about the practicalities of a peer supervision group as we understand them. We will facilitate us all meeting each other and discussing our wants, needs and expectations. If sufficient people appear interested, we will ask for your permission to take any final decision about membership, should that be needed. Otherwise, someone else may wish to volunteer to take that role. In any event, our initiator respons-ibility will come to an end when we have arranged a first peer group meeting. We will start at 7 and finish at 8.30. Tea, etc. will be laid on. Whatever the outcome, we hope you will come – at least it will give us all a chance to meet new colleagues.

This is not a prescription – just an attempt to headline the issues of responsibility.

Contract and working agreement

As with a led group, the Russian frogs are aids to the management of peer groups. The sketch plan of purpose is a starting place. Members have to fill in the detail. What will be the parameters of our shared supervisor tasks? Will we be the people who fill in the supervisor form for professional accreditation or for references? At what point do we know each other well enough to give informed consent to such responsibilities? Do we all have altern-ative supervisors if this is not to be our role?

As supervisees, what are our rights and responsibilities? How will we identify if we are doing the 'supervisor/supervisee' dual role well enough for each other? When will we review? Should we bring in a consultant from time to time?

How will we co-operatively manage time; task; group formation, maintenance and repair? What ground rules and good manners can we identify and agree on that would create a safe and challenging enough culture for us, collectively?

What will be the pattern of our meetings? A luxurious time to arrive, have tea, check in and update each other on 'life', followed by two hours of evenly divided supervision time? A minimum of chat time? Work first, tea after? Go with the mood of the day? Will we work in the group all the time, or spend some time in pairs or threes – supervisor/supervisee and possibly observer/feeder back?

Will we rely on our ability to develop organically as a group – we are all very experienced? Or shall we have a rotating chairperson, designating one member each week, who can facilitate agenda-building and be time-keeper and trouble-shooter? Or should there be more varied designated roles?

Options for management

Figure 8.1 illustrates some of the changes which can be rung. The issue of designated or 'emerging' leader is present at the start of contracting. Will the initiator continue to take responsibility for bringing some suggested ground rules? Or for facilitating the process of creating ground rules from scratch? Since no one can officially answer that question at this stage, the group may follow some leader to 'just start working and see'. It will have 'been led', however unconsciously.

So if moves are to be intentional, someone has to 'show' as leader, and offer choices. The worst that can happen is that the group openly or covertly decides not to follow his lead. Once more pragmatism and courage reign. If I want a good group, and no one else seems to be taking effective leadership, then – if not me, who? If not now, when? The chances are that people will be grateful for any lead, even if only as something to throw up a counter-lead that is more acceptable. A member's right and responsibility to express frustration needs to be validated. It is often through the expression of frustration by one member that the group shifts to a new level of effectiveness. In a led group, the leader can manage that. In a peer group, individual members have to risk being authentic.

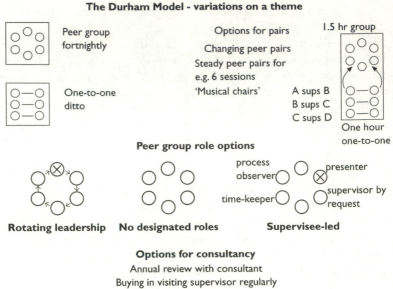

Figure 8.1   *Peer group arrangements*

Doing the work

The following chapters suggest the rich possibilities that groups have for doing economic and moving supervision work. All these possibilities are available to peer groups. However, like all groups, a peer group can easily become routine in its methods and expectations. It can be helpful if some members want to be creative and adventurous, to make that clear at the outset.

An effective management aid is giving the supervisee the responsibility for how he wants to do his 'piece of work'. If he wants some structure to be used, he can ask for volunteers or designate a 'manager'. Alternatively, the 'manager of the day' can be responsible for making a mini-contract with the presenter and suggesting or deciding how the work is to be done. As well, during the agenda-building, someone can ask to have the chance to set up and manage some creative exercise; or do some live supervision, one-to-one, within the group, and get feedback. In these ways a peer supervision group also serves the purpose of a supervisor development group.

Reviews and consultants

Groups that continue on from working together in other capacities often develop organically. Leadership rotates unselfconsciously, at best. At worst, hierarchies have become sneakily established, and therefore cannot easily be challenged. Whether a group decides to designate rotating leadership or to follow the organic route, reviews are essential. Inviting an occasional consultant can be helpful, if scary. Things that are difficult to say can be said more safely. If the consultant is offered a clear contract, he can also help the group reconsider its ground rules and procedures if they have proved inadequate for good supervision work.

Leaving and joining

Reviews offer the opportunity for people to say that they wish to change supervision or leave the group for some other reason. Of course, this can happen at any time, but the review offers some protection if the decision or the announcement is difficult. Deciding on replacements for leaving members is not so difficult as deciding membership in the first place. Members know each other; they have the chance to discuss privately and recruit intentionally. They can identify lacks – of cultural and sub-cultural variety, experience, expertise or personal qualities – and know more clearly what diversity the group can sustain and still work well.

Hot issues

Not all hot issues can wait until a review or a consultant is present. Controversy and conflict; drama triangles and the aftermath of parallel process; prejudice and stereotyping; bad or unethical practice; any of these can happen in a peer group and they are hard to speak about and resolve – if they are resolvable.

Ground rules that spell out responsibility for group maintenance and repair, as well as co-responsibility for 'good enough' practice, give permission for any member to address what is problematic if it is interfering with good work. Beyond that lies, once more, the capacity for each person to determine which core condition is missing – empathy, respect or authenticity – and to speak about the lack. This may be in relation to herself, or in relation to another group member. That means taking leadership, while not allowing oneself to become stuck as unofficially designated Challenger, Victim, Persecutor or Rescuer.

It is for all these reasons that members of peer groups have greater opportunity to develop, in balance, the capacity for leadership, assertion and trusting others' leadership. My totally unscientific equation is that if 51 per cent of each member is able to trust the other members for 51 per cent of the time, then the group will work – its pot, in Virginia Satir's (1972) metaphor, is more than half full. Which is not all that much to ask.

In summary

Peer groups are *restorative* in ways that are different from led groups. They can be extremely *formative* because of the demands they make for balanced personal qualities and abilities, group sophistication and communication skill. In requiring members to take full *normative* responsibility for their own work and that of fellow members, they call for the development of ethical courage and judgement.

They seem to work well if they grow naturally out of a previous working relationship. If members of such a group are to grow and develop together, it will help if they make an overt working agreement, and review it from time to time. Creating a new group is problematic, and benefits from careful thought and clear statements about taking and relinquishing particular responsibilities. It can work well and have a challenging edge which an established group could miss.

All the management aids and supervisor and supervisee skills which have been spoken about in previous chapters are at the disposal of peer group members if they can summon up some leadership in 'getting going' and breaking through difficulties. Correspondingly, any of the free-flowing or structured possibilities for doing supervision that are spoken of in subsequent chapters are at their disposal if they find ways of accessing and introducing them.

Members will need courage, skill, and clarity about supervision priorities, if they are to risk leading and trusting others' leads. If an enabling culture is well enough established in the first place, members can experiment and develop as group members and co-supervisors. If they succeed in doing mutually satisfying supervision they are helping the profession realize its aspiration as a self-monitoring body of colleagues. They will also be in position to pioneer ways of extending peer accountability beyond the face-to-face group.

III Supervising in groups

9 The harvest

I sometimes wonder how group supervision would go if no attention were paid to thinking about groups, theories, purposes, roles, responsibilities – if the supervisor just came in and started to engage the group in doing supervision. Would Martin's experience be typical? Even if that is an unduly cautionary tale, in principle participants have a right to know their rights and responsibilities. In addition, clarity provides relative safety so that they are more likely to bring what really concerns them in their work, and risk talking about it freely.

Economic and effective supervision

The previous chapters have concentrated on ways of providing a safe climate and the clear intention for counsellors to share their work with colleagues as freely as possible. They have dwelt on the importance of the supervisor (or peer supervisors)

- believing that a group is potentially richer as a resource than an individual, however expert;
- knowing clearly what are her own responsibilities to the twin tasks of supervision and group facilitation;
- conveying to the participants what are their responsibilities and rights within their particular context;
- having care for each individual;
- conveying to participants their responsibility for
    saying what is helpful and unhelpful
    remembering the expressed needs of others
    taking shared responsibility for their own and each other's development as counsellors and co-supervisors.

Previous chapters have also emphasized the differing amounts of teaching, training and 'bossing' that group participants may need before trusting and using their own talents appropriately. All of this is to prepare the ground for the development of excellent and economic supervision within a setting that is often considered less generous in time than individual supervision.

Case study 3 – Christine

Christine's group had ten minutes of supervision time in hand at the end of the session. During the check-in time, Phil, a member of the group, had said he 'could bring something but it didn't matter if there was no time'. Christine offered him the remaining ten minutes – he demurred because the time was so short, but agreed to try an experiment. Christine asked him to tell each member of the group one brief reason why this case was not urgent to bring. He went round:

'I'm not really stuck.'
'You have heard this one before and I don't want to bore you.'
'Nothing dramatic is the matter with him.'
'It seems a real effort to think of what I want to say.'

Christine then asked him to go round again, saying the same things but pretending that the other members were the client he was speaking about. So:

'I am not really stuck with you.'
'They've heard about you before and you/I will bore them.'
'Nothing dramatic is the matter with you.'
'I can't get my head around what I want to say about you.'

There was a good deal of embarrassed laughter during the round and the counsellor mockingly buried his head at the end. Christine then asked each person in turn to respond in some way to what had been said – as if they were his client.

'Well, I feel stuck and I'm not sure what we are meant to be doing.'
'I worry that I am a bore and yet I don't know how to interest you.'
'It seems so silly me coming – it's not as if anything is really the matter with me.'
'I want you to bother to think about what you could do to help me.'

Six minutes had gone and Christine asked Phil how he would like to spend the remaining four minutes. He replied that he now felt immensely sad and helpless. Would each in turn say, from their experience of the exercise, what they thought might help him connect with the client. One replied, taking the role of client:

'I think it might help if you somehow came alongside me and asked me about what would feel helpful to focus on today. Give me some purpose.'

The others spoke as themselves:

'Perhaps you could acknowledge the feelings of sadness and helplessness which seem covered up in the session by the depression.'
'I wonder if you could suggest that he may feel frustrated by knowing things are not right for him, but not knowing what is wrong or why.'
'I think it might help for you to bring him to the peer group next week and start from what you are feeling now – just give him more time and attention, and forbid us or you to be bored!'

The final minute was spent in silence; on the dot of ten minutes Phil sighed deeply, looked up, smiled and said 'Thank you all – that was moving and helpful.' Christine made a note to ask for a brief report back next month – the session was clearly helpful to Phil and riveting for the whole group – would it be helpful for the client? Christine also noted that she herself had done no supervision with Phil – purely facilitated the exercise. She too felt moved – she had noticed how she often seemed to say the last word in any exercise, and had made an intention to risk not speaking unless she really thought something needed saying. On this occasion, she had not even noticed that she had not spoken until after the group had had five minutes processing the whole group session and said goodbye.

This group had eventually been constituted as a Type 3 group – the members already operated as a peer group once a month and took part in a case study group fortnightly. Christine had contracted to do some pretty forceful leading. Each member wished to develop as a supervisor and was eager for stimulating and creative methods of supervision. Their self-discipline improved markedly within a few meetings, and paid off in the way they could respond to ideas and use small bites of time fruitfully. In the processing time after this exercise, one member commented how powerful it was to speak to the client rather than about the client. She would remember to do that in the peer group sometimes.

Brief creative exercises like this show how a well working group can:

- do economic supervision;
- make space for clients who might otherwise fall between the cracks;
- work spontaneously when invited;
- make overt the parallel process rather than spending time guessing about it;

- learn useful devices for self-supervising and supervising others;
- deepen the respect and trust of the group in each other and in the supervisor;
- be fully involved and engaged as a group without interfering with the counsellor's reflective space;
- furnish opportunities for the supervisor to be inventive (Christine made up that exercise 'out of her head' and on the spot);
- offer a learning opportunity for the progressive development of supervisor, facilitator and supervisee skill.

The useful ten minutes built on six months of preparation, teaching, encouragement and self-discipline.

Moments of choice

This chapter and Chapter 10 offer a guide to the possibilities for doing effective supervision with a group. They map options that may be useful in guiding the process. In addressing Frog 4 (Figure 4.1, p. 61) – the individual counsellor's reflective space – we have reached the heart of the matter. The roles of supervisor and facilitator overlap. Since this is supervision work, the *supervisor* has prior regard for the counsellor. The *facilitator* is aware of the Shadow Frog – the appropriate roles for other members to take as co-supervisors. They will learn from their colleague's work even if they are the audience. The potential is also there for them to learn in other dimensions.

The time allocation will probably be taken care of in the session agenda. The 'headline' for the piece of work may also have been offered then. 'I want to talk about M. I got in a real mess last week.' ' I need to go over my last session with J. She brought up some new material.' 'My session with P was very moving and I want space to talk about it – I think I will probably end up weeping.' 'I need help.' 'I haven't had time to think what I want, but something may be triggered by other people's issues.' In groups of trainees, each may routinely bring his or her 'client/s'.

In any case, the outline issue will emerge if the presenter is asked for a mini-contract for her piece of work. The supervisor then needs to prepare for a series of choices which she will have to make, spontaneously or with forethought. How long will she let the story run without interjecting? Will she protect the presenter's space to tell his story? Will she suggest a structured exercise, or

encourage a random discussion? Will she delegate some responsibilities or do all the management herself? In her mind she will
have some sense of the meaning of this bit of work for the
presenter, and of its place in the rhythm of the session. She will
also have a wider sense of its place in the development of the
individual counsellor and of the group as a supervising system.
Some of the possible options are set out in Table 9.1.

The helping process

The underlying map is an adaptation, for use in group supervision, of the Egan Helping Process (1994). It consists of:

- contracting
- laying out the issue
- exploration
- focusing
- deeper understanding
- pulling together
- action planning
- reflecting

Individual supervisors may prefer a variant of this process or
another model altogether. It is necessary to have *some* shape in
mind, when there is a participating group and a time limit. The
time acts as a boundary within which the full process may be
contained. Otherwise, suitable stopping points can be identified
which round off a 'part process'.

Christine's exercise allowed a speeded version of the full process. She addressed Phil's 'headline' for his work; made a mini-
contract; provided for an exploratory round which was already
focused and a round which offered the potential for deeper
understanding; she re-contracted with Phil, who, after internally
pulling the material together, asked for an action round and then
reflected. We know that Christine made up this exercise spontaneously – she did not plan to follow a set process and neither
did Phil. Her experience in inventing exercises led her to an
'intuitive' structure, which could contain an effective supervision
process. Phil and the participants 'knew' how to use it. He might
well have opted for a further exploratory round, in which case the
time boundary would have required that he settle for a 'part
process'. He would still have had time for pulling together and
reflection.

Table 9.1   *Menu of 'choices'*

Time allocation
- predetermined in working agreement
- presenter requests
- some negotiation between those wanting 'time'

Responsibility for time holding
- supervisor
- volunteer from group

Contracting
- hard contract, including what the supervisee specifically wants
- soft contract

Laying out issue: considerations
- the contract
- the available time

Exploration
- clarifying
- empathic responses: first- and second-level empathy

Choices:
- supervisor only
- group in structured way
- free group

This exploration may be all the presenter needs/has asked for. If so, summarize, end and reflect on the piece of work.

Focus
- presenter invited to choose
- in accordance with contract
- supervisor chooses/suggests
- group offer variety
  - in structured way
  - by free responding

Deeper understanding
- presenter continues/supervisor responding
- structured exercise: suggested by
  - presenter/supervisor/group member
  - conducted by presenter/supervisor/group member
- free group responses

This may be all the presenter needs/wants. If so, summarize as above.

Pulling together
- noticing any parallel process
- summarizing:
  - supervisor
  - presenter
  - group
- debriefing

Action planning, if necessary
- rehearsal/role-play
- group suggestions
- supervisor suggestion or direction

Reflecting
- group comments
- supervisor comments
- presenter comments

Source: Inskipp and Proctor (1995)

Often a presenter will want to unpack and talk about a client's 'story'. As counsellors, we are party to stories which outrage, delight or move us to tears. We cannot use the human outlet of gossiping to discharge our grief, anger, gratification or impotence. An attentive group is a marvellous medium for silently witnessing such narratives, receiving them and gently offering them back. Exploration and the assurance of being heard is all that is needed. The table suggests some other suitable stopping-off places.

Whose responsibility?

At various stages in the process, the supervisor can allocate (or ask for a volunteer to offer) part responsibility for some managerial function. Designated *time-keeping* can free the supervisor to focus on other aspects of her role/s and can encourage shared responsibility. The presenter, or another member, can be asked to suggest a *form* for the supervision. Someone can volunteer to practise *managing an exercise* when the group is familiar with it. *Focus* can be decided by the presenter or the supervisor, or a variety of foci can be offered by members for the presenter's choice. *Deeper understanding* will almost always be participative, as will *pulling together, action planning* and *reflecting*. What is appropriate sharing will, of course, depend on the type of group, and on the developmental stage of the group as a whole. The supervisor will also be keeping in mind the needs of the particular client, the counsellor, and the interactive mood of members.

Random or structured

An early choice is whether the group will respond randomly to the counsellor or in some structured way. Probably the most traditional form of response in a participative group is random responding which just 'happens'. The nature of the responses could be analysed in terms of individual, interpersonal or group dynamics. (Probably no set of responses is truly random.) The responses may also be representative, in tone and content, of some unconsciously identified client/counsellor dynamic (in other words, useful in identifying some parallel process). However, on the face of it, the responses are random and will be useful to the counsellor in proportion to the degree of skill, good manners and intuition of group members.

Case study 4 – Martin

In the fifth group session, the student counsellor in Martin's group spoke about a client who was causing him considerable anxiety. The story raised the temperature in the group. Members were falling over themselves to speak. One quite sharply inquired if the student client had been given a psychiatric assessment. While the counsellor was responding to that, Felicity broke in to object to the way that 'the group' was talking about the student. She felt it was unduly diagnostic, rather than empathic. Martin asked Felicity to say how she might talk about the student. She did that, and immediately the first speaker gave a little lecturette on how important it was to recognize dangerous or pathological behaviour and take it seriously. The marital counsellor, probably seeking to lower the temperature, cut across that debate, asking about the managerial support and consultation that the student counsellor had access to. He found it helpful to consider that. When he had ruminated aloud for some little time, Martin asked him what he next wished to think about/work on. He said he really wanted to have an opportunity to talk further about his anxieties in his own terms, so Martin rather diffidently suggested he be given five minutes without interruption. Felicity and her antagonist concurred in this, but their way of sitting did *not* communicate high-class attention to the counsellor. The faces and bodies of Martin and the two remaining members were, in contrast, almost rigidly trained on the counsellor. It was in the session after this that the group review, described earlier, was due.

This example shows the pitfalls of random responding when the supervisor has not contracted

- his own leadership role
- the supervisee's responsibilities to himself as supervisee
- the members' responsibilities to each other's reflective space

and, therefore, members of the group are insufficiently aware or self-disciplined in their responses, have not acknowledged and addressed differences in theoretical assumptions and professional style, and are at the mercy of the dynamics of storming and of competing.

In contrast:

Case study 2 – Carmel

After the first review, Carmel had continued to keep the group on a tight rein, which they seemed to enjoy. They experienced the supervision as very productive. However, anyone speaking 'out of turn' would usually be ignored and this gentle sanction aided the development of a rather compliant group. Members were being gently dissuaded from more honest and adventurous interactions. Their full potential as co-supervisors might never be realized. Carmel discussed the situation with her consultant and reflected that she was in danger of creating a dependent group.

In the session after her consultation, she informed the group that she would like them to be more spontaneous with each other. To help them in that, she wished to set up an exercise in which she would act as 'holder' of the supervision, while they practised their skill as co-supervisors. Did the idea appeal to them? Farah asked if she could come back to Carmel if she wanted more help after her session. Carmel promised to make herself available in the processing time at the end of the session if anyone felt unfinished. When she asked again if they were prepared to try the exercise, the response was wholehearted.

Carmel reminded them to be aware of allowing sufficient reflective space for the presenting supervisee and promised extra time at the end to reflect on their own and each other's experience. She invited a different member to be time-keeper for each mini-session and clarified the order in which each would present. At the start of each mini-session, she asked the presenter to say something about what they wanted from their time. She did not attempt to get a 'hard contract' – she was mainly interested in helping the other members have some focus for their interventions. She then sat back until the start of the following presentation, when she clarified the next agenda.

The first presentation was rather subdued and members were very tentative and polite. Kate, when asked for feedback at the end of her time, said that she appreciated the space and respect, but, in accordance with what she had asked for, would have liked to hear more of what people really felt about her work with the client.

Stephen, the next presenter, said forcefully that he wanted to get some feel for what the counselling might be like for his client. He found her hard to understand. He started to present the client, his voice getting lower and flatter. Farah interrupted and said that she was finding it really hard to concentrate. Could he say what his client looked and sounded like instead of telling her rather repetitive story. Stephen shifted in his chair and began to describe his client in words and gestures. Kate commented how much the client came to life for her now, and that it made her wonder how the client felt when she came to see a man who was young enough to be her son. Mary laughingly added that she wondered what it was like for the young man to try and help someone old enough to be his mother. Carmel noted this shift of emphasis from the original contract. She saw that the counsellor became immediately engaged in exploring that issue (his counter-transference, though that term was never used). Since her objective for the session was to let the group find its own voice, she considered it unnecessary to intervene. At this comparatively early stage, it seemed unhelpful to limit the focus to what, after all, was still inexperienced contracting.

Kate and Farah went on to identify with the client and Mary clearly identified with Stephen and his difficulty, of which he was now aware. Stephen subsequently said that he had found the session helpful and enlivening. At the following meeting of the group he reported that the sense of rapport with this client was quite different. 'It almost feels as if we are playing a quite expert game of catch now – I think she really enjoyed the session and I felt as if I was confident in being able to support and help her.' The group reported that they had really enjoyed the whole session – both Farah's and Mary's presentations had been quite spontaneous – though Farah thought that more time had been 'wasted'. No one asked for Carmel's added contribution.

Carmel found that, from then on, she was consciously choosing when to suggest structures or free flow, and was also more conscientious in asking supervisees how they would prefer their mini-session to be conducted. Her consultant pointed out that the whole experience could be seen as an undeclared parallel process in reverse – as the group became confident in their own usefulness and therefore more spontaneous, Stephen was able to 'play' with his client. Carmel reflected that that particular piece of work could just as easily be seen as a reflection of the issues of age and gender in the group. She hoped that, in addition to doing good supervision, the members would feel safer to acknowledge and enjoy their diversity.

This session was not all free flow. It was lightly structured in order to create a 'nursery slope' for these trainees in proactive participation. As there are advantages and disadvantages to free flow, so there are to using structures in the group. We will consider these when we look at creativity.

Table 9.2 suggests guidelines for good practice when helping a group become effective in free-flowing supervision discussion. As the case studies show, supervisees need to communicate empathy and respect if they are to be more help than hindrance to the presenter – this takes skill as well as good-will. The supervisor will, hopefully, model these skills consistently, but he can also teach them intentionally – or remind the group members to use

Table 9.2   *Guidelines for good supervisor practice for free-flow discussion*

Make clear ground rules at the outset.
Teach and model non-evaluative and evaluative feedback.
Teach and model empathic and non-judgemental responses.
Teach choice of focus.
Encourage members to share what is real and important for them (authenticity).
Value, and model valuing, responses.
If responses are well meant but clumsy, judgemental, etc., reflect, summarize or re-frame.
Challenge unempathic, judgemental, unclear, projective, jargon responses when appropriate.
Encourage members to give feedback on such responses.
Set and keep time boundaries.
Allow time for reflection/processing which includes monitoring usefulness of responses for the presenter.

Source: Adapted from Inskipp and Proctor 1995

the skill they have in the service of supervision. Increasingly, they will also use and develop skill in challenging, and this too needs modelling and teaching. The degree of challenge and feedback about the effectiveness of comments has to be geared to the robustness of group members, and their stage of development as supervisees and co-supervisors. However, preserving reflective space for the presenter is always a priority, and this may necessitate challenge that may feel premature. Learning about what is or is not helpful takes place most appropriately after the discussion. It is important to preserve time for processing, giving feedback and reflecting on what was of interest to all members, as well as to the presenter.

Ordered focus or random focus

In individual supervision there is always an issue of where and how to focus on the material brought by a supervisee. In a group, this issue is more complex. Carroll's research (1996) showed how experienced supervisors tend to have a favoured focus. If a group supervisor does not realize this, she can condition a group to focus on one particular aspect of a case – the potential for benefiting from a wide variety of perspectives can be lost. Even if the supervisor is aware of her bias, each individual member, too, will have a favoured focus. Benefiting from that variety, while preserving reflective space for the presenter, is problematic. In addition, responsibility to the development of each counsellor as self-supervisor and co-supervisor of colleagues requires encouraging flexibility of perspective.

Hawkins and Shohet (1989) offer their process model of supervision (in my terminology, this would be a 'framework for focusing' rather than a model) which Inskipp and Proctor (1993, 1995) have amended and called the Seven-Eyed Supervisor. Figure 9.1 shows what these seven perspectives are.

Key

1 The client's life and experience
2 The interventions, techniques and goals
3 The process and relationship between client and counsellor
4 The internal experience of the counsellor
5 The here-and-now relationship and process between counsellor and supervisor
6 The internal experience of the supervisor
7 The systems in which all or any may be engaged, for instance:

   – client's systems
   – counsellor's systems
   – supervisor's systems
   – agency systems
   – cultural, sub-cultural systems
   – professional, economic systems

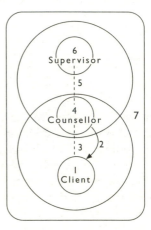

Figure 9.1   *The Seven-Eyed Supervisor (adapted from Hawkins and Shohet 1989)*

Fairly early on in the life of even a relatively unsophisticated participative group, the members can be introduced (most helpfully by an imaginative enactment) to these perspectives. This enables them to

- become more aware and imaginative about what they want to focus on in their own mini-session;
- be choiceful and aware of their own favoured focus;
- practise their less-favoured foci;
- act concertedly to hold a single focus or to offer a variety of foci from which the presenter can choose.

Case study 3 – Christine

The team that Christine worked with had between them a variety of theoretical perspectives. In the early stages of the group, their proffered observations, reflections or questions were quite skilled, and also somewhat predictable. One, being used to case discussion groups, would usually focus on the client – especially her history (eye 1).

Another, from a person-centred tradition would focus on the feelings and thinking of the counsellor in relation to the client (3). The psycho-dynamically trained counsellor would either focus on the relationship and interaction or on the defence system of the client (4 or 1). While Maria, the manager, was part of the group, her most usual responses seemed to flow from anxiety about issues of organizational protocol – the issues she raised were systems issues (7). Christine appreciated that at first, because she knew little about organizational and systems issues in the particular setting, but she later became irritated, considering that this fixity of focus inhibited and frustrated the other counsellors.

Christine herself had two different favoured foci. While she still knew little of the work of individuals, she was concerned to know what a counsellor actually said to a client, and what were the intentions of their interventions (2). She was also aware of her own emotional and physical responses to the presentation and, if no one else in the group mentioned their own reactions, she would often offer hers. She might have a hunch that these reactions were to the material in general – her own counter-transferential responses (6). Sometimes, however, she suspected that they were reactions to the way the supervisee was interacting with the group during this particular bit of work – that is, paralleling the client/counsellor relationship (5).

After discussing with her supervisor development group, she decided to do some straightforward teaching and development work on the seven eyes. In the fifth session, when the group were putting forward their menu items for the day, she ascertained that there were two urgent cases and two other counsellors who definitely wanted time. She negotiated to have twenty minutes for her agenda after they had done one of the urgent pieces of work.

In the event, she was faced with a dilemma because that piece of work proved uncomfortable. The counsellor had been upset by some instructions she had been given about meeting the bereaved spouse of a patient who had died in unfortunate circumstances. She wanted to take the matter up with Maria in the presence of the supervisor. This was the first time that there had been a direct challenge to the manager in the group (though such challenges had been the implicit sub-plot of several pieces of work). Christine intervened to ask the counsellor what, specifically, she wanted to come out of her session. The counsellor said that she wanted Maria to hear and understand how difficult it had been to respond naturally to a distressed and newly bereaved spouse, while also juggling with what she was meant to say to protect the rights of the hospital and the patient's family. Christine asked her if she would like her (Christine) to manage the piece of work by just reflecting and paraphrasing the experience the counsellor wanted to talk about. The counsellor would talk to Christine, not to Maria – how much Maria listened or heard would be up to her. The managerial issue belonged in the monthly managerial case discussion group rather than in the supervision group. The counsellor agreed, saying that she understood the distinction. Christine then checked with Maria if that would be all right with her, and she agreed, although it was clear that she felt criticized and put on the spot. Christine knew that it was not 'informed consent' but felt that this device was the best she could offer. It would allow some communication and also possibly stand future clients, counsellors and agency in good stead.

When the counsellor had spoken about the incident, wept about it and reflected on how she had managed the dual role, Christine asked each group member to offer in turn one empathic or identificatory response. This they did, including Maria who spoke very simply and warmly.

Christine then made a swift decision about whether to change the agenda and talk about the organizational issue. She quickly recognized that she had not thought through what her appropriate role would be, or what helpful outcome could be aimed at. She did not want the group to use her as 'the goodie' and Maria as 'the baddie' (or vice versa if things did not go well). She was also unsure how much the anger at 'the manager' was preventing the group members from accepting their own power and responsibility in the supervision. She therefore decided to pursue the original agenda. At least it would offer the safety of sticking to an agreed agenda; at best, it might offer a vehicle for addressing some of the tension in an indirect way.

Using the five group members as representative of the seven eyes, she enacted the choices of focus available. Three of the members represented, respectively, client (eye 1), counsellor (eye 4) and supervisor (eye 6). To illustrate the counsellor's intentions and interventions with the client, (eye 2) one member sat on the floor between them. For the relational foci, she asked counsellor and client to do a little dance together (eye 3) and supervisor and counsellor to do a dance (eye 5). The fifth member wove in and out, representing systems issues that might be affecting client, counsellor and/or supervisor, severally or collectively (eye 7). When they had clarified the different foci, she asked each one in turn to identify what they thought was their own most favoured focus; and then the one they seldom or never found themselves employing.

She was impressed with how readily they were able to do this, and it was clear that the exercise was both stimulating and relieving after the tension of the last piece of work. Among other comments, Maria said how hard she found it to relinquish her sense of managerial responsibility and that she would like to practise favouring other foci. Christine acknowledged that and stressed that it would be important for others to carry that focus if she relinquished it. After the coffee break, the group went on to do three more pieces of work. The first one Christine structured and organized by negotiating that each member would comment from one unfamiliar focus and that the presenter would then choose which she wanted to respond to. Of the remaining two, she asked the first presenter to choose a single focus that he would like to hold to, and asked the group to discipline themselves to holding that focus; and for the second she offered no suggestion and let the group free-flow. There was quite a lot of laughter as members recognized familiar or new interactions. The presenters reported that each session had been helpful.

Sharpening up a group's awareness of focus issues can, therefore, serve several purposes. It can release potential. It can be formative both for the whole group and for the counselling and self-supervision of individuals. It can help individuals challenge themselves about their own inflexibility. It can act as an exercise in cross-tribal empathy – perspectives which people have learned through their training to think of as 'right' and sometimes exclusively right, can be reviewed and extended in the light of fresh understanding. The supervisor, by sharing the responsibility of where and how to focus with the others, shifts 'transferential' responsibility. She is also protected from, and protects the group from, her own blind spots and favoured foci.

Supervisor-led, group member-led, counsellor-led

One remaining dimension of choice is the question of who decides how any bit of supervision will be done. The previous examples have shown the supervisor choosing to suggest how bits of work should be done. In one case this has been because of a wider agenda – the seven eyes; in another case – Christine's ten-minute quickie – time and the immediate issue determined the choice of method. However, the supervisor can ask the presenter how he wants to work and what he wants from the group. At a later stage of a co-operative group, either the presenter or another member of the group might suggest the method. As with other dimensions, there is seldom one 'right' choice – whatever choice is made will have implications for the individual presenter and her client; for the empowering or disempowering of individuals and the group as a whole; or for longer-term policies and strategies for group and individual development.

Case study 4 – Martin

By the end of their first year together, Martin's group was becoming increasingly proactive. He had facilitated an exercise in which they had explored their theoretical differences, declaring their beliefs and understanding about 'good practice'. This had shown up some strong differences – as much in style and personal preference as in theoretical orientation. Paradoxically, acknowledging these seemed to increase respect, trust and honesty with each other. The second review had been successfully completed. This time it included the opportunity for feedback to each other on their counselling style and skill. In addition, Martin introduced a devil's advocate exercise – 'If I were a client of yours I would like more x and less y.'

Martin continued to have an agreement that was essentially a co-operative one, though he had again emphasized that he wanted the members to take more responsibility, especially for what they wanted from their supervision. He had regularly initiated role-plays or exercises to involve them actively in co-supervising, while allowing plenty of free-flowing participation. This had given members a range of possibilities of how they might be helped to get what they were wanting.

Following the second review, Martin decided to facilitate the shift he hoped for. When the first presenting supervisee, Paula, had said what she wanted from supervision, and had talked a bit about her client issue, Martin broke in. Did she want to talk and get comments from the group, or would it be helpful to use one of the other methods he had shown them? Paula looked a bit disconcerted and said that she would be happy if Martin suggested one. He replied that he was wondering if there was one that she thought would match her mood or the issue. After thinking for a few seconds, she said that she would love to sit out and listen to the others talking about her and/or her client. She was finding the complexity of the case exhausting. Martin asked her if she wished to allocate different 'bits' of the case to different group members, but she said she would just like to describe her situation and problem and then sit back and listen.

After she had talked for some time, with group members occasionally clarifying some meaning or fact, Martin checked if she had said enough to trust the group to address salient issues. Both she and the group members said 'yes'. Martin asked Paula to sit well away from the group, and to listen as much or as little as she wanted to their discussion. He gave the group ten minutes to discuss what they had heard in the light of what Paula had said she wanted. The discussion was lively and people spontaneously took differing but complementary perspectives. There was a good deal of identification with Paula but two members also identified with the client and with the client's family, and wondered about the client's apparent inability to use her considerable resourcefulness in her own interest.

When Paula returned to the group, she said she was touched by their empathic understanding. It was such a relief to hear things spread out and it was as if the relationship had been defused for her. In fact, she now realized that she wished to focus on helping her client take action, however small, to gain some control in her life. Martin asked if she wanted to think about how she would make that shift in focus. Paula decided that her fresh understanding was enough for the time being – there was still a lot for her to think about. Felicity – laughingly, but speaking very directly to Paula – said that she expected the client might reply like that. Would Paula bring that client back to the next supervision group so that they could check if their work had been helpful, and encourage Paula if she was finding the switch of focus unrealistic? Paula groaned, and said she supposed she would if she had to – and everyone laughed.

Martin had to make quite a strong challenge to move Paula into taking responsibility for her own supervision. This is typical. One of the advantages of having a working agreement for active leadership is the permission it gives to push that little bit more than may feel 'respectful'. The agreement is in the service of co-ownership – an agreement which by this time in a group's life, has been made with informed consent. Evidence had shown Martin that such pushes had worked in the past with this rapidly developing group. That again validated the challenge he made.

It is tempting to speculate that Paula's initial reluctance was paralleling her client's process. Even after agreeing to take responsibility for her own session, she opted for a relatively passive structure. Perhaps the choice also said something about her identity and behaviour in the group. Would commenting on these processes have been an effective tactic in Martin's current strategy for the group, or for his overall strategy in relation to Paula's development as a counsellor?

To comment or not to comment on process?

Whether, when, and how to make process comments are recurring issues for a sophisticated group supervisor. There are frequently absorbing parallels between counselling and supervision process – reflections which can mirror in both directions. Supervision work can also seem to parallel issues in the group-as-system and individuals' roles and identities in the group.

Looked at analytically, members of Carmel's group, while identifying appropriately with client/counsellor issues, were also 'speaking' their identity issues in the group-as-system. They could be regarded as doing some gentle storming amongst themselves while experimenting with norming. Some supervisors might have pointed this out. Such opportunities are their 'bright spot' (Penny Henderson, in an unpublished paper, refers to Mary Burton's categorization of 'supervisor spots') – the thing they naturally focus on and cannot bear not to say. For others, it could be a 'blind spot' – something they failed to notice; or a 'dumb spot' – something they had never heard of as a possibility. Carmel noticed it, in retrospect, because she did know about such parallel processes. At the time her focus was on her identified task, and the emerging highlights which came to the fore against that background. If she had noticed, she would probably have chosen not to comment on it. How do supervisors choose whether and when to comment?

Strategically unhelpful comments

Carmel had a strategic aim for the session – to help individuals and the group become more self-confident and unselfconscious in co-supervising. Her tactical aim was to provide an open challenge in a protected space. Paradoxically, this would entail initial self-consciousness (the stage in the learning cycle of self-conscious incompetence). To change the learning focus by raising self-consciousness about individual identity in the group, or the process of the group-as-system, was not a priority. More, it would probably have detracted from their growth into unselfconscious competence.

She remarked to her consultant that she hoped the group would be more at ease with their age and gender differences after that piece of work. This indicates her assumption that learning in one system (the supervision system) unconsciously interacts with similar needed learning in related dimensions or systems. The choice of whether to make a process comment would not be problematic. She had enough learning agendas for group members for one session. They had their own learning to digest from each piece of work. She could check at a later date if transfer of learning, from the supervision session to group understanding, had been effected. Observation would show if Kate, Farah, Stephen and Mary were more at ease with each other. If difficulties with age and gender popped up in a new guise, interfering with their work, it would have to be addressed in that 'system'. In Stephen's piece of work, the dynamic was of use to him.

Another supervisor might work on the assumption that learning takes place mainly through conscious insight – bringing the unconscious into the conscious. The issue for that supervisor would also be 'How many insights can a person have at one time and learn from them?' and 'Which are my priorities for their/his/her learning?' Martin did not comment on Paula's choice of supervision method. As a Gestalt practitioner, he would value the development of process awareness for supervisees in general. However, his aim was to move the group into taking responsibility for what they wanted from supervision and how they wanted to do it. He had chosen Paula as his first 'mark' and received a tentative consent. She had taken her, albeit limited, plunge and gained fresh understanding. This was a first for the group and a first for her. A process comment about her reluctance, and how that might mirror her client's reluctance to use her resources in her own interest, might have been experienced as disrespectful to both. It would probably not have encouraged her to be more adventurous in future. Felicity, however, did make an oblique process comment – that the client might make the same reply as Paula – and followed it up by asking Paula to bring the client to the next group. As peer, the comment might be received without the transferential charge attaching to 'the leader'. That Felicity could make the comment, apparently spontaneously, was a sign that the group was on its way to being a co-operative group. It would be crucial, since that was what Martin wished for, that he did not enter into that exchange, or be triggered into competitive process commenting. The interchange should stand in its own right – and it would give information, consciously or unconsciously, about preparedness of group members to accept each other's leadership.

'There is anecdotal and empirical evidence that counsellors who are meeting their first clients, "learning to walk" and disentangling "content", can find process comments confusing' (Holloway 1995). The wish to grasp the erudite knowledge of the supervisor can interfere with their more immediate concerns. They can become competitive in being the first to 'spot a process' and take their eye off the task of making respectful and empathic relationships with clients, and with colleagues in the group.

Process comments as useful tactics

However, there will be times when process comments are valuable. If a supervisor is seeking to enlarge the group's outlook, to help them to an understanding of group and family dynamics, or, in the middle stages of their counselling work, sharpen their process awareness, they can be enlightening and exciting. When the group is well into norming and performing, the supervisor may want to share his sense of awe at the connectedness of systems. He may feel himself to be plodding and earth-bound and judge that members of the group are anxious for stretching. If process is his bright spot, it is depriving to keep it permanently under wraps. With such priorities, process comments can be magical. And, of course, process awareness is an internal and external skill which is an important part of any counsellor's vocabulary.

How to process comment

The 'how' of making process comments differs according to assumptions. If the person-to-person relationship is being fostered as the main vehicle for development, then process comments need to be personally owned – 'I've lost the thread – I thought we were addressing something which felt lively, but it's gone away . . .', rather than 'the group is avoiding the issue'. Also, to be considered by group members, process comments usually need to be offered tentatively as a personal hypothesis rather than as 'the Truth'. 'I keep wondering if your/our ideas or stereotypes about "the young" (or "older women" or "black women" or "men") are interfering with us discovering who each other is in a wider sense and also with your understanding of your client/s.' This example ties the comment in with the overall purpose of the supervision – this is not a therapy or process group.

Words only or more than words?

In her decision, Paula opted for her colleagues to discuss what she had presented to them. She could have accepted Martin's suggestion, and asked members of the group to represent different 'voices'. This could have been a discussion between voices which represented a variety of systems in which Paula and her client were enmeshed:

- differing strands of the client–counsellor interaction
- Paula's internal voices
- the imagined sub-personalities of her client
- different members of the client's family system
- the family and counselling system.

An alternative suggestion could have been that group members took 'roles' rather than 'voices'. Instead of a discussion, they could have enacted a mini-psychodrama. In this, they would have been using words, but accompanying them with actions. Or, taking more charge, Paula could have used her colleagues to 'sculpt' the differing personalities, sub-personalities, family dynamics, counselling relationship or whatever focus she chose. In that case, she would put them into position while they remained silent – only speaking when asked to say what they were experiencing in that position.

These four possibilities illustrate a spectrum of options for using colleagues:

- discussion within a light structure while she listened at a distance (Paula's choice);
- discussion taking imaginary voices of the presenter's choice – the dialogue staying in the hands of the non-presenting supervisees;
- enacting, still leaving the process and content in the hands of colleagues;
- sculpting, with the content and process in the presenter's hands.

The veracity with which these apparently imaginary discussions, dramas or sculpts dependably represent the counsellor's sub-conscious knowledge of the situation is startling. We do not know if the client material would have veracity for the client – some people believe such mini-dramas are products of projection rather than accurate projective identification. The only evidence of effect-iveness as a supervision technique is whether the counsellor goes back and is facilitative to the client. And, of course, she may have been in any case. The suggestion that Paula should report back at the following session, as well as being good support and chal-lenge to Paula, also provides information for informal research. Does supervision, and in this case playful group supervision, really work?

Freeflow and structure

All these examples of supervision work indicate that there is no such thing as unmanaged free flow or random discussion. Mostly, the supervisor will set the parameters in which the group oper-ates. At other times the group will develop a habit which goes unchallenged. As the group develops, or if it starts as a co-operative or peer group, any member will be empowered to lead or set limits to time, task or manners. The choice to use methods which are more structured and which intentionally use 'more than just words' to explore and reflect on client and counsellor issues, is the subject of the next chapter.

In summary

Table 9.1 (p. 152) suggests the different dimensions of choice which are offered to a group supervisor and facilitator when he is 'doing the work'. It is built around a version of Egan's Helping Process (1994), though any other model of supervision process could serve as well. The table is a map which can act as a reminder of choices that are not apparent in the heat of the moment, under pressure of time and conflicting demands. It is not a formula to be systematically and consciously followed. A developing supervisor can look at it from time to time as a reminder to be more varied and choiceful. In a co-operative group (Type 3) the supervisor could also consider and discuss this chart with the group in order to encourage devolving power and skill.

Random discussion is a supervision choice which requires management and skill in order to be effective. In groups, a major problem for presenter and supervisor can be confusion of focus. Like other responding skills, focus can be consciously taught and practised.

The choice of whether, when and how to make process comments is a continuing issue. Unlike some choices, it is more problematic as a supervisor becomes experienced and sophisticated. Reviewing strategic aims helps to clarify the 'whether' and the 'when'. Process comments, like any action taken (or not taken) in a group, are tactics to be used in the service of priorities.

As a group develops, members have access to a greater range of ways that colleagues can participate in their supervision. This allows temporary leadership to be taken by, or given to, the presenter or other group member.

10 Inviting creativity

Structures as catalysts

Free or random discussion elicits words – brainstorms. Ideas and imagination are sparked. Structured exercises are devised to elicit information that lies behind words. The story, about client or issue, is spread as a backcloth. The presenter, the supervisor and the group members give attention to this story. A structured exercise focuses their attention and offers a channel for accessing and expressing information which is not in conscious awareness. When this fresh and unexpected information interacts with the story, the story is transformed. The structure has been a catalyst.

Words can do this but they can also represent stereotypical ideas and mental frameworks that may preclude fresh understanding. We understand in terms of our maps of the world, and they are limited and sometimes limiting. In Christine's group, Phil thought that it was 'not important' to talk about his client. Those words, and the idea represented by them, prevented him exploring further. Although she had heard similar words many times, Christine decided to focus on them within a particular structure. Subsequently, she asked his colleagues to 'be' someone different for Phil – his client. This engaged their ability to take the role of another and 'know' fresh information from that position. In speaking *to the client* – an imaginative leap which engaged his ability for internal travel through time and space – Phil's words had a different significance. They elicited sensations and emotions of which he had been unaware. In imagination, he was with his client and recognized the interaction differently. In turn, this freed him to behave differently.

'Creative structures' can focus attention on any or all of the senses – sight, sound, sensation, smell, taste. They can invite fresh contact with external stimuli – what does she *really* look like? How might I draw her? What impulses do I have – to run, to touch, to shake, to embrace? What are the pitch, the tones and rhythms of her speech? If we were physically fighting, what would be happening? They can turn attention to the inner world of experience – self-talk, imagination and sensation, and the blend which is emotion. They can invite the transposition of any of this information to different contexts of time and place. They may encourage almost infinite mixing and matching within the boundaries of real time and task.

Predictability and unpredictability

'To create' means 'making something'. The adjective 'creative', or the noun 'creativity', usually carry extra connotations. They imply an act of imagination. Something new will emerge as a result of putting pieces together – either pieces not usually associated with each other, or traditional pieces put together in different ways. In a simple *act of creation*, the maker may scrupulously put together known ingredients to obtain predictable results. A person seeking to be *creative* will expect the overall results to be relatively unpredictable. The *creation* of anything usually entails craftsmanship – which may be highly skilled, aspiring or poor. The *process of creativity* also builds on craftsmanship and the quality of the resulting innovation will probably be in proportion to skill. Art emerges from craft.

In counselling and psychotherapy, the effects of interactions between person and person are relatively unpredictable. Our models of human behaviour are still quite primitive as is our ability to map and measure complex psychology and physiology. Attempts to research effective practice often result in oversimplification in the interests of replicability or comparability. Supervision of an individual within a participating group is even less likely to be predictable. To that extent, all group supervision will be creative – it will be putting only partially known ingredients together to obtain relatively unpredictable results.

Desirability and additional skill

Intentional creativity is desirable in a group because it allows into awareness what is known, by the counsellor and the group members, about the client and the counsellor. Each group member will know far more than she realizes. In addition, she may consciously know some things that she would not like to express in ordinary group discussion. Creative methods access both kinds of intelligence.

Group discussion can become stereotyped (as Christine found in the example quoted in the previous chapter). Moreover, if there are unacknowledged dynamics and agendas within the group, words can be used to conceal or compete. Creative methods focus attention on the supervision issue. At other times they can be used to focus on building, maintaining and repairing the working alliance.

However, the power to break through self-protectiveness and take defences by surprise can be experienced as destructive. This *may* be helpful to the task or to the development of the working group, if members are respected and encouraged to know when they want to say 'no'. ('There is no re-construction without de-struction' (Perls 1947).) Since the agreed goal of supervision is increased counsellor competence and confidence, intentionally working in a creative way has to be within limits and boundaries of the task and of individual capability and consent.

Using all the available potential of the group calls for creative facilitation and the ability to think and work creatively as a supervisor. It brings both challenge and tension. Unpredictability is anarchic. The unexpected falls outside immediate rules and structures. So a creative supervisor – and creative supervisees – have to develop additional skills. They need to be able to think about ways 'to reach parts other methods do not reach', while monitoring what is effective for time and task. They also have to become adept at responding appropriately to the unexpected within these limits.

The enabling unconscious

In a recent radio discussion, Jonathan Miller was mourning the loss of the idea of the 'enabling unconscious'. This was apparently being developed in the nineteenth century but was overtaken by Freud's perspective on the unconscious. Humanistic psycho-therapies, and more recent developments from those – Kagan (1980) and Gendlin (1978), for instance – have reverted to the idea of the unconscious as friend (1, 2). This chapter assumes, as spelt out in Chapter 1, that:

- holding to the agreed focus of the task, while respecting boundaries, creates space for inquiry, play and discourse;
- functional and dysfunctional Child states and behaviour will surface in Adult group work;
- individuals, and the group-as-system, can have a playful and easy relationship with the 'unconscious';
- unconscious material demands profound respect.

Dimensions of creativity – the matrices

Free flow/structure

The last chapter identified that free-flowing discussion will always take place within some holding 'structure' or ground rules. This may be the widest remit of the overall working agreement or it may be within a more closely holding structure agreed on the spot. Structures can also be used to elicit and contain information or interaction which is predominantly non-verbal. The structure – like the structure of a country dance – is the boundary which contains and encourages energetic freedom.

Figure 10.1 suggests dimensions of creative structures. These are drawn as matrices. Any creative structure used could probably be mapped on one or more of these matrices. The device is offered as an aid to skilful and intentional creativity.

Intention

In each case, the vertical continuum remains the same. When the supervisor suggests a creative structure he may at first do so on an intuitive hunch. However, he should become progressively aware whether

- he has a clear and specific intent which he is pursuing in some creative way (the top of the continuum);
- he has an agenda, but expects or hopes for some unexpected learning (the midpoint on the continuum);
- he is offering a creative play-space, with no specific intent beyond the overall aims of supervision, whether for the individual or for the group.

If the supervisor believes that a supervisee 'needs' to see or think about a particular issue, he will intentionally employ methods for the supervision work which could achieve that result. If there is a

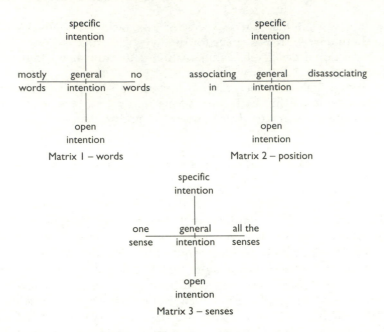

Figure 10.1   *Mapping creative structures*

general group agenda, as in the example below, the method needs to be carefully geared to that learning aim.

Matrix 1 – words

Matrix 1 suggests a horizontal continuum which starts with reliance on the spoken word; which, at the mid-point, uses more than words; and at the extreme end, uses few or no words.

In the example of Carmel's group (Chapter 7), she had a dual linked agenda. She wished the group to 'grow up' and become less compliant. She also wanted them to become more spontaneous and proactive as co-supervisors. She used minimal structure to encourage free-flowing discussion, by

- reminding them of their shared agreement to offer reflective space;
- asking for a 'soft' mini-contract from each presenter;
- asking someone to be time-keeper in order to devolve her responsibilities;
- promising them time to give and get feedback at the end.

The simple structure allowed increasingly energetic and playful engagement. On Matrix 1, it would fall on the far left – it relied entirely on words. On the vertical axis it would be at the top – Carmel had two clear intentions.

Developing counselling skill

Skills exercises are structures. Simplicity can be very powerful.

Case study 3 – Christine

In Christine's supervisor development group, a fellow member, David, who was supervisor to trainees, wanted to help them improve their ability to listen and respond with 'first-level empathy' – no interpretations, hunches, premature connections, reframing. Particularly, he wished them to be more accurate in 'hearing' what emotions were being spoken of, and better at noticing subtle degrees of emotion. He asked the development group to let him try an experimental exercise with them called the Noddy Jackpot.

David managed the exercise. One member spoke about a client for a few minutes until David noticed a natural break. Members in turn had to pick up one 'piece' of the story, giving it back without alteration or embellishment. 'She came in looking fraught.' 'You had overrun the last client and were busy writing up your notes.' 'She is a single parent and has three children.' 'Last session, she told you she had been hit frequently by both father and mother.' And so on. If the statement was absolutely accurate, the presenter nodded vigorously. If it did not quite 'ring true' she made facial expressions or physical movements which indicated the degree of accuracy. The respondent would have one more try and if that was inaccurate the presenter could remind her what she *had* said.

That went on until the whole 'story' had been covered (not necessarily in its original order). David then asked the presenter for the next chapter and the process was repeated.

He stopped the exercise after the second round and asked for feedback. His fellow supervisors were shocked at how hard they found it to stay with such simplicity of response. They commented on their embarrassment when they 'got it wrong' and some frustration at what seemed simplistic. They could see it could be useful for trainees. The presenter shook her head. She had found it useful and refreshing, despite the apparent 'messiness'. Half of what she had said in her 'story' she had forgotten – it was like hearing it afresh, with a chance to really 'hear' it. When the respondent got it even slightly 'wrong' she was amazed at how important the inaccuracy was to her – 'No, not 'depressed' – I said she was 'harassed and chronically fatigued'.

Christine thought about her own group and decided that they were getting a bit 'too clever'. It would be interesting to see if they found it hard to go back to basics. She realized, ruefully, that she did.

Trainees obviously have the task of developing counselling skills through supervision (3). Experienced counsellors may have as much to learn. Their skill has become automatic, and new skills learning creates self-consciousness. 'Games' can be amusing and informative, while remaining respectful to client and practitioner.

David's exercise forced respondents to focus on words with unusual intensity. Breaking the story into small pieces stopped the presentation becoming a screen for projections. Focusing on exact words prevented each piece being 'tweaked' because of the respondent's bright, deaf, blind and dumb spots. Indeed, these were rather mercilessly exposed. By hearing back the accurate and inaccurate story in this way, the presenter disassociated from it, and heard it afresh.

On Matrix 1 the exercise lies at the top of the vertical axis, and at the centre of the horizontal. It also engaged hearing and disassociation.

Matrix 2 – associating in and disassociating

Matrices 2 and 3 indicate additional resources, other than words, which can be harnessed for supervision. Matrix 2 reminds us of our capacity to position ourselves – psychologically – in different places in relation to an issue we may be exploring. (Such a change of view is greatly helped when we actually move our bodies to different positions.)

At one end of the continuum is an invitation to *associate in* to their own, or another's experience – 'be your client' or 'if you were the counsellor, what would you be experiencing?' The middle axis represents the differing distances that it is possible to take from the experience being explored. At the end is the 'helicopter position', beyond the gravitational pull of inhibiting forces in the client/counsellor field – intentionally disassociating. (This is different from our capacity to *unintentionally dissociate* when an event is too traumatic for us to experience physically.) Paula's session in Martin's group harnessed this potential. By sitting well away from the group she disassociated herself and could 'rise above' the interpersonal dynamics to see and feel what might be helpful for her client. Had she asked her colleagues to use role-play, she would have been asking them to *associate in* to a 'voice' or sub-personality.

Structures that allow changes of viewpoint and experience can also be simple.

Case study 1 – Ruth

In the third term of their supervision, Ruth's trainee counsellors were expected to be able to talk about their relationship with their clients in terms of transference and counter-transference. Most of them still found it difficult to do that. Ruth prepared a written form with some simple headings –

- What do I particularly notice about the way the client speaks to, or interacts, with me?
- Who do I imagine she might have been this way with before?
- Who might I 'be' for her? What might I represent for her?
- How do I feel in response to this?
- How do I find myself interacting with her?
- Is this the way I usually feel if people relate to me in a similar way?
- If so, is it unhelpful to the client? (Note: Bring this issue to supervision to find how other people might react – is this a therapy/counselling issue for you?)
- If this is an unusual reaction for me, what information does it give me that could be helpful in the counselling?

She gave each supervisee a copy and asked them to fill it in for every client they were seeing. When they met, she first dealt with urgent issues in her normal supervision way. She then asked one or two of the group to present their client from their forms. She allowed time for other members to say how they tended to react to similar behaviour.

Pieter said that his client bragged a good deal. He found himself wanting to put him down. Everyone in the group felt the same. Ruth pointed out that this was probably counter-transference and he could surmise that his client met this response regularly.

Rosa said that her client remained sad and seldom looked up when she talked about her grief. This had gone on over the weeks she had known her and it had the effect of making Rosa want to shake her. Others in the group felt differently. Ruth did not take up these differences, but asked Rosa if she felt she might have difficulties around loss and grief. Looking embarrassed, she replied that she thought there was a time for grieving and a time for getting on with life. She knew she should not make that kind of judgement as a counsellor, but that was what she thought and it was difficult to change deeply held beliefs.

Ruth was clear that within her stated supervision model, acknowledging a counselling difficulty belonged in supervision; 'working' on it belonged in counselling. She acknowledged Rosa's embarrassment, saying that discovering an issue like that was a milestone in a counsellor's development. It was in order to facilitate such development that this course required trainees to have a therapeutic space for themselves throughout their training. She suggested that Rosa talked about her thinking and feeling around loss and mourning with her counsellor. She might find that there were some unresolved issues which she could fruitfully work on, or she might discover that her impatience was a counter-transferential response to the client.

In this example, Ruth had a clear learning agenda for the trainees. The written form was her way of helping them, economically, with their required learning. It was helpful for all group members – it brought difficult concepts to life. Her method was creative. It used words in a written and spoken form. In asking themselves specific questions about behaviour, thinking and emotional reaction, they had to practise 'going in' to self-scan their reactions to their clients, and also distance themselves in order to 'look at' their relationship from a specific point of perspective.

The grey zone

Perls, Hefferline and Goodman (1972) reportedly said that we live our lives in the 'grey area' – neither 'in' our experiencing nor at an effective distance from it. Using the written form required the counsellors to break out of the grey zone. It broke through their habit of 'telling the story'. An information-giving session on complex concepts would not have necessitated a change of perspective.

Because it utilized information which was previously out of the awareness of group members, its outcome was unpredictable. Rosa made an unexpected discovery and suffered some embarrassment. Since this was a Type 1 group – supervision by the supervisor supplemented by members as invited – Ruth was able to take back the reins cleanly and manage the supervision in accordance with her stated model. She was sensitive to Rosa's embarrassment, pointed to a suitable resource and noted for herself the unexpected outcome of her device. That was the extent of her contracted responsibility.

On Matrix 1 the method would lie at the top of the vertical axis. She had a teaching agenda. Horizontally, it would lie in the middle of the left-hand side – Ruth used words only, but experimented with using the written word as an additional resource.

On Matrix 2, the self-scanning would lie somewhere to the left of the mid-line. She wished her supervisees to become aware of the experience they had with the client. The reflecting part of the exercise would lie to the right of the mid-line. She did not want them to observe their interaction from outer space but she did want them to be freed from unconscious reactions.

Matrix 3 – engaging the senses

Matrix 3 maps the potential for using our senses intentionally. To the left, only one sense is specifically engaged. So, for instance, asking a supervisee to draw expressively, or make a figure of the client's family would be engaging *sight* specifically. (It is worth noting that expressive drawing also engages movement and invites the drawer to *associate in* to his own experience; while 'mapping', or making a diagram, also entails a 'sense of position' and invites the mapmaker to *disassociate* or look from outside the system he is addressing.) At the centre-point, asking someone to move about and make a sound would be engaging *sound and movement*. To the right, the exercise would actively engage *all the senses* in exploration.

Case study 4 – Martin

After his first punishing review, Martin became aware that the working agreement he had offered the group had effectively disempowered him. He had deprived the group members of his experience and expertise and frustrated himself. He remembered their competitive discussions, and how he had longed to 'bring them to their senses'. The new contract following the review gave him permission to lead, and also stung him into showing his paces.

In negotiating the agenda for the day, three counsellors said they wanted to introduce new clients to the group and have a chance to think about them. Martin asked if they were prepared to experiment by engaging their senses in exploration, and they all agreed. He asked each to pair with another member or with him. He spoke privately with the non-presenting members, asking them to write down a simple list of questions to ask their supervisee. He told them to hold the focus of the question and not to let the counsellor waffle. He informed everyone that there were three minutes for this part of the exercise. They paired off, and did the task. The questions were:

- What flower does your client look like?
- What animal does he sound like?
- What substance would he smell like?
- What dance does he move like?
- What material does he have the texture/feel of?
- What food would he taste like?

There was a good deal of laughter during the three minutes. Martin then asked the 'listener' to give a feeling reaction to the information she had heard, and the counsellor to take five minutes to reflect on what he had taken from the exercise. The following ten minutes was spent in processing the exercise in the group. One of the presenters said that he had thought the exercise would be disrespectful to his client. However, on reflection, he had surprised himself by his answers and had become aware of a gracefulness and dignity in his client which her rather anxious manner had disguised. Another was struck by the incongruity of her own answers – her client now seemed more complex than she had realized. The student counsellor suggested that they add a further ground rule – 'In this group, we will give anything that is suggested, one try.'

This structured exercise could be plotted on the middle of Matrix 1. Martin had a clear general intention – to engage the senses of his group. He had no specific aim for individuals. The exercise used words extensively – in exploring and in reflecting. It also relied on 'more than words'.

On Matrix 2, it falls on the extreme left – the exercise invited the counsellors to associate into their 'felt senses' of the client.

On Matrix 3, it would be mapped at the extreme right of the horizontal continuum. It actively engaged each sense.

Every exercise affects the life of a group. Pairing up gives privacy to each presenter, serving to lower competitiveness. It offers less exposure. This may have been Martin's intention. It certainly signalled his change of *leadership style*, while demonstrating that he was not going to take over as sole or even active *supervisor*. He stayed true to his wish for the group to *become* a co-

operative Type 3 group, while acting in a way that was appropriate to a mature participative Type 2 group.

Sensory acuity

Sensory acuity is the ability to be fully alive to all our senses – to let
them inform us in our life and work. Maps for appreciating and
using sensory capabilities have improved. The self-supervising
technique of Interpersonal Process Recall (Kagan 1980) suggests
inquirer questions that cover most of the internal and external
reactions it is possible to have to another person. Neurolinguistic
Programming (NLP) and the sensate focus work of Gendlin (1978)
have uncovered processes for storing and recalling our experiences through the variety of sensory channels. All of these draw
on the pioneering work of Fritz Perls and neurolinguists and
neurophysiologists. Developmentally, we are on a cusp. Behind
us lie intuitive skills described in terms of metaphor. Ahead
lie explanations based on neurophysiological processes. Writing
about sensory acuity, I am self-consciously aware of my ignorance
of neurology and also of mistrust for previous metaphorical
constructs. I have tried to map the understanding I have drawn
from the sources I have had access to in as simple terms as
possible. My object is to offer a reminder of the brilliance of our
human abilities for gathering, storing, processing, retrieving and
using sensory information. This brilliance can be masked in a
group, or it can be liberated and used.

Case study 2 – Carmel

Carmel wanted to raise the awareness of the trainees in her group. Since
they were on different counselling courses, and had different life experiences, the extent to which they were self-aware varied considerably. She
looked up Interpersonal Process Recall (IPR) questions and then compared them with NLP formulations she had encountered on a short
course. During the check-in, she 'booked' half an hour for an exercise.
She likened the exercise to a workout in the gym – some of the sensory
muscles they would be invited to use would respond quite well; others
might be stiff. She asked if they had any questions and if they were
interested/prepared to do the workout. In answer to questions about
the purpose and nature of the exercise, she said that the purpose was to
help them audit their current awareness so that they could, if they
wished, create an exercise programme for themselves. She wished them

to be in trim for doing creative supervision work together. As to the content of the exercise, she asked them to take it on trust. Farah said that she was feeling rather vulnerable that day and said she would rather not join in. Carmel took her statement at face value and suggested that she sat a little outside the group, within earshot of Carmel's instructions. She could switch off from them entirely if she wished. Farah said, wryly, that she might go to sleep. Carmel said that she was welcome to do that – and meant it.

She then ran an awareness exercise with the others. Inviting them to relax and sit comfortably, she asked them to be aware of their breathing, and to respect it; to skim over the counselling sessions they had had in the previous week, noting incidents that came to mind and letting them go; to notice a particular incident that they were curious about and to hold it in their mind. She then slowly went through the following 'inquirer prompts'.

- As you look at the client's face, what specifically do you notice?
- What colour are you aware of?
- What texture?
- Does that remind you of anything you have noticed before in your life?
- What do you imagine the client would look like as a child of eight?
- What might your client look like in ten years' time?
- If you were to look in through the window at both of you, what would you see?
- What would you notice about the way you were sitting?
- Can you recollect what you were experiencing as you sat in that manner?
- What was your breathing like?
- How did your face feel? Your stomach? Your bottom? Your legs and feet?
- If you were experiencing any emotion, what would it be? And another?
- How do you know that was what you were feeling?
- As you notice that, recollect your client's voice – notice the pitch of voice, the speed of voice, the rhythm of the words.
- Does the voice remind you of anything you have heard before in your life?
- As you hear that voice, become aware of what you are saying to yourself in your head.
- Where in your head is any conversation going on?
- Is there more than one voice?
- What is the pitch of your main inner voice?

- As you are aware of any inner conversation, recollect what you were saying to the client.
- If you were listening as a fly on the wall what would you notice about your conversation?
- Back in your seat, if there were to be a smell in the room, what would it be?
- And if there were a taste in your mouth, what would it be?
- If you were back there and could move around freely, what movements might you want to make?
- How do you imagine your client might react?
- Notice anything that you might want to say to the client as a result of this exercise and imagine saying it.
- How does the client respond?
- What response does your body have to that conversation?

At the end, Carmel invited them to come back slowly into present awareness, moving gently from their own inner world to become aware of their present surroundings and, when and as they felt ready, making eye contact with other people. She noticed that Farah also seemed to 'come to' at the same time. She asked her if she wished to join in the processing of the exercise and she replied that she would like to be part of it, though she might not join in.

Carmel then suggested that anyone could say anything they wanted to say about the experience. Kate said that she had 'wandered off' early on, but that she had 'come back' when asked what she might want to do and say. She knew that she wanted to move closer to her client and tell her that she felt extremely sad for her. Mary reported staying with the exercise most of the time but she found herself 'making up' answers to some of the questions. Her client did not really remind her of anyone, but she told herself that she might have been like an aunt she could hardly remember. Stephen said that he had become aware that he had been in internal conversation with himself throughout the exercise – doing it on one hand and talking to himself about it on the other. Farah said that she had been in a delightful reverie – she could not remember the content but she felt very refreshed. Perhaps that was what 'restorative' supervision was! Desmond, a new member of the group, asked what use the exercise would be for his counselling work. He didn't imagine that Carmel would want him to feel free to do and say what he wanted. Carmel asked the others what they thought about that and a lively discussion followed. At the end, Carmel summarized that being more aware did not give licence to act or speak thoughtlessly. As sensory muscles became more active and attuned, the possibilities for respect, empathic understanding and congruent communication increase.

In this exercise, Carmel was setting up a marathon sensory workout. She suggested a visit to all five senses – visual, auditory, kinaesthetic (physical awareness), smell and taste. She focused on external sight and the inner eye of imagination; external hearing and hearing the inner voices; specifying internal sensations and linking those with named emotions. She presumed on an ability for time travel – to be in the recent past, the further past, the future and the immediate present – all in seconds. She encouraged space travel – in and out of the room, on the wall, in the chair, imaginary moving around. She drew attention to 'movement' in perception, will and understanding as a result of increased awareness. No doubt she returned to the exercise at a later date – helping participants identify what had been easy and what hard for them.

She had been prepared for some distress. Perhaps because she was sensitive and respectful of people's choices, this did not occur. She had underestimated the time the exercise would take, and had someone become distressed, she would have had to choose whether to renegotiate the final piece of supervision work, or over-ride the distress in some way.

Everyday pieces

This chapter cannot do justice to the potential of creative group supervision. When supervisors in training are asked to brainstorm every possible creative exercise they have used or could imagine (with clients or supervisees) the list is endless. Many have never thought of using familiar devices in a supervision context. Creativity is helped by a conducive location – spacious, relatively comfortable, with potential for using, for example, paper, colour, clay, soft toys as props; better still if it is sound-proofed or isolated from other users. Even in cramped and cramping circumstances, there are props to hand. The contents of handbags and briefcases; clothing and jewellery; all can be used as projection objects – as metaphors or to elicit comparisons. Bowls of pebbles or buttons can be used to map or 'stand for' different aspects of client/counsellor relationships.

Simple role-play and enactment need little space. 'I would like to off-load. Will you shoulder my frustration? You hold my boredom at arm's length. You carry some of my sadness, and you sit over there and represent my sneaking scepticism.'

Case study 3 – Christine

Sometimes Christine's group members were hesitant in volunteering to 'go first'. 'Who's going first then?' Silence, followed by demurring. 'Right, each in turn mime the issue you are going to bring.' Two very heavies, one bouncy ball and another laid-back and stretched out. The fifth scrunched up in a foetal position. 'So how do we decide the order?' Each says who should go first and why. Three takers for a heavy first and fourth, interspersed by the bouncy ball and the scrunch, ending up with the laid-back. 'OK? Off you go then, number 1.'

Developing creative practice

Intentionally creative practice calls for similar skill on the part of the supervisor as any participative group supervision. To recap on Chapter 5, this requires:

- flexible ability for active leadership, receptivity, 'followership', and assertiveness;
- the ability to develop a climate of empathy, respect, authenticity and purposefulness;
- a trust in the body's sense and the reliability and literalness of physical imagery;
- a developed capacity for spontaneity, balanced by rapid self-scanning;
- ready maps for processing;
- ability to use and develop those maps in the light of experience.

The skills are the same but additional maps are needed for the particular tasks of initiating, facilitating and managing creative structures. The dimensions and matrices explored earlier in the chapter are offered as useful mapping devices. In addition, there are rules of thumb for good practice. The table is not definitive but is intended as a starting point for new group supervisors, or as a checklist for the experienced supervisor.

Creative exercises – when?

Many of the examples of creative work have illustrated a supervisor's wish for the group as a whole to learn some specific skill:

Table 10.1   *Guidelines for good practice for setting up and managing creative structures*

'Trawl the water' in order to get a sense of whether the presenter/group are in the mood for an exercise.

Make clear the purpose and structure of the exercise (at the outset or when it has become clear to you).

Make clear your expectations of members, at the start and subsequently.

Demonstrate/model what is meant/expected.

Share, or get volunteers for, tasks, e.g. time-keeping, roles in exercise.

Be respectful and empathic when reframing or correcting responses which do not accord with 'rules' of the exercise.

Do not let by too many 'wrong' responses – the group will be uneasy if you patronize or over-protect.

Keep to time and role boundaries.

Negotiate (or at least 'flag') when you want to alter boundaries.

Always, always, always debrief.

Allow sufficient time for debriefing according to the powerfulness of the exercise, so that no one is knowingly left 'holding' feelings from the case; and so that participants have a chance to express disengagement or anger, etc. with the exercise.

Check in the following session if you suspect there may be 'leftovers': share thoughts you have had in the interim.

Leave sufficient free dialogue presentations between 'bossy' exercises.

Source: Adapted from Inskipp and Proctor 1995

- Martin wanted his group, as counsellors, to develop sensory awareness;
- Christine wanted her participants, as co-supervisors, to develop variety in focusing;
- Ruth wanted her members, as supervisees and as counsellors, to develop psychodynamic understanding;
- Carmel wanted her group, as co-supervisors and as counsellors, to become more responsive to their sensory knowledge.

In all instances, they thought that an experiential exercise would be immediate as a learning medium and congruent with the desired learning.

In every case the supervisor sought the consent of the presenter and/or group. If either are not potentially in an experimental mood, they will not be open to 'play'. The exception was when Christine 'risked' playing with focus when an uncomfortable incident between Maria and a team member had just been aired. Perhaps the signal in that case was that Maria had ended the exercise with a warm and empathic response to the team member. The worst of the anger had been dissipated through expression. Because Christine deliberately shielded her from having to face the account directly and respond personally, Maria was able to listen to and hear her colleague's experience. In that instance, the playful exercise acted as a relief from tension.

On other occasions, the complexity of a presentation, or the dispirited delivery of the presenter may invite some creative response. Often, the impulse will spring from the nature of the session – it seems to 'call' for a break from talk. As we have seen, time may indicate some swift, creative gesture. Group occasions may merit a response which penetrates beyond words. The supervisor may feel in a playful mood, or she or a group member may want to 'try something out'. If the timing is appropriate, such energy is infectious and induces a special kind of learning.

Balancing free flow and structure

Within a session, or over time, freedom and structure should be in balance. Within each structured or experiential exercise, the same is true. 'Knowing' about the appropriate dance between structure and free flow is primarily a sensory knowing. If a supervisor has not been engaged in creative exercises during his training or other development, he may not have a sense of rhythm and boundaries 'in his bones'. He will almost certainly have some comparable sense of other dances. I suggest that this is a 'deep structure'. The initially self-conscious development of skill in creative supervision elicits that sense of deep structure. (If you are sceptical about this, think back to the introduction of 'helping micro-skills' programmes, such as those of Truax and Carkhuff (1967) or Egan (1994). Traditionalists feared that such programmes would breed counsellors who permanently worked by rote. What usually happens is that micro-skills elicit buried treasure. For those who 'have' helping skill at some deep level, the micro-skills provide a flexible 'vocabulary', which allows the development of personal style and abilities.)

Tight and loose structures

Some structures are fairly loose. When Paula sat out and listened to her colleagues' discussion, there was a considerable freedom of time and focus within general boundaries. On the other hand, a structure may be extremely tight – for instance, Martin's three-minute exercise, which invited participants to say such things as what animal their client sounded like. Tightness serves a purpose

– by constricting space and time, it aids focus, which in turn elicits the ejection of unexpected sensory (or in another terminology, subconscious) material. His instructions to the 'inquiring partner' were exact – 'write down the words I want you to use'; 'three minutes only'; 'no waffle'. From experience of using such exercises in a training context, he 'knew' that such a tight exercise needed to be carefully set up. It also required at least double the length of time for reflection and processing. Awareness which is 'ejected' is dense – it requires unpacking and sorting if it is to be an aid to improved practice.

Clear, specific, positive

In setting up and managing structures, the 'director' – usually the supervisor but sometimes another group member – needs to be exact in giving directions. The words used are building a psychological arena within which new information can emerge, be safely contained and played with. Words, and how they are laid, matter as much as the bricks used by a builder in a physical structure. (Luckily, that does not require perfection.) They need to speak to the 'unconscious'. In such exercises work is done in an altered state – a mild trance. Time is experienced as longer or shorter than 'reality'. Group members 'happen' for themselves without conscious decision. They can do this if they are clear what is expected of them and have been given boundaries of role, time and space. If they are unsure or unsafe, they will stop themselves becoming so engaged. The unconscious does not recognize a negative. If you invite someone not to imagine an elephant, they cannot but imagine it. So participants should be given instructions in the positive rather than the negative.

Coming up for air

'Coming out', if the exercise has been powerful, is a strange experience. When participants are fully in awareness, they may want to make contact and check out 'where they are' in relation to other participants. Group members who have not engaged in shared trance will feel painfully or angrily out of it. The supervisor, or director of an exercise, holds, or loses, the group through the power of words. He cannot hope to hold all of the group all of the time. However, he has the responsibility of being aware when he has lost individuals or members, and of noticing when the group is aware or unaware of such losses. This is particularly necessary when he sets up an exercise or supports a group member to do so. This is someone's opportunity for presenting. It is other members' opportunity to engage usefully as co-supervisors. He has to be mindful and curious about what words help to create an engaging and useful exercise. He has also to continue to develop theories about what helps who and why – including how specific words helped or hindered people participating effectively for themselves and in the service of the task.

Cathartic experience

At the start of the chapter, creative exercises were described as catalytic. It was also suggested that, in using them, supervisor and group need to become able to respond appropriately to the unexpected. Participants can be moved to tears or to anger by their experience. If, for instance, the role, or position (in a sculpt), that they take touches upon an experience of their own, the emotion which follows is deeply personal as well as identificatory. They may not be able to shake off the emotion when the exercise is at an end. In the early stages of a group, they and/or fellow participants may be embarrassed by strong personal emotions, and fear or shame may intensify an already confusing experience.

Before using creative methods, supervisors should know what their attitude to such incidents is. Ruth would take care not to provide the circumstances in which they happened. If, by chance, she had, she would have treated the supervisee with empathy and respect and suggested that she take the issue to her counsellor. Carmel and Christine would probably have allowed space for some 'dis-stressing' (Christine's ground rules included 'cry if you want to' and Carmel was happy for a supervisee, on occasion, to sit out and go to sleep if she wanted to.) They would probably choose to negotiate some extra time for the distressed participant to debrief. Martin, a Gestalt and transpersonal practitioner, might believe that bringing such material into the open and acknowledging it as an important part of 'life's rich tapestry' is crucial learning for developing counsellors. Cathartic expression, for him, might be a valuable personal and group experience to be encouraged rather than guarded against. As in all situations, stated and intentional priorities determine appropriate responses to events.

For any supervisor, it might feel appropriate to encourage the person to share in the group personal material which the exercise had thrown up. There would be learning in this for members and supervisor. However, since this is a supervision group, such sharing should not be pressured in any way.

The supervisor's responsibility remains with supervision work, and reflective space for each participant. If further supervision work remains, it might be appropriate to suggest that one other group member take time out with the person who is distressed while the supervisor and the rest of the group continue the work. If one member frequently becomes overcome by experiential work, this is information which will affect the supervisor's judgement about appropriate supervision methods. She will need to consider her own skill at initiating and managing exercises. She may also need to decide if the supervisee has personal issues which are unresolved and might affect her ability as a counsellor. As we saw earlier, some people can experience extraordinary vulnerability in groups. Their distress does not necessarily imply general dysfunction. Supervisors need to take these questions to their own consultant or group and reflect on the implications for supervisor practice and the supervisee's welfare and that of her client.

Debriefing

Because anyone can get caught in a role or a trance-like state, debriefing is essential. It can take a simple form. 'I am Felicity. I am with Martin in X and I can see Ben sitting opposite me.' If the exercise has included role-play, it helps personal awareness to add, 'I can identify with the client whose part I took because I can be sulky and feel hard-done by: I am different from her, because I am now aware when I am doing it and have some choice.'

Sometimes, moving about, 'shaking out' or chatting with each other for a few minutes serves to bring individuals and the group into 'real time'. If there is light 'bubbling' in the group it is important to honour it and go with the flow. If there is a sombre reflective mood, that too needs to be honoured and allowed expression.

Semi-detached reflection – no re-supervising

Whether the supervision work has consisted of discussion or experiential work, it is always desirable to take time for shared reflection on the piece of work when the presenter's 'time' is finished. This defines a separate but linked space – one might call it semi-detached – which allows each member to speak about her experience of the work – 'How was it for you?' In this time, new material may emerge. Frequently the group will revert to re-supervising, but that piece of work is finished for today. The stated purpose of processing allows counsellor or supervisor to assert the right of proper protection. The counsellor is now in a different role – that of group member – and shares the task of co-processing.

Words as transitional objects

A final comment on the power of words and the skill of mindfulness with words. Words are, in Winnicott's (1974) imagery, transitional objects. They are *outward, social, shared, relatively objective* expressions of *inner, subjective, private, personal* experience. As suggested earlier, they can as well be used to disguise as to reveal. They tie together the personal culture and the shared culture, or they spectacularly fail to do so. If supervision is a major learning and developmental forum for beginning and experienced counsellors, language is crucial. The supervisor has a special responsibility for using lively language that expresses her meaning as closely as possible. She also has to take care to clarify meaning and to encourage group members not to make assumptions about personal meanings.

In summary

When a group supervisor intentionally uses creative methods he is intending to elicit information which lies behind words. The information is vested in our senses. Structured exercises are built around aspects of awareness and, through focusing attention, act as catalysts for fresh understanding. By nature the fresh information is anarchic and can be unpredictable. It draws on the enabling unconscious, and can also elicit the distressed unconscious.

Supervisors need to become increasingly able to build structures which enable, and also need to respond appropriately to, unexpected results of their work. The three matrices are a first attempt (by the author, that is) to map some well-used dimensions of creative work. They are intended as aids to more skilled and intentional exercise building. Some identified guidelines for good practice are offered which complement the guidelines for managing free discussion. When creative work goes wrong it is almost always because one or more of those guidelines has been ignored. When it goes right, our human potential for 'knowing' is released in awesome ways. Clients, supervisees and supervisor benefit and are helped and healed through the supervision process.

End note

Case study 2 – Carmel

Their year together had come to an end for Carmel's group. They had formed and, briefly, stormed before discovering shared norms. They had had, painfully, to change their shape to include an additional member and with some difficulty find a new accommodation. They had developed into a close-knit and well-working group. They would mourn the loss of each other and of Carmel, as well as the opportunity for supervision in a special group.

Carmel reminded them of the review, which would happen on their penultimate meeting. Together they planned how that would be carried out. Then they talked about their final meeting. Mary had recently been on an art therapy weekend where they had made a group painting. Each member had painted their sense of the group on one portion of a huge piece of paper. They had then gradually interacted with each other's 'territory' until a single painting had emerged. She said that it had succeeded in representing each person's individuality and that of the group as a whole (Silverstone 1993). She would like to do the same in this group. Everyone seemed enthusiastic. Carmel promised to provide materials. Stephen said he would bring his camera and photograph the results. Kate said she would bring a tape recorder and tape a comment from each member. Farah said she would like to bring some snacks to eat. Desmond commented that he seemed to have been left with bringing liquid refreshment.

Carmel commented to her consultant that she thought they could now consider themselves members of a co-operative group. She herself felt real grief. It had been her 'first' and she had learned so much with them and from them and their clients. She found it hard to believe that there would ever be a group like them. And yet, at the start, they had not seemed very promising. And as for her . . .

IV   Development

11 Groups for developing supervision

Sauce for the gander

The millennium is upon us. An arbitrary date in the short history of the counselling and psychotherapy profession/s but metaphorically useful. In this final chapter, I would like to look at the importance of supervisors, including group supervisors, meeting in groups for a variety of personal and professional purposes as we move into the twenty-first century. As we saw when looking at peer groups, there are many purposes around which peers can associate. The major theme of this book has been that well-working groups are more than the sum of their parts. They act as catalyst for the development of the participants. It is also true of groups as systems of wider influence. Development, change and innovation – cultural, social, professional – spring out of people getting together. First they find shared hopes and dissatisfactions; then they imagine the 'what' and the 'how-tos' of changing the unsatisfactory or implementing new ideas.

If group supervisors do appreciate, or come to appreciate, the richness of group potential, they will want to be in groups with their supervising colleagues for the monitoring and development of their work. In addition, in taking on the role of supervisor, they have taken on a responsibility for their professional associates. For part of their working lives, they assume the role of 'official monitor' for particular counsellors or psychotherapists. This role implies responsibilities to the profession as a whole.

They should be rendering regular account of their work, to check that they, like their counsellors, are satisfactorily self-monitoring. They need to be open to feedback from their supervising peers, who can speak from experience. They have also undertaken to keep their knowledge and understanding regularly refreshed, so that they can be a formative resource for their supervisees. Meeting with other lively, curious and grounded colleagues offers an opportunity for exchange of learning and mature discourse – as well as refreshment. Together, they need to notice trends, problems, shortfall in the working life of their supervisees. This can only happen by meeting to exchange experiences. They have a responsibility to register these publicly in some way. This should be through established channels of communication to professional associations, trainers of counsellors and supervisors and managers of agencies and services. It could be through writing and informal research. Networking with other groups might throw up other possibilities.

Groups as a resource for supervisor development

Training – one-to-one in group

Starting with the personal, what are the needs and opportunities of supervisors, and especially group supervisors, at different stages of their development (1)? Firstly, training. Counsellors who are training as supervisors may well concentrate initially on one-to-one supervision. Practice will probably be in pairs, possibly with an observer. However, the opportunity to practise in front of a group and hear feedback from a variety of observers is obviously an added resource. Most courses require trainees to be 'in supervision of supervision' outside the course. This can be with an individual supervisor, but I would suggest that a group offers greater stimulation. At this stage, a led group may well be the necessary choice. A group offers all the opportunities of variety in style and orientation, and experiences as supervisor and supervisee can be exchanged as added information.

> I think the best part of my training was our development group. There were six of us. We worked in threes, doing one-to-one supervision with feedback and then finished off each session back in the group. We had to struggle with 'group dynamics' initially – I had not been prepared for the diversity of ideas and practice which I found there, nor the competitiveness which our anxiety generated. The staff members visited regularly as consultants and we used them to help us address some sticky issues. By the end of the course we could challenge each other without 'dramas' and the speed with which all our practice improved was amazing. The trust was such that our self and peer assessment was quite a profound experience – I felt I had been seen, appreciated and also 'seen through' in both senses of that expression. We are still meeting twice yearly – that amount of trust is rare. One group did not

manage to gel, but their feedback was that they had still learned a lot from the variety.

Group supervision for group supervisors

For those in training who are, or will be, working as group supervisors, group supervision seems essential. The group offers experience as a group supervisee. Many people will have had that experience before but there is an added edge when, at the same time, they are supervising a group themselves. Empathic understanding is greatly enhanced by recent experience. The meaning behind group theories will emerge experientially. As supervisees, participants have to learn how to present group work for supervision – itself complex; and risk the exposure of presenting in a group.

Supervisors in training are vulnerable, perhaps more so than beginning counsellors. They have stuck their heads above the parapet and, initially, self-selected themselves as suitable to move into Parental roles for and on behalf of their colleagues. Many of them may not have developed a range of skills which matches their experience and intuitive development. They may not have been in participative or co-operative groups. Earlier training courses may not necessarily have offered intermediate technology (see Chapter 8) to help them develop sophistication and good manners as group members. They can suffer from a sense of appallingly self-conscious incompetence. Meanwhile, other, younger colleagues may have been in more or less self-managed groups throughout their counselling training. Strange hierarchies and painful competition can be present in supervisor training.

Most trainees can benefit from being at the receiving end of a sensitive Type 2 group if they are to have a model of how to engage supervisees in their own development and that of others. I imagine training courses can presume on a level of experience and expertise which supervisors in training may not have. At the same time, these are adult learners who will rightly resent being patronized or babied. Supervisors in training and trainers of supervisors need to give careful thought as to how the requisite skills and abilities can best be developed in limited training time.

One thing is certain, a group is the only forum which can offer the opportunity for trying out the group supervisor role. Feedback on leadership style and on particular interventions is immediate – effects do not have to be imagined. Creative structures can be tried in a relatively safe environment. The supervisor can facilitate the naming and handling of hot issues, and his methods for doing this can subsequently be processed by the group. When group supervision issues are presented for supervision, members can role-play different participants in the presented group. The interactions in the group presented will often be mirrored in the supervision group. The possibilities are endless.

Post-training – accountability

I prefer not to use the term 'supervisor of supervision' once a supervisor is out of training. It begs the question of where responsibility ends. Supervisors will not be asking their 'supervisors' to carry the buck for them – they will seek consultation on thorny ethical issues; they will continue to use consultation as an opportunity for learning, development and refreshment. By choosing to offer supervision, they have identified themselves as willing and able to carry Parental roles within the profession (which is different from 'being the parents'). If they have been assessed by their training course, or become accredited, they have the endorsement of their colleagues. They can be youthful in the roles or highly experienced but they will carry ultimate responsibility for encouraging self-monitoring and challenging bad practice.

It is not very clear how supervisors render an account of their work to their peers, and get feedback. Presumably, this is through their consultancy, though accountability suggests a more systematic arrangement than the 'occasional consultancy' required by most Codes of Ethics (ACES 1993; BAC 1995). In the case studies, Martin, Carmel and Ruth all had one-to-one consultancy. All three were new to group supervising and used their consultant as mentor. This has probably been the most prevalent arrangement. Christine had a supervisor development group with whom she discussed her work. We do not know what their working agreements were, and, in my experience, this is seldom talked about. Hopefully, it will become usual, if not required, for consultation to include some regular accountability.

A supervisor may continue to want an individual mentor – that is a great treat and offers something that a group cannot offer, even if it has a leader/consultant. I do not advocate a group as the

only resource for supervisor development. Rather, it is one necessary resource for group supervisors.

Supervisor development groups

An audit of the developmental needs of group supervisors reveals
complexity.

> There are a lot of things I need, having started working with my
> agency group. I need support, help, advice. I want an opportunity to
> talk about individuals and the group as a whole. There are tricky
> supervision issues that have already come up and the group can feel
> rather heavy weather. I worry about the training course that one
> supervisee is on. The agency is not very clear about what it expects
> from the supervision and I need to think about how to address that
> with the manager. Is that enough to start with?

As an individual consultant, I can feel doomed by such a presentation. It is hard not to turn into a non-stop teacher. In a supervisor
development group it is different.

> Presented to four supervisors with varying experience in individual
> and group supervision, the concerns are metaphorically spread out
> immediately. One holds the tricky supervision issue; another the heavy
> group; a third the agency and a fourth the individuals. As facilitator, I
> offer to take the role of the supervisor's *alter ego* – that will hold me to
> empathic understanding and respect while the structure lasts. Any
> teaching that might be useful can come at a later stage. Where does the
> presenter want to start? A huge sigh, a straightening of the back and a
> decision to speak very briefly to each member about the issue they are
> holding. Following that, a decision to explore the supervision issue,
> because that seems urgent. The group put down what they are holding
> for the time being and clarify, summarize and offer information. The
> presenter checks out with them what he thinks he will say to the
> counsellor back in his group.
>   Does he want them to take up the issues again? No, they can stay on
> the floor. All can wait except the heaviness of the group and his
> feelings of helplessness and dread. On second thoughts, not quite that
> bad. Frustration and irritation as he comes to think about it. The time-
> keeper says that there are five minutes of his presentation left – does he
> want more? He doesn't. I offer to hold his recessive respect and
> empathy while he vents his irritation. He stands up and goes round
> telling the people who held individuals, agency and group what he
> wants of them, with amazing clarity and brevity. He then stands and
> looks at me, and says 'OK, I'll have them back now.'

And that's it. No teaching, practically no words, a silent role. Give
me a group any time. A supervisor development group can be a
led group or a peer group, or alternate between the two. It can,

with benefit, contain supervisors in various stages of their development, and be a forum for sharing individual and group supervision. In making a working agreement members can make the boundaries as wide or as narrow as they wish. Some people may want to have a chance to practise live one-to-one supervision and get feedback. Others may wish to bring a tape from time to time. Since it is not a supervision group, people may want to think about shared issues; ask the group to monitor their overall counselling, supervision and training practice; give feedback on relevant writing. Each meeting it is likely that there will be 'supervision of supervision'. Needs vary considerably according to different stages of development (1). The previous example was of a young man who was a newly trained supervisor starting his first group.

In some groups of experienced practitioners, each member may work in a wide range of settings, carrying varied responsibilities. It is not unusual for such a group to become a valued and highly personal opportunity for overall professional monitoring, development and accountability. However, if the group is designated a supervisor development (or consultation) group, members should remember to relate back learning from the professional development aspects of the group's work to their role as supervisor and to its consequences for the tasks of supervision.

Cross-professional groups

Although this book has focused on supervision of counsellors and psychotherapists, many supervisors also supervise groups of related professionals – nurses, doctors, psychologists, managers, social workers and, increasingly, groups of mixed professional workers. In Europe, supervisors are engaging in 'Intervision' (Themanummer 1998, de Hoop and Kuiper 1993) within organizations, supervising in one group, for instance, doctor, nurse, counsellor and manager. Supervisor development groups may include members who are working in these contexts and this serves to challenge professional insularity.

Groups as clearing houses

So groups are restorative, formative and normative for individual supervisors. However, their importance goes well beyond that. As people meet, they begin to recognize common strands, identify issues that have their roots in wider systems than the client–

counsellor dyad or even the triad which includes the supervisor. They begin to share and recognize issues that have impact on the profession as a whole, and on the service offered to clients in general. It seems strange, once one is in a group, not to have connections to other developing supervisors. How could they become feeder groups to a larger network?

Monitors in a self-monitoring profession?

The last decade has been marked by supervisor accreditation – for individual and group supervisors, and supervisors who offer both. There has been an extraordinary mushrooming of supervisor training courses, some concentrating on individual supervision and others on group supervision – and some on both (2). All British counsellors and psychotherapists who belong to a professional association are required, by their Codes of Ethics, to be in regular on-going supervision. All British supervisors are required to have consultation available to them. Supervision is a necessary requirement as a training resource on all accredited courses. The growing profession, if such it can be called, prides itself on its self-monitoring and accountability – primarily by means of supervision.

And yet, apart from one or two networks, and an annual Standing Conference (British Association for Supervision Practice and Research), there is no regular meeting ground for supervisors – group and/or individual; there is no formal channel of communication between supervisor training courses nor between trainers and professional associations, let alone between supervisors and associations. There is no forum where counselling trainers and supervisors and their trainers can meet to exchange mutually useful information. We all subscribe to shared Codes of Ethics (3, 4, 5), but otherwise, with so little exchange and so little access to each other's work, the extent to which we are a self-monitoring body has to be called in question.

Tribalism and other anachronisms

There are a great many questions facing the profession at the turn of the century. My personal hope is for a state of post-tribalism. By that, I mean a condition in which clients have the likelihood of working with a counsellor or psychotherapist who practices in a way which is geared to them, and their issues, in their social and economic contexts. At present, all too frequently, clients still encounter counsellors who only want (or are able) to offer a particular way of working – person-centred, psychodynamic, gestalt, cognitive behavioural or other. These models of working are passed on through trainings which incorporate codified wisdom and also quasi-tribal norms, myths and taboos which may or may not be functional for client or counsellor.

There is wisdom in most traditions and tribes and many trainers and writers are developing their own integrative models. Practitioners are often motivated – even forced – to become 'integrative' by working in settings where their particular model is clearly inappropriate for some of their clients, and may not accord with the culture and economics of their agency or service. In my imagination, there is a step beyond 'integration', which would result in a simplified model of good practice, incorporating and subsuming the major tribal wisdoms. This may be wishful thinking – tribal identity offers security and status, and is often demanded by employers and professional associations. My belief is that it can interfere with active 'cross-tribal' engagement with each other in the service of best practice for our clients. While supervisor trainers and supervisors seldom meet amongst themselves, tribalism is not strongly challenged. Supervisors, especially group supervisors, working at whatever is the modern equivalent of the coal face, know that tribalism no longer works.

Trainees from different courses meet in agency groups and have to wrestle with what is 'core good practice'. Carmel and her fellow new group supervisors have to find ways of determining that for themselves – not everyone is in Integrative training as she is. The Martins have to work to help their groups find common ground and shared commitment. Some members struggle to adapt long-term work, in which they have been trained, in order to offer effective time-limited counselling. They are challenged by fellow supervisees who, to some degree, fear and belittle brief work. Meanwhile, the marital counsellor has to explain systems thinking to other members of the group. Christine works with a team predominantly trained in a variety of long-term orientations, now working within the economic demands of an Employee Assistance Service. They enjoy offering counselling to a range of employees who would never normally come near a counsellor. They resent the constant constraints of time and money, and of seeming to be working for two masters. They go off to a variety of short courses on brief, focused or time-limited work and come back to wrestle with trying to integrate new ideas with tried and familiar rhythms and systems of work. Specific contexts may call for specialist knowledge. 'Supervisors need to be flexible specialists or specialists in flexibility' (Proctor and Inskipp, in Lawton and Feltham (eds) 2000). For neither is a dedication to a single theoretical orientation useful.

Tribalism is my particular Aunt Sally (probably because I have not found a sub-tribe I wish to belong to. That is a bit lonely and gloriously freeing. I am happy to be named a counsellor, and accept clients calling me 'my therapist' – it does sound more impressive.) But tribalism is only one of the complex issues which are being worked and fought out on the ground, and which supervisors are uncomfortably aware of. Too many trainees chasing too few placements; inappropriate clients for new counsellors; Codes of Ethics which do not reflect organizational issues; academic excellence not translating into skilled practice; self-awareness losing out to theoretical ideas; intuitive workers who are unable to talk about what they do and why they do it – a welter of leftovers from traditional systems, codes and trainings which cannot easily be resolved given the exponential rate of internal and external change.

Supervisors – potential communication centres with no outlet

Of course, others know about these issues, from their individual experience. However, supervisors in general, and group supervisors in particular, have access to a wealth of information from all the limbs of the body of counselling and psychotherapy. They know about training courses – their strengths and their shortcomings. They may have access to agencies. They will be aware of agencies' effectiveness for clients, and also their policies and practices for trainees' induction and placement, and how they compare with other agencies. They have information about a wide range of client problems, and how individual clients are and are not helped. They are potentially major communication centres through which information should be transmitted to and fro. And yet they seldom meet to form a clearing-house for that welter of information; nor do they have formal channels for transmitting it out.

Writing and research

In addition to lacking meeting grounds, they have no dedicated public forum. There is no British supervision journal and little research on supervision effectiveness (in America there are two journals dedicated to supervision: *The Clinical Supervisor* and *Counselor Education* and *Supervision*). (I do not wish to belittle the refreshing trickle of native research projects which are beginning to emerge from Masters and Doctoral programmes – they are an oasis in the desert which I hope will blossom.) There is a welcome explosion of books and articles on general and specialist supervision. Unless supervisors are regularly meeting with each other, formally and informally, the useful learning to be taken from them will mainly influence training courses and individuals. It will not be discussed between practising supervisors and cannot affect professional policies.

Writing and research, both formal and informal, needs to emerge from the field as well as from academic institutions. There is so little written about group supervision and practically no research in this country. I assert it is a good thing for supervisees and for clients when it is well run. Anecdotal evidence supports this, as it does the assertion that there are many unhelpful or bad supervision groups. Supervision is expensive – even group supervision – and often comes under fire. If research is not available, it would be good to have some systematic case studies to quote. Since supervisors are usually busy people, perhaps another purpose for meeting in groups could be to develop some such materials.

Readiness for the call

It is up to professional associations to find ways to communicate with their supervisors. If supervisors have a network of groups (6), which have been meeting to exchange information; to monitor each other's work; to do writing and research – they will be in a better position to act as a pressure group and to inform the development of channels of communication. Many counselling and psychotherapy practitioners who are active and who wear influential hats in professional associations are also supervisors when they are wearing another hat. It remains puzzling why this has not resulted in the formation of a supervisor/supervision forum (at the time of writing).

My fear is that supervisors may come to see themselves as separate from the profession of counselling and psychotherapy. Instead of being members of those professions, who have undertaken a certain role on behalf of their peers, they could see themselves as different. They would be supervision experts offering a 'tendered out' service, like consultants. There are those who might prefer that option. It gives relief from the anxiety of holding the dual roles of colleague and monitor; peer and expert. To my mind it buys off the opportunity to struggle, as a 'people' profession, with this universal human dilemma. It would destroy the basis of a self-monitoring profession.

In conclusion

Group supervision makes a challenge which individual supervision does not make. It requires supervisees to take some shared responsibility for the development of their colleagues. It also requires them to share their work publicly and be open to, at least, supervisor feedback in a public forum. In most groups, they will also become accustomed to receiving feedback, support, challenge and criticism from their peers. These are the necessary experiences for professionals who belong to, or are training to be, members of a so called self-monitoring profession.

If this process is to be more creative than destructive, supervisors have to develop group-work skills that are geared to the central tasks of supervision. Group leadership and facilitation require the ability to move between quite different 'ways of being' with increasing elegance and confidence. Whatever role or decision the group supervisor is taking, her intention for respect and empathic understanding of each individual, and authenticity in undertaking her contracted duties, are the underlying bedrock. This is her best hope for developing a climate in which each supervisee can grow in ethical confidence, competence, compassion and creativity as a counselling practitioner.

Glossary

This is a glossary of how certain words and expressions are used in this text. It is not necessarily what might universally be recognized as 'correct usage'. Words in *italics* have their own glossary entry.

acting out, enacting, acting into – These expressions all suggest that people can 'do themselves' in different ways, both voluntarily for creative exercises, and involuntarily, through action, expressing emotions and beliefs about which they are unaware.
> **Acting out** is a pychodynamic expression for the process of acting on impulses and emotions of which the person is unconscious – a substitute for considered thought and action.
> **Enacting** is used to suggest that some people may learn about their impulses and emotions by first acting on them and then reflecting. Such enactments are seen as valuable in their own right.
> **Acting into** is a way of deliberately trying on some behaviour or idea about behaviour, 'taking a role' in order to learn more about the thinking, emotions and experience which give rise to the behaviour.

advocacy – client, professional, devil's – A supervisor may often need to take an advocacy stance for some person not present in the supervision.
> **Client advocate** – 'If I were your client, I might feel/think . . .'
> **Professional advocate** – 'How might your counselling colleagues think or feel if they knew you were making that decision?'
> **Devil's advocate** – An exercise used to assist when a group may not have the courage to say or ask what is uncomfortable or potentially threatening to group cohesion. 'If I had to identify one thing that I would like more (or less) of from you, it would be . . .'

alter ego – A psychodrama term, meaning to take, or role-play, some 'part' of another person, in order that he can temporarily relinquish that part of himself and fully identify with some other 'part'. For example, the *alter ego* may 'hold' the caring part of a colleague, allowing the colleague to give vent to his frustration.

Aunt Sally – A fairground game in which a coconut is set up for people to knock off – hence a subject introduced in order to 'have a go' at it.

authoritative group supervision – A group in which the supervisor makes an agreement with group members to supervise them one-to-one within a group setting – the other group members acting as a more or less participating audience. This is also called Type 1 or supervision *in* a group.

Beneficial Triangle – See **Drama Triangle**. From Transactional Analysis, and devised by Jill Hunt, it suggests how the truth about fearful situations can be addressed by seeing VPR roles as potential resources. Issues are not addressed, because people are, and feel, Vulnerable; fear their own and others' Potency; and are Responsive to the difficulties in the situation. If this can be acknowledged, hot issues can be addressed sensitively.

collusion – An unacknowledged 'agreement' not to notice certain unpleasant or difficult facts of group life. This may be conscious for some or all members, or entirely out of everyone's awareness.

contracts – hard and soft – From Transactional Analysis, a hard contract expresses in exact and behavioural terms what is wanted from, for example, the supervision session. A soft contract outlines in general terms what the supervisee wants to focus on or wants to explore.

co-operative group supervision – A group in which the supervisor makes an agreement with members that they will take responsibility for co-operating with her and with each other to deliver good supervision. The supervisor remains ultimately responsible for the overall quality of supervision and group well-being. This is also called Type 3 or supervision *by* the group.

cross-tribal empathy – The ability to work for empathic understanding of colleagues' working values and practices which may spring from a theoretical orientation (or 'tribe') different from one's own.

debriefing – The process of enabling people who have taken on roles in the group – usually in a voluntary manner for the purpose of a creative exercise, but sometimes involuntarily as a result of, for example, parallel process – to de-role and return to 'being themselves'. Without this, they may unwittingly stay in role and *act out* situations which are not relevant to the present task.

disassociating – The voluntary and intentional process by which someone can see or hear themselves and others as if from outside.

dissociating – An involuntary process which is experienced when a situation is too frightening for a person to stay 'present' – often described as 'out of body' experience. Not to be confused with *disassociating*.

Drama Triangle (or VPR Triangle) – From Transactional Analysis, the triangle was devised by Steve Karpman as a way of analysing *psychological games*. It describes the favoured and stereotyped roles which we take when faced with issues which, consciously or unconsciously, we find too difficult or painful to confront. The roles are Victim, Rescuer and Persecutor. These differ from the same words with small letters, which describe real situations in which there are protagonists who are powerless in the face of real force; others who use their power oppressively; and brave onlookers who work to stop that happening. With capital letters, Victims choose at some level to see themselves as helpless; Rescuers choose to perceive others as helpless; and Persecutors (bullies) are encouraged to imagine they have more power than they really have. Players in the Triangle usually have a preferred role, but they can slip in and out of the three roles rapidly – blaming, feeling hard done by, and overprotecting. The outcome is that the 'hot issue' which they need to address is not spoken. See **Beneficial Triangle**.

dysfunctional group – A supervision group which cannot provide good enough supervision for its members, because it lacks the core conditions of trust and safety which allow its members to give others access to their counselling work and receive help and feedback.

Employee Assistance Programme – Services which may operate nationally, regionally or in-house to offer counselling and specialized advice to employees of organizations which contract with the service.

family stage organization – In organizational systems terms, an organization which is still largely dependent on the way it was set up by its founding members. Many organizations fail (or go through internecine struggles) when interaction is no longer face-to-face, and formalized procedures and written agreements become necessary.

fight or flight – From the Bion group framework, which describes how therapy groups can fail to address the task by fighting or fleeing from contact rather than engaging. The unhealthy equivalent of the *storming* phase.

foreground – See **gestalt formation**.

forming – From the *group-as-system* framework, as expounded by Tuckman. It is the first stage of necessary group psychological development. Groups may form satisfactorily on their own without facilitation. Most task groups (such as a supervision group) which have limited time available to them will need help and support in forming well and quickly. (See also **norming, performing, storming**.)

framework (for supervision) – A *model*, or cognitive map, within an overall model of supervision; or the way of describing a partial task or process.

gestalt formation – A way of understanding human processing which originated with the Gestalt psychologists, but which was therapeutically developed by Fritz Perls and his followers. It suggests that human beings apprehend and experience in 'wholes' rather than 'bits'. Out of a perceived 'whole' (the group, for instance) a perceiver who is psychologically open and aware will be led to notice a salient feature that is unsatisfying. This becomes foreground for him. In paying attention to that, and doing something to complete the unfinished 'need', the cycle can be completed. The foreground, once attended to, slips into the background, and some new salient feature emerges. People can grow rigid or obsessive in this cycle. In this value system, fluidity is always desirable, and is essential for group supervisors.

good enough/well enough – From the child psychotherapist Donald Winnicott. He asserted that a mother/carer did not need to be perfect in order for a child to develop healthily – only good enough. The child is programmed to survive well. In this, Winnicott is similar to Carl Rogers, who asserted that '*to the extent* [my italics] I can offer . . . [the core conditions)] . . . the person will be able to . . .'

good manners – Traditional social etiquette has loosened considerably and would never be appropriate in the context of counselling training and supervision. Good manners, here, is used humorously to suggest that a different, and not always familiar, etiquette is necessary for doing good group work (see **ground rules**).

GP practice – General Practitioner practices (or surgeries) are the basic primary care points of the British National Health Service.

ground rules – The behaviour and attitudes which supervisor and group supervisees agree to aim for within the group in order that they can work well together.

group-as-system – See '**thinking group**'. Systemic thinking suggests that, for example, groups, families, organizations, have a life of their own, with identifiable processes which are mediated by individuals within them. Since they consist of individuals, individual behaviour can appropriately be seen as doing or expressing something for the system of which they are a sub-system. At the same time it can be seen as acting on behalf of the enacter's personal system which exists before and after any particular supervision group-system.

group maintenance – The responsibility or task of ensuring that the members of the group become established as a group (see **group-as-system**) and are self-nurturing and self-challenging in a way which is suitable to their stage of group development.

group working agreement – The working agreement made between supervisor and supervisees to help create a fruitful working alliance. This is bounded by the terms of the overall *supervision contract*. It includes administrative arrangements, behavioural and attitudinal ground rules, and personal/professional learning agendas for individual members.

helicopter position – The psychological position in which a person can be detached and disassociated from a perplexing or anxiety-creating situation. If he has first been able to identify with his own and others' experience of the feelings and thinking from within, this position allows the appreciation of the full situation.

integrative orientation – A term used to supersede previous attempts at 'trans-orientational' descriptions of practice. Unfortunately, by itself it does not indicate what is being integrated. Sometimes it may be a truly 'meta-model' (see **relational model**). At other times, what is being integrated may be specified, for example, person-centred and Gestalt.

intermediate technology – Based on the idea of helping developing countries produce simple technology (for example, agricultural) suited to their needs and economy. In this context, a way of expressing the need for simple methods to help people from dependency and hierarchy to interdependence and co-operation.

inquirer prompts – See **Interpersonal Process Recall**.

Interpersonal Process Recall (IPR) – A method devised by Norman Kagan to help develop interpersonal awareness and self-supervision. It is based on the roles of experiencer and inquirer. The experiencer listens to an audio-taped situation in which she was active. The inquirer asks questions, or offers prompts, which help the experiencer to recall what she was experiencing, out of her awareness, during that session.

Karpman Triangle – See **Drama Triangle**.

leaderful – A 'leaderless (peer) group' suggests that no one is leader and this often results in fear of taking initiatives – a leadership vacuum that can interfere with good work. A 'leaderful group' suggests that leadership is shared rather than absent.

maps of pathology – Frameworks which concentrate on what is going wrong, or has developed dysfunction, in any system: as opposed to frameworks which offer the healthy intention behind behaviour and interactions.

mini-contract – The contract that an individual supervisee makes with the group and supervisor as to what she wants from her particular piece of supervision work.

model (of supervision) – A comprehensive cognitive system for describing the tasks and processes of supervision, built around a central unifying concept or value system.

NLP – Neurolinguistic Programming – a complex model for describing how people develop excellence, or inhibit their potential abilities. First developed by John Bandler and Richard Grindler, and modelled on the work of, among others, Fritz Perls, Virginia Satir and Milton Erickson.

normative, formative, restorative – The way of categorizing the complex tasks of supervision, within the Supervision Alliance Model:
>   **Normative** are those tasks which have to do with monitoring standards and ethics – one's own and one's colleagues'.
>   **Formative** are those tasks which have to do with developing competence, confidence, compassion and creativity.
>   **Restorative** are those which have to do with discharging stress and tension and recharging professional and personal batteries.

norming – See **forming, performing** and **storming**. The stage in which a group, having come to establish basic trust and having discovered its realistic power and constraints, takes ownership of its own special way of doing things and develops its own distinct personality.

parallel process – Sometimes called 'mirroring', this is a phenomenon in which people can unconsciously pick up and enact behaviour and interaction which is being talked about. This may happen in a supervision group where the group members find themselves acting in ways which mirror the client–counsellor interaction being described. It can also happen that a counsellor's subsequent behaviour with a client can unconsciously mirror the experience in the supervision group.

Parent, Adult and Child states – Taken from Transactional Analysis, originally developed by Eric Berne. The description of these 'states' has changed through the years. Here the words are used to indicate:
>   **Adult** – the psychological state in which a supervisee may be trusted to manage his life and actions realistically from moment to moment. This takes account of his Child wishes and his Parental value system.
>   **Parent** – the state in which he judges what are his responsibilities for himself and for others with whom he has working relationships.
>   **Child** – the state in which he is aware of and responsive to his wants and needs.

participative group supervision – A group in which the supervisor makes an agreement with group members that they will participate in supervising each other, with the help, tuition and leadership of the supervisor – the supervisor being responsible for the quality of supervision and the well-being of the group. This is also called Type 2, or supervision *with* a group.

performing – See **forming, norming** and **storming**. An optimal stage or condition in which a task group, having established trust, and come to terms with diversity in power, culture, and competence can co-operate in doing excellent, or *good enough*, work in an autonomous rather than merely compliant manner.

Persecutor – See **Drama Triangle**.

practical placement – In Britain, trainees are usually responsible for finding their own opportunities for working with clients, and this is expected to be within some formal setting – agency, organization or service.

preference stating – A 'may' intervention. 'I would like you to think more about that and maybe do some reading around the issue.' A negotiable suggestion which remains in the choice of the receiver.

projection object – Any object which is used to trigger some thought, feeling or imagination which would otherwise remain out of awareness. The projection process may often be unconscious or unintentional, but in creative work it is used as a deliberate aid to awareness.

psychological games – From Transactional Analysis, originated by Eric Berne and his followers. 'Games' are established interpersonal rituals which serve to keep individuals in known, safe psychological territory, at the expense of their own and other people's openness to each other and to new experience. The basis for games is the *Drama Triangle* with its roles of Victim, Rescuer and Persecutor.

purpose stating – A 'must' intervention by, for example, the supervisor or agency manager; stating a non-negotiable requirement.

reframe – To offer a perspective on a set of 'facts', different from that which is presently being used. 'Interpretations' are reframes. The word is usually used when what is being thought of as negative or pathological is 'reframed' as having a positive intention or outcome.

Relate trained – Relate is a major, nationally organized marital and relationship counselling service of the UK.

relational model – An integrative model which uses, as its unifying concept, the potential for establishing different helping relationships for different clients, for example, the working alliance relationship, the transferential relationship, the developmentally needed relationship, the I–Thou relationship.

Rescuer – See **Drama Triangle**.

re-supervision – Slipping back into supervising the counsellor after her piece of work is 'officially' finished (see **mini-contract**).

reverse parallel process – As well as the interaction of counsellor/client being mirrored unconsciously by the supervising group (see **parallel process**), the counsellor can unconsciously parallel the group supervisory relationship when working with the client.

Russian frogs (dolls) – A metaphor for the series of contracts and agreements within which a supervision group works – each one shaped by the pre-existing ones – professional and organizational contracts; group working agreement; session agenda; *mini-contracts*.

sculptures – A method of creative supervision in which a supervisee uses the bodies of other members of the group to represent a client in all his aspects. The sculpt could also represent the client's family, or the counsellor–client relationship. If invited, those sculpted may speak about what it is like to be in that position.

self-scanning – Focusing on one's internal experience, and noticing thoughts, bodily sensations, emotions, imaginings, internal dialogue and how that experiencing interacts with external happenings.

semi-detached reflection – A semi-detached house is one that is joined to its neighbour on one side while being a separate abode. The group needs time to process and reflect together after an individual piece of supervision work. This work is separate from the supervision while being linked to it. (See **re-supervision**.)

storming – See **forming, norming** and **performing**. The stage of psychological development when the group, as a system in its own right, is testing and discovering the extent and limits of its power in its context. Equivalent to the adolescent stage of individual development.

strategic thinking – A way of thinking 'long-term', as opposed to *tactically thinking*. A supervisor thinking strategically will (temporarily) have regard for overall intentions and agendas rather than for immediate outcomes – for example, for the group's development in self-management, rather than acting as referee.

sub-cultural – Behaviour, attitudes and expectations which follow from experience in a shared sub-culture such as gender, ethnic origin, theoretical orientation, etc.

supervision contract – The overall supervision contract with a training course or agency, within Codes of Professional Ethics.

supervisor development group – A group in which practising supervisors meet and share experience and practice. It may serve as a forum for co-accountability and/or for live practice and feedback.

tactical thinking – A way of thinking about 'what to do now'. A supervisor thinking tactically will (temporarily) be thinking short-term – how to achieve the immediate intention he may have for the group, or the group may have for itself; this is opposed to *strategic thinking*.

target communications – A way of saying something that connects with the thinking, responsible Adult state of the recipient, as well as with the Parental ethical values and the feeling, intuitive Child. (See **Parent, Adult and Child states**.)

theoretical orientation – The counselling or psychotherapeutic model which informs a practitioner and by which she may identify herself, for example, 'I am psychodynamic (or person-centred, or cognitive behavioural)'.

'thinking group' – See **group-as-system**. An invented term for reminding of the difference between thinking in terms of individual development, health, pathology, etc., and thinking in terms of the group as a living system in its own right. Individual behaviour is thought about in the *context* of its purpose for the group.

tribalism – A word which suggests that practitioners from particular theoretical orientations are members of a tribe – carrying its wisdom and also liable to be unquestioningly limited by its traditions and taboos.

Victim – See **Drama Triangle**.

voices – In this context, role-playing different strands of internal messages and imaginings of which a counsellor is aware, or at which she hints; or which she or her colleagues may intuit that a client is experiencing.

References

Adair, J. (1987) *Effective team building*. Gower Publishing.

Association for Counselor Education and Supervision (ACES) (1989) *Standards for Counseling Supervisors*. Alexandria, VA: ACES.

Association for Counselor Education and Supervision (ACES) (1993) *Ethical Guidelines for Counseling Supervisors*. Alexandria, VA: ACES.

Berne, E. (1961, reprinted 1993) *Transactional Analysis in Psychotherapy*. Souvenir Press.

Bion, W. (1961) *Experiences in Groups*. New York: Basic Books.

British Association for Counselling (BAC) (1990) *Code of Ethics and Practice for Counsellors*. Rugby: BAC.

British Association for Counselling (BAC) (1995) *Code of Ethics and Practice for Supervisors*. Rugby: BAC.

Carroll, M. (1996) *Counselling Supervision: Theory, Skills and Practice*. London: Cassell.

Clarkson, P. (1998) 'Intermind Dialogue', *Dialogue*, 1 (2).

de Hoop, A. and Kuiper, P. (1993) *Supervise en intervisie in het voortzezet, onderwis*. In: Docentengids, aflevering 19, December.

Egan, G. (1976) *Interpersonal Living*. Monterey, CA: Brookes/Cole.

Egan, G. (1994) *The Skilled Helper* (4th edition). Pacific Grove, CA: Brooks/Cole.

Egan, G. and Cowan, M. (1978) *People in Systems: A Model for Development in the Human Resource Professions and Education*. Monterey, CA: Brookes/Cole.

Gendlin, E.T. (1978) *Focusing*. New York: Bantam.

Gilmore, S.K. and Fraleigh, P.W. (1980) *Communication at Work*. Oregon: Friendly Press.

Hawkins, P. and Shohet, R. (1989) *Supervision in the Helping Professions*. Buckinghamshire: Open University Press.

Heider, J. (1986) *The Tao of Leadership*. England: Wildwood House.

Holloway, E. (1995) *Clinical Supervision: A Systems Approach*. Thousand Oaks, CA: Sage.

Houston, G. (1995) *Supervision and Counselling*. London: The Rochester Foundation.

Inskipp, F. and Proctor, B. (1993) *The Arts, Crafts and Tasks of Counselling Supervision. Part 1. Making the Most of Supervision*. Middlesex: Cascade Publications.

Inskipp, F. and Proctor, B. (1995) *The Arts, Crafts and Tasks of Counselling Supervision. Part 2. Becoming a Supervisor*. Middlesex: Cascade Publications.

Kagan, N. (1980) 'Influencing human interaction: 18 years with IPR', in A.K. Hess (ed.), *Psychotherapy Supervision: Theory, Research, Practice*. New York: Wiley.

Karpman, S. (1968) 'Fairy Tales and Script Drama Analysis', *Transactional Analysis Bulletin*, 7 (26): 39–43.

Lawton, B. and Feltham, C. (eds) (2000) *Taking Supervision Forward: Trends and Dilemmas*. London: Sage.

Lieberman, M., Yalom, I. and Miles, M. (1973) *Encounter Groups: First Facts*. New York: Basic Books.

Mattinson, J. (1977) *The Reflection Process in Casework Supervision*. London: Tavistock Institute of Human Relations.

Page, S. and Wosket, V. (1994) *Supervising the Counsellor: A Cyclical Model*. London: Routledge.

Perls, F. (1947) *Ego, Hunger and Aggression*. New York: Vintage Books.

Perls, F., Hefferline, R. and Goodman, P. (1972) *Gestalt Therapy: Excitement and Growth in the Human Personality*. Harmandsworth: Penguin.

Randall, R., Southgate, J. and Tomlinson, F. (1980) *Cooperative and Community Group Dynamics*. London: Barefoot Books.

Rogers, C. (1961) *On Becoming a Person*. London: Constable.

Satir, V. (1972) *Peoplemaking*. Palo Alto, CA: Science and Behavior Books.

Schulz, W.C. (1989) *Joy*. Berkeley, CA: Ten Speed Press.

Sills, C. (ed.) (1997) *Contracts in Counselling*. London: Sage.

Sills, C., Fish, S. and Lapworth, P. (1995) *Gestalt Counselling*. England: Winslow Press Ltd.

Silverstone, L. (1993) *Art Therapy: The Person Centred Way*. London: Autonomy Books.

Themanummer, (1998) *Supervisie in opleiding en beroep*. Tijdschrift van de LVSB. Secretariaat: Stationsstraat 12, 5431 CC Cuijik.

Truax, C. and Carkhuff, R. (1967) *Towards Effective Counseling and Psychotherapy*. Chicago: Aldine.

Tuckman, B.W. (1965) 'Developmental sequences in small groups', *Psychological Bulletin*, 63 (6): 384–99.

Winnicott, D.W. (1965) *The Maturational Processes and the Facilitative Environment*. London: Hogarth Press and the Institute of Psycho-Analysis.

Winnicott, D.W. (1974) *Playing and Reality*. Harmondsworth: Pelican Books.

Burke, W.W. (2005). 'Implementation and continuing the change effort'. In: W.J. Rothwell and R.L. Sullivan (eds), *Practicing Organization Development* (2nd edn). San Francisco, CA: Pfeiffer, 313–326.

Burns, T. and Stalker, G.M. (1961). *The Management of Innovation*. London: Tavistock.

Byars, L.L. and Rue, L.W. (2011). *Human Resource Management* (10th edn). New York: McGraw-Hill.

Cameron, K. (2008). *Positive Leadership*. San Francisco, CA: Berrett-Koehler Publishers.

Cameron, K. (2014). The personal management interview program: A technique for enhancing engagement, empowerment, and positive deviance. Paper presented at the Positive Organizations Conference. Johannesburg: Knowledge Resources.

Cameron, K. and Spreitzer, G.M. (2012). 'What is positive about positive organizational scholarship?' In: K. Cameron and G.M. Spreitzer (eds), *The Oxford Handbook of Positive Organizational Scholarship*. New York: Oxford University Press, 1–16.

Campion, M.A. and Berger, C.J. (1990). Conceptual integration and empirical test of job design and compensation relationships. *Personnel Psychology*, 43, 525–553.

Caprara, G.V., Barbaranelli, C., Hahn, R. and Comrey, A.L. (2001). Factor analysis of the NEO PI-R inventory and the Comrey Personality Scales in Italy and the United States. *Personality and Individual Differences*, 30, 217–228.

Cartwright, S., Cooper, C. and Earley, C. (2001). *International Handbook of Organizational Culture and Climate*. New York: Wiley.

Carver, C.S. and Scheier, M.F. (2002). 'Optimism'. In: C.R. Snyder and S.J. Lopez (eds), *Handbook of Positive Psychology*. Oxford: Oxford University Press, 231–243.

Cascio, W.F. (2001). Knowledge creation for practical solutions appropriate to a changing world of work. *South African Journal of Industrial Psychology*, 27, 14–16.

Castellana, M.J. (2013). 'Teamwork in financial institutions: Does it really matter?' In: E. Salas, S.I. Tannenbaum, D.J. Cohen and G. Latham (eds). *Developing and Enhancing Teamwork in Organizations: Evidence-based Best Practices and Guidelines*. San Francisco, CA: Jossey-Bass.

Cattell, R.B. (1965). *The Scientific Analysis of Personality*. London: Penguin Books.

Cederblom, D. and Pemerl, D.E. (2002). From performance appraisal to performance management: One agency's experience. *Public Personnel Management*, 31, 131–140.

Chamorro-Premuzic, T. (2007). *Personality and Individual Differences*. London: Blackwell.

Chen, C., Gostafson, D. and Lee, Y. (2002). The effect of a qualitative decision aid on group polarization. *Group Decision and Negotiation*, 11, 329–344.

Cheung, F.M., Leung, K., Zhang, J.X., Sun, H.F., Gun, Y.G., Song, W.Z. and Xie, D. (2001). Indigenous Chinese personality constructs: Is the five-factor model complete? *Journal of Cross-Cultural Psychology*, 32, 407–433.

Cheung, F.M., Van de Vijver, F.J.R. and Leong, F.T.L. (2011). Toward a new approach to the study of personality in culture. *American Psychologist*, 66(7), 593–603.

Church, A.T. and Lonner, W.J. (1998). The cross-cultural perspective in the study of personality: Rationale and current research. *Journal of Cross-Cultural Psychology*, 29, 32–62.

Clarke, S. and Robertson, I. (2005). A meta analytic review of the big five personality factors and accident involvement in occupational settings. *Journal of Occupational and Organizational Psychology*, 78, 355–376.

References

Adams, J.S. (1963). Toward an understanding of equity. *Journal of Abnormal and Social Psychology*, 67, 422–436.

Agars, M. and Kotke, J. (2005). 'Innovations in diversity management'. In: R. Burke and C. Cooper (eds), *Reinventing Human Resource Management*. London: Routledge.

Ajzen, I. (2001). Nature and operation of attitudes. *Annual Review of Psychology*, 52, 27–58.

Ajzen I. and Fishbein, M. (1977). Attitude-behavior relations: A theoretical analysis and review of empirical literature. *Psychological Bulletin*, 84, 888–918.

Ajzen, I. and Fishbein, M. (1980). *Understanding Attitudes and Predicting Social Behaviour*. Upper Saddle River, NJ: Prentice Hall.

Allport, G.W. (1961). *Pattern and Growth in Personality*. London: Holt, Rinehart & Winston.

Amunkete, S. and Rothmann, S. (in press). Authentic leadership and psychological capital in state-owned enterprises: Effects on job satisfaction and intention to leave. *International Journal of Human Resource Management*.

Anderson, L. (2012). *Organization Development: The Process of Leading Organizational Change* (2nd edn). Thousand Oaks, CA: Sage.

Argyris, C. (1970). *Intervention Theory and Method: A Behavioral Science View*. Reading, MA: Addison-Wesley.

Argyris, C. (1990) *Overcoming Organizational Defenses: Facilitating Organizational Learning*. Boston, MA: Allyn & Bacon.

Argyris, C. and Schön, D.A. (1978). *Organizational Learning: A Theory of Action Perspective*. Reading, MA: Addison-Wesley.

Argyris, C., Putnam, R. and Smith, D.M. (1985). *Action Science*. San Francisco, CA: Jossey-Bass.

Armstrong, M. and Taylor, T. (2014). *Armstrong's Handbook of Human Resource Management Practice* (13th edn). London: Kogan Page.

Armstrong, M., Cummins, A., Hastings, S. and Wood, W. (2003). *Job Evaluation: A Guide to Achieving Equal Pay*. London: Kogan Page.

Arnold, J., Cooper, C.L. and Robinson, I.T. (1995). *Work Psychology: Understanding Human Behaviour in the Workplace* (2nd edn). London: Pitman Publishing.

Aronsson, G. and Gustafsson, K. (2005). Sickness presenteeism: Prevalence, attendance-pressure factors, and an outline of a model for research. *Journal of Occupational and Environmental Medicine*, 47, 958–966.

Aronsson, G., Gustafson, K. and Dallner, M. (2000). Sick but yet at work: An empirical study of sickness presenteeism. *Journal of Epidemiological Health*, 54, 502–509.

Aronsson, G., Svensson, L. and Gustafson, K. (2003). Unwinding, recuperation, and health among compulsory school and high school teachers in Sweden. *International Journal of Stress Management*, 10, 217–234.

Arthur, D. (1995). The importance of body language. *HR Focus*, 72, 22–23.

Arvey, R.D. and Faley, R.A. (1988). *Fairness in Selecting Employees* (2nd edn). Reading, MA: Addison-Wesley.

Arvey, R.D. and Murphy, K.R. (1998). Performance evaluation in work settings. *Annual Review of Psychology*, 49, 141–168.

Ashforth, B.E. and Mael, F. (1989). Social identity theory and the organization. *Academy of Management Review*, 14, 20–39.

Axtell, R.E. (1991). *The Dos and Taboos of Body Language Around the World*. New York: Wiley.

Azar, B. (1996). People are becoming smarter: Why? *APA Monitor*, 27, 20.

Bales, R.F. (1953). 'The equilibrium problem in small groups'. In: T. Parsons, R.F. Bales and E.A. Shils (eds), *Working Papers in the Theory of Action*. Glencoe, IL: Free Press, 111–161.

Bandura, A. (1977). Self-efficacy: Toward a unifying theory of behaviour change. *Psychological Review*, 84, 191–215.

Barker, R.T., Johnson, I.W. and Pearce, G. (1995). Enhancing the student listening skills and environment. *Business Communication Quarterly*, 58, 28–33.

Barkhuizen, N., Rothmann, S. and Van de Vijver, A.J.R. (2014). Burnout and engagement of academics in higher education institutions: Effects of dispositional optimism. *Stress and Health*.

Barling, J., Kelloway, K. and Zacharatos, A. (2002). 'Occupational safety'. In: P. Warr (ed.), *Psychology at Work* (5th edn). London: Penguin Books, 253–275.

Barnard, C.I. (1938). *The Functions of the Executive*. Cambridge, MA: Harvard University Press.

Barnes-Farrell, J. (2001). 'Performance appraisal'. In: M. London (ed.), *How People Evaluate Others in Organizations*. London: LEA, 135–150.

Bar-On, R. (1997). *BarOn Emotional Quotient Inventory*. Toronto: Multi-Health Systems.

Barrick, M.R. (2001). Personality testing: Controversial no more. Paper presented at the 4th Annual Conference of the Society for Industrial Psychology, Pretoria, South Africa, June.

Barrick, M.R. and Mount, M.K. (1991). The big five personality dimensions and job performance: A meta-analysis. *Personnel Psychology*, 44, 1–26.

Barrick, M.B. and Mount, M.K. (2005). Yes, personality matters: Moving on to more important matters. *Human Performance*, 18, 359–372.

Barrick, M.R., Mount, M.K. and Judge, T.A. (2001). Personality and performance at the beginning of the new millennium: What do we know and where do we go next? *International Journal of Selection and Assessment*, 9, 9–30.

Barry, B. and Stewart, G.L. (1997). Composition, process and performance in self-managed groups: The role of personality. *Journal of Applied Psychology*, 82, 62–78.

Bass, B.M. (1981). *Stogdill's Handbook of Leadership: A Survey of Theory and Research*. New York: The Free Press.

Bass, B.M. (1985). *Leadership and Performance Beyond Expectation*. New York: Free Press.

Bass, B.M. (1990). From transactional to transformational leadership: Learning to share the vision. *Organizational Dynamics*, 18, 19–31.

Bass, B.M. (1997). 'Concepts of leadership'. In: R.P. Vecchio (ed.), *Leadership: Understanding the Dynamics of Power and Influence in Organizations*. Notre Dame, IN: University of Notre Dame Press, 3–23.

Bass, B.M. (1998). *Transformational Leadership: Industrial, Military, and Educational Impact*. Mahwah, NJ: Erlbaum.

Baumeister, R.F. (1982). A self-presentational view of social phenomena. *Psychological Bulletin*, 91, 3–26.

Bell, G. (2013). Cary Cooper on engagement, wellbeing, and the persistence of the glass ceiling. *Human Resource Management International Digest*, 21(4), 41–44.

Berry, J.W. (1989). Imposed etics-emics-derived etics: The operationalizations of a compelling idea. *International Journal of Psychology*, 24, 721–735.

Berry, J.W., Poortinga, Y.P., Segall, M.H. and Dasen, P.R. (2002) *Cross-cultural Psychology: Research and Applications*. Cambridge: Cambridge University Press.

Bion, W.R. (1961). *Experiences in Groups*. London: Tavistock Publications.

Blake, R.R. and Mouton, J.S. (1964). *The Managerial Grid*. Houston, TX: Gulf.

Block, J. (1995). A contrarian view of the five factor approach to personality description. *Psychological Bulletin*, 117, 187–213.

Boehm, J.K. and Lyubomirsky, S. (2008). Does happiness promote career success? *Journal of Career Assessment*, 16(1), 101–116.

Borman, W.C. and Motowidlo, S.J. (1997). Task performance and contextual performance: The meaning for personnel selection research. *Human Performance*, 10, 99–109.

Bormann, E.G. (1996). *Effective Small Group Communication* (5th edn). Minneapolis, MN: Burgess.

Bormann, E.G. and Bormann, N.C. (1988). *Effective Small Group Communication*. Minneapolis, MN: Burgess.

Bowling, N.A., Eschleman, K.J. and Wang, Q. (2010). A meta-analytic examination of the relationship between job satisfaction and subjective well-being. *Journal of Occupational and Organizational Psychology*, 83, 915–934.

Brayfield, A.H. and Crockett, W.H. (1955). Employee attitudes and employee performance. *Psychological Bulletin*, 52, 396–424.

Breckler, S.J. (1984). Empirical validation of affect, behavior, and cognition as distinct components of attitude. *Journal of Personality and Social Psychology*, 47, 1191–1205.

Brewerton, P. and Millward, L. (2004). *Organisational Research Methods*. London: Sage.

Brodsky, C. (1976). *The Harassed Worker*. Lexington, MA: D.C. Heath and Company.

Brown, D.R. (2011). *An Experiential Approach to Organization Development* (8th edn). Upper Saddle River, NJ: Prentice Hall.

Brown, M.E., Treviño, L.K. and Harrison, D.A. (2005). Ethical leadership: A social learning perspective for construct development and testing. *Organizational Behavior and Human Decision Processes*, 97, 117–134.

Bryson, J. and Hosken, C. (2005). What does it mean to be a culturally competent I/O psychologist in New Zealand? *New Zealand Journal of Psychology*, 34, 69–76.

Bundel, T. (2004). *Effective Organizational Communications*. London: Prentice-Hall.

Burke, R. and Cooper, C. (2004). *Leading in Turbulent Times*. Oxford: Oxford University Press.

Burke, R. and Cooper, C. (2006). *Inspiring Leaders*. London: Routledge.

Clawson, J. (2006). 'The inspirational nature of level three leadership'. In: R. Burke and C. Cooper (eds), *Inspiring Leaders*. London: Routledge, 105–116.

Clegg, S., Kornberger, M. and Pitsis, T. (2005). *Managing and Organizations*. London: Sage.

Conger, J.A. and Kanungo, R.N. (1987). Toward a behavioral theory of charismatic leadership in organizational settings. *The Academy of Management Review*, 12, 637–647.

Conner, M. and Clawson, J. (2004). *Creating a Learning Culture*. Cambridge: Cambridge University Press.

Cooper, C. (2005). *Leadership and Management in the 21st Century*. Oxford: Oxford University Press.

Cooper, C.L. and Dewe, P.J. (2004). *Stress: A Brief History*. Oxford: Blackwell.

Cooper, D., Robertson, I. and Tinline, G. (2003). *The Psychology of Personnel Selection*. London: Routledge.

Costa, P.T. and McCrae, R.R. (1988). Personality in adulthood: A six-year longitudinal study of self-reports and spouse ratings on the NEO Personality Inventory. *Journal of Personality and Social Psychology*, 54, 853–863.

Coyle-Shapiro, J., Shore, L., Taylor, S. and Tetrick, L. (2004). *The Employment Relationship*. Oxford: Oxford University Press.

Cummings, J.N., Kiesler, S., Zadeh, R.B. and Balakrishnan, A.D. (2013). Group heterogeneity increases the risks of large group size: A longitudinal study of productivity in research groups. *Psychological Science*, 24, 880–890.

Cummings, T.G. and Huse, E.F. (1989). *Organization Development and Change* (4th edn). St. Paul, MN: West Publishing Company.

Cummings, T.G. and Worley, C.G. (2005). *Organization Development and Change* (8th edn). Cincinnati, OH: South-Western College Publishing.

Daniels, A.C. (2000). *Bringing Out the Best in People: How to Apply the Astonishing Power of Positive Reinforcement*. New York: McGraw-Hill.

Dawis, R.V. and Lofquist, L.H. (1984). *A Psychological Theory of Work Adjustment: An Individual Differences Model and its Applications*. Minneapolis, MN: University of Minnesota Press.

Deci, E.L. and Ryan, R.M. (2000). The "what" and "why" of goal pursuits: Human needs and the self-determination of behavior. *Psychological Inquiry*, 11, 319–338.

Deci, E.L. and Ryan, R.M. (2008a). Self-determination theory: A macrotheory of human motivation, development, and health. *Canadian Psychology*, 49, 182–185.

Deci, E.L. and Ryan, R.M. (2008b). Facilitating optimal motivation and psychological well-being across life's domains. *Canadian Psychology*, 49, 14–23.

Demerouti, E., Nachreiner, F., Bakker, A.B. and Schaufeli, W.B. (2001). The job demands-resources model of burnout. *Journal of Applied Psychology*, 56, 499–512.

Derlega, V.J., Winstead, B.A. and Jones, W.H. (2005). *Personality: Contemporary Theory* (3rd edn). Belmont, CA: Wadsworth.

Diedericks, E. and Rothmann, S. (2014). Flourishing of information technology professionals: Effects on individual and organisational outcomes. *South African Journal of Business Management*, 45(1), 27–41.

Diener, E., Suh, E.M., Lucas, R.E. and Smith, H.L. (1999). Subjective well-being: Three decades of progress. *Psychological Bulletin*, 125, 276–302.

Dienesch, R.M. and Liden, R.E. (1986). Leader-member exchange model of leadership: A critique and further development. *The Academy of Management Review*, 11, 618–634.

Digman, J.M. (1989). Five robust trait dimensions: Development, stability, and utility. *Journal of Personality*, 57, 195–214.

Digman, J.M. (1997). Higher-order factors of the Big Five. *Journal of Personality and Social Psychology*, 73, 1246–1256.

Donaldson, S.I. and Ko, I. (2010). Positive organizational psychology, behavior, and scholarship: A review of emerging literature and the evidence base. *The Journal of Positive Psychology*, 5, 177–191.

Drennan, D. (1992). *Transforming Company Culture*. Berkshire: McGraw-Hill.

Drucker, P.F. (1954). *The Practice of Management*. New York: Harper & Row.

Duckitt, J. and Foster, D. (1991). Introduction to the special issue: Race, social attitudes, prejudice. *South African Journal of Psychology*, 21, 199–202.

Dunbar, E. (1993). The role of psychological stress and prior experience in the use of personal protective equipment. *Journal of Safety Research*, 24, 181–187.

Dunette, M. (1976). *Handbook of Industrial and Organizational Psychology*. Chicago: Rand McNally College Publishing Company.

Dyer, W.G., Dyer, J.H. and Dyer, W.G. (2013). *Team Building: Proven Strategies for Improving Team Performance* (5th edn). San Francisco, CA: Wiley.

Einarsen, S. (1999). The nature and causes of bullying at work. *International Journal of Manpower*, 20, 16–27.

Einarsen, S., Hoel, H., Zapf, D. and Cooper, C.L. (2003). 'The concept of bullying at work: The European tradition'. In: S. Einarsen, H. Hoel, D. Zapf and C.L. Cooper (eds), *Bullying and Emotional Abuse in the Workplace: International Perspectives in Research and Practice*. London: Taylor & Francis, 3–30.

Eysenck, H.J. (1992). Four ways five factors are not basic. *Personality and Individual Differences*, 6, 667–673.

Faragher, E.B., Cass, M. and Cooper, C. (2005). The relationship between job satisfaction and health: A meta-analysis. *Occupational Environmental Medicine*, 62, 105–112.

Feldman, D.C. (1984). The development and enforcement of group norms. *Academy of Management Review*, 9, 47–53.

Feldman, J. (1992). The case for non-analytic performance appraisal. *Human Resource Management Review*, 2, 9–35.

Festinger, L. (1957*). A Theory of Cognitive Dissonance*. Evanston, IL: Row, Peterson & Co.

Fiedler, F.E. (1967). *A Theory of Leadership Effectiveness*. New York: McGraw-Hill.

Fishbein, M. (ed.). (1967). *Readings in Attitude Theory and Measurement*. New York: Wiley.

Fishbein, M. and Ajzen, J. (1975). *Belief, Attitude, Intention and Behaviour: An Introduction to Theory and Research*. Reading, MA: Addison-Wesley.

Fitzgerald, L.E. (1995). Sexual harassment: Violence against women in the workplace. *American Psychologist*, 48, 1070–1076.

Fitzgerald, L.E., Drasgow, F., Hulin, C.L., Gelfand, M.J. and Magley, V.J. (1997). Antecedents and consequences of sexual harassment in organizations: A test of an integrated model. *Journal of Applied Psychology*, 82, 578–589.

Fogli, L. and Whitney, K. (1991). ServiceFirst: A test to select service oriented personnel. Symposium conducted at the Annual Meeting of the American Psychological Association, San Francisco.

Frederickson, B.L. (1998). What good are positive emotions? *Review of General Psychology*, 2, 300–319.

French, J.R.P. and Raven, B. (1959). 'The bases of social power.' In: D. Cartwright (ed.), *Studies in Social Power*. Ann Arbor, MI: Institute for Social Research, 150–167.

French, W.L. and Bell, C.H. (1999). *Organizational Development: Behavioral Science Interventions for Organization Improvement* (5th edn). Englewood Cliffs, NJ: Prentice Hall.

Fry, L.W. (2003). Toward a theory of spiritual leadership. *The Leadership Quarterly*, 14, 693–727.

Fry, L.W. and Cohen, M.P. (2009). Spiritual leadership as a paradigm for organizational transformation and recovery from extended work hours cultures. *Journal of Business Ethics*, 84, 265–278.

Gagné, M. and Deci, E.L. (2005). Self-determination theory and work motivation. *Journal of Organizational Behavior*, 26, 331–362.

Galbraith, J., Downey, D. and Kates, A. (2002). *Designing Dynamic Organizations*. New York: AMACOM.

Gelfand, M.J., Fitzgerald, L.F. and Drasgow, F. (1995). The structure of sexual harassment: A confirmatory analysis across cultures and settings. *Journal of Vocational Behavior*, 47, 164–177.

Gelfand, M.J., Erez, M. and Aycan, Z. (2007). Cross-cultural organizational behaviour. *Annual Review of Psychology*, 58, 479–514.

Gerber, P.D., Nel, P.S. and Van Dyk, P.S. (1995). *Human Resources Management* (3rd edn). Halfway House: Southern Book Publishers.

Gersick, C.J.G. (1988). Time and transition in work teams: Toward a new model of group development. *Academy of Management Journal*, 31, 9–41.

Glińska-Neves, A. and Stankiewicz, M.J. (2013). 'Key areas of positive organisational potential as accelerators of pro-developmental employee behaviours'. In: M.J. Stankiewicz (ed.), *Positive Management: Managing the Key Area of Positive Organisational Potential for Company Success*. Toruń Scientific Society for Organization and Management, 17–32.

Goffman, E. (1959). *The Presentation of Self in Everyday Life*. New York: Doubleday.

Goldberg, L.R. (1990). An alternative 'description of personality': The big five factor structure. *Journal of Personality and Social Psychology*, 59, 1216–1229.

Goldberg, L.R. (1993). The structure of phenotypic personality traits. *American Psychologist*, 48, 26–34.

Goleman, D. (1995). *Emotional Intelligence*. New York: Bantam Books.

Graen, G.B. and Uhl-Bien, M. (1995). Relationship-based approach to leadership: Development of leader–member exchange (LMX) theory of leadership over 25 years: Applying a multi-level multi-domain perspective. *Leadership Quarterly*, 6, 219–247.

Grant, A.M. (2008). Designing jobs to be good: Dimensions and psychological consequences of prosocial job characteristics. *The Journal of Positive Psychology*, 3, 19–39.

Grant, A.M., Passmore, J., Cavanagh, M. J. and Parker, H. (2010). The state of play in coaching today: A comprehensive review of the field. *International Review of Industrial and Organizational Psychology*, 25, 125–167.

Gray, J.L. and Starke, F.A. (1980). *Organizational Behavior: Concepts and Applications* (2nd edn). Columbus, OH: Charles E. Merril Publishing Company.

Greenberg, J. (2011). *Behavior in Organizations* (10th edn). Upper Saddle River, NJ: Prentice Hall.

Hackman, J.R. and Oldham, G.R. (1976). Motivation through the design of work: Test of a theory. *Organizational Behaviour and Human Performance*, 16, 250–279.

Hall, J.A. (1985). 'Male and female nonverbal behaviour'. In: A.W. Siegman and S. Feldstein (eds), *Multichannel Integrations of Nonverbal Behavior*. Hillsdale, NJ: Lawrence Erlbaum, 195–226.

Hall, D.T. (1976). *Careers in Organizations*. Glenview, IL: Scott, Foresman.

Halpin, A.W. and Winer, B.J. (1957). 'A factorial study of the leader behavior descriptions'. In: R.M. Stogdill and A.E. Coons (eds), *Leader Behavior: Its Description and Measurement*. Columbus, OH: Bureau of Business Research, Ohio State University.

Hambleton, R.K. and Oakland, T. (2004). Advances, issues and research in testing practices around the world. *Applied Psychology: An International Review*, 53, 155–156.

Harter, J.K., Schmidt, F.L. and Keyes, C.L. (2002). 'Well-being in the workplace and its relationship to business outcomes: A review of the Gallup studies'. In: C.L. Keyes and J. Haidt (eds), *Flourishing: The Positive Person and the Good Life*. Washington, DC: American Psychological Association, 205–224.

Harter, S. (2002). 'Authenticity'. In: C.R. Snyder and S.J. Lopez (eds), *Handbook of Positive Psychology*. London: Oxford University Press, 382–394.

Heneman, H.G., Schwab, D.P., Fossum, J.A. and Dyer, L.D. (1989). *Personnel/Human Resource Management* (4th edn). Homewood, IL: Irwin.

Hersey, P.H., Blanchard, K.H. and Johnson, D.E. (2013). *Management of Organizational Behavior: Leading Human Resources* (10th edn). Boston, MA: Pearson.

Herzberg, F., Mausner, B. and Snyderman, B.B. (1959). *The Motivation to Work* (2nd edn). New York: Wiley.

Hoag, B. and Cooper, C. (2006). *Managing Value-Based Organizations*. Cheltenham: Edward Elgar Publications.

Hoel, H., Faragher, B. and Cooper, C.L. (2004). Bullying is detrimental to health, but all bullying behaviours are not necessarily equally damaging. *British Journal of Guidance and Counselling*, 32, 367–387.

Hofstede, G. (2001). *Culture's Consequences: Comparing Values, Behaviors, Institutions and Organizations*. Newbury Park, CA: Sage.

Hogg, M.A. and Terry, D.J. (2000). Social identity and self-categorization processes in organizational contexts. *Academy of Management Review*, 25, 121–140.

Holland, J.L. (1997). *Making Vocational Choices* (3rd edn). Odessa, FL: Psychological Assessment Resources.

Hough, L. and Furnham, A. (2003). 'Use of personality variables in work settings'. In: W. Borman, D. Ilgen and R. Klimoski (eds), *Handbook of Psychology*. New York: Wiley, 131–169.

Hough, L.M. and Oswald, F.L. (2000). Personnel selection: Looking toward the future – remembering the past. *Annual Review of Psychology*, 51, 631–664.

Hsueh, Y. (2002). The Hawthorne experiments and the introduction of Jean Piaget in American industrial psychology, 1929–1932. *History of Psychology*, 5(2), 163–189.

Hulin, C.L. (1991). 'Adaptation, persistence and commitment in organisations'. In: M.D. Dunette and L.M. Hough (eds), *Handbook of Industrial and Organizational Psychology* (2nd edn). Palo Alto, CA: Consulting Psychologists Press, 445–507.

Illies, R., Mogeson, P.F. and Nahrgang, D.J. (2005). Authentic leadership and eudaimonic well-being: Understanding leader-follower outcomes. *The Leadership Quarterly*, 16, 373–394.

Infante, D.A. and Gorden, W.I. (1985). Superiors' argumentativeness and verbal aggression as predictors of subordinates' satisfaction. *Human Communication Research*, 12, 117–125.

Ivancevich, J.M. and Konapaske, R. (2013). *Human Resource Management* (12th edn). New York: McGraw-Hill.

Ivey, A.E. (1988). *Intentional Interviewing and Counseling: Facilitating Client Development*. Pacific Grove, CA: Brooks/Cole.

Jang, K.L., Livesley, W.J. and Vernon, P.A. (1996). Hereditability of the big five personality dimensions and their facets: A twin study. *Journal of Personality*, 64, 577–591.

Janoski, T., Luke, D. and Oliver, D. (2014). *The Causes of Structural Unemployment: Four Factors that Keep People from the Jobs they Deserve*. Cambridge: Polity Press.

Jennifer, D., Cowie, H. and Ananiadou, K. (2003). Perceptions and experience of workplace bullying in five different working populations. *Aggressive Behavior*, 29, 489–496.

Johnson, D.W. (2014). *Reaching Out: Interpersonal Effectiveness and Self-Actualisation* (11th edn). Boston, MA: Pearson.

Johnson, D.W. and Johnson, F.P. (2014). *Joining Together: Group Theory and Group Skills* (5th edn). Boston, MA: Pearson.

Judge, T.A. and Ilies, R. (2002). Relationship of personality to performance motivation: A meta-analytic review. *Journal of Applied Psychology*, 87, 797–807.

Judge, T.A., Thoresen, C.J., Bono, J.E. and Patton, G.K. (2001). The job satisfaction–job performance relationship: A qualitative and quantitative review. *Psychological Bulletin*, 127, 376–407.

Kahn, W. (1990). Psychological conditions of personal engagement and disengagement at work. *Academy of Management Journal*, 33, 692–724.

Kahn, W. and Heaphy, E.D. (2014). 'Relational contexts of personal engagement at work'. In: C. Truss, R. Delbridge, E. Soane, K. Alfesand A. Shantz (eds), *Employee Engagement in Theory and Practice*. Abingdon: Routledge, 163–179.

Karasek, R.A. (1979). Job demands, job decision latitude and mental strain: Implications for job redesign. *Administrative Science Quarterly*, 24, 285–308.

Katz, D. and Kahn, R.L. (1978). *The Social Psychology of Organizations* (2nd edn). New York: Wiley.

Kepes, S. and Delery, J. (2006). 'Designing effective HRM systems'. In: R. Burke and C. Cooper (eds), *The HR Revolution: Why Putting People First Matters*. Oxford: Elsevier, 55–78.

Keyes, C.L.M. (2002). The mental health continuum: From languishing to flourishing in life. *Journal of Health and Social Behavior*, 43, 207–222.

Keyes, C.L.M. (2007). Promoting and protecting mental health as flourishing: A complementary strategy for improving national mental health. *American Psychologist*, 62, 95–108.

Keyes, C.L.M. and Annas, J. (2009). Feeling good and functioning well: Distinctive concepts in ancient philosophy and contemporary science. *Journal of Positive Psychology*, 4, 197–201.

Kidd, J.M. (2002). 'Careers and career management'. In: P. Warr (ed.), *Psychology at Work* (5th edn). London: Penguin Books, 178–202.

Kirkpatrick, D.L. (1959). Techniques for evaluating training programs. *Journal of the American Society of Training Directors*, 13, 3–26.

Kivimaki, M., Head, J. and Ferrie, J.E. (2005). Working while ill as a risk factor for serious coronary events: The Whitehall II studies. *American Journal of Public Health*, 95, 98–102.

Klein, C., Derouin, R.E. and Salas, E. (2006). 'Uncovering workplace interpersonal skills: A review, framework, and research agenda.' In: G.P. Hodgkinson and J.K. Ford (eds), *International Review of Industrial and Organizational Psychology*: Vol. 21. Chichester: John Wiley & Sons.

Klikauer, T. (2007). *Communications and Management at Work*. London: Palgrave.

Kluckhohn, F. and Strodtbeck, F. (1961). *Variation in Value Orientations*. Evanston, IL: Row, Peterson.

Kraiger, K., Ford, J. and Salas, E. (1993). Application of cognitive skill based and affective theories of learning comes in new methods of training evaluation. *Journal of Applied Psychology*, 78, 311–28.

Kraut, A.I. (1976). 'New frontiers for assessment centres.' In: K.M. Rowland, M. London, G.R. Ferris and J.L. Sherman (eds), *Current Issues in Personnel Management*. Boston, MA: Allyn & Bacon.

Labriola, M., Christensen, K.B., Lund, T., Nielsen, M.L. and Diderichsen, F. (2006). Multilevel analysis of workplace and individual risk factors for long-term sickness absence. *Journal of Occupational and Environmental Medicine*, 48, 923–928.

Landy, F.J. (2005). Some historical and scientific issues related to research on emotional intelligence. *Journal of Organizational Behavior*, 26, 411–424.

Langan-Fox, J., Cooper, C. and Klimoski, R. (2007). *Research Companion to the Dysfunctional Workplace*. Cheltenham: Edward Elgar.

Latham, G.P. and Mann, S. (2006). 'Advances in the science of performance appraisal: Implications for practice'. In: G.P. Hodgkinson and J.K. Ford (eds), *International Review of Industrial and Organizational Psychology*. Chichester: Wiley, Vol. 21, 295–337.

Latham, G.P. and Pinder, C.C. (2005). Work motivation theory and research at the dawn of the twenty-first century. *Annual Review of Psychology*, 56, 485–516.

Lawrence, K.A. (2004). Why be creative? Motivation and copyright law in a digital era. *IP Central Review*, 1, 2.

Lawrence, P.R. and Lorsch, J.W. (1986). *Organization and Environment*. Boston, MA: Harvard Business School Press.

Lazarus, R.S. and Folkman, S. (1984). *Stress, Appraisal, and Coping*. New York: Springer.

Levinson, D.J. (1978). *The Seasons of a Man's Life*. New York: Ballantine Books.

Lewin, K. (1952). *Field Theory in Social Science*. New York: Harper & Row.

Lewis, S. (2011). *Positive Psychology at Work: How Positive Leadership and Appreciative Inquiry Create Inspiring Organizations*. Chichester: Wiley-Blackwell.

Leymann, H. (1990). Mobbing and psychological terror at workplaces. *Violence and Victims*, 5, 119–126.

Liden, R.C., Martin, C.L. and Parsons, C.K. (1993). Interviewer and applicant behaviours in employment interviews. *Academy of Management Journal*, 36, 372–386.

Linley, P.A., Garcea, N., Harrington, S., Trenier, E. and Minhas, G. (2011). 'Organizational applications of positive psychology: Taking stock and a research/practice roadmap for the future'. In: K.M. Sheldon, T.B. Kashdan and M.F. Steger (eds), *Designing Positive Psychology: Taking Stock and Moving Forward*. New York: Oxford University Press, 365–384.

Locke, E.A. (1976). 'The nature and causes of job satisfaction'. In: M.D. Dunette (ed.), *Handbook of Industrial and Organizational Psychology*. Chicago: Rand McNally, 1297–1349.

Locke, E.A. (2005). Why emotional intelligence is an invalid concept. *Journal of Organizational Behavior*, 26, 425–431.

Locke, E.A. and Latham, G.P. (1984). *Goal Setting: A Motivational Technique That Works?* Englewood Cliffs, NJ: Prentice Hall.

Locke, E.A. and Latham, G.P. (2002). Building a practically useful theory of goal setting and task motivation: A 35-year Odyssey. *American Psychologist*, 57, 705–717.

Loden, M. (1996). *Implementing Diversity*. Chicago, IL: Irwin.

Lombardo, M.M. and Eichinger, R.W. (2000). *For Your Improvement: A Development and Coaching Guide* (3rd edn). Lominger, 389.

Lonner, W.J. and Malpass, R.S. (1994). *Psychology and Culture*. Boston, MA: Allyn & Bacon.

Loveday, B. (2006). Policing performance: The impact of performance measures and targets on police forces in England and Wales. *International Journal of Police Science and Management*, 8, 282–293.

Lu, L., Cooper, C.L. and Lin, H.Y. (2013). A cross-cultural examination of presenteeism and supervisor support. *Career Development International*, 18(5), 440–456.

Luft, J. (1984). *Group Processes: An Introduction to Group Dynamics*. Palo Alto, CA: Mayfield.

Luthans, F. (2002a). Positive organizational behavior: Developing and maintaining psychological strengths. *Academy of Management Executive*, 16, 57–72.

Luthans, F. (2002b). The need for and meaning of positive organizational behavior. *Journal of Organizational Behavior*, 23, 695–706.

Luthans, F. (2012). 'Psychological capital: Implications for HRD, retrospective analysis, and future directions'. *Human Resource Development Quarterly*, 23(1), 1–8.

Luthans, F., Youssef, C.M. and Avolio, B.J. (2007). *Psychological Capital*. New York: Oxford University Press.

McClelland, D. (1955). *Studies in Motivation*. New York: Appleton-Century-Crofts.

McClelland, D. (1984). *Motives, Personality, and Society*. New York: Praeger.

McClelland, D. (1987). *Human Motivation*. Cambridge: Cambridge University Press.

McCrae, R.R. and Costa, P.T. (1997). Personality trait structure as human universal. *American Psychologist*, 52, 509–516.

McCrae, R.R. and Costa, P.T., Jr. (1995). Trait explanations in personality psychology. *European Journal of Personality*, 9, 231–252.

McGregor, D. (1960). *The Human Side of Enterprise*. New York: McGraw Hill.

Mabey, C. and Iles, P. (2001). *Managing Learning*. London: Thompson Learning.

Mani, B.G. (2002). Performance appraisal systems, productivity, and motivation: A case study. *Public Personnel Management*, 31, 141–159.

Mann, R. (1959). A review of the relationship between personality and performance in small groups. *Psychological Bulletin*, 56, 241–270.

Margerison, C.J. and McCann, D.J. (1990). *Team Management: Practical New Approaches*. London: Mercury Press.

Martin, D.C., Bartol, K.M. and Kehoe, P.E. (2000). The legal ramifications of performance appraisal: The growing significance. *Public Personnel Management*, 29, 379–405.

Maslow, A.H. (1971). *The Farther Reaches of Human Nature*. New York: Viking.

Mathews, G. (2012). Happiness, culture and context. *International Journal of Well-being*, 2, 299–312.

May, D.R., Gilson, R.L. and Harter, L.M. (2004). The psychological conditions of meaningfulness, safety, and availability and the engagement of the human spirit at work. *Journal of Occupational and Organizational Psychology*, 77, 11–37.

Mayer, J.D., Caruso, D.R. and Salovey, P. (1999). Emotional intelligence meets traditional standards for an intelligence. *Intelligence*, 27, 267–298.

Mayer, J.D., Salovey, P. and Caruso, D. (2000). 'Competing models of emotional intelligence'. In: R.J. Sternberg (ed.), *Handbook of Human Intelligence*. New York: Cambridge University Press, 396–420.

Mayer, R.C., Davis, J.H. and Schoorman, F.D. (1995). An integrative model of organizational trust. *Academy of Management Review*, 20, 709–732.

Middaugh, D.J. (2006). Presenteeism: Sick and tired at work. *Medsurg Nursing*, 15, 103–105.

Mikkelsen, G.E. and Einarsen, S. (2002). Basic assumptions and symptoms of post-traumatic stress among victims of bullying at work. *European Journal of Work and Organizational Psychology*, 11, 87–111.

Mintzberg, H. (1983). *Structure in Fives: Designing Effective Organizations*. Englewood Cliffs, NJ: Prentice Hall.

Moorhead, G. and Griffin, R.W. (2012). *Organizational Behaviour: Managing People and Organizations* (10th edn). Boston, MA: Houghton Mifflin.

Napier, R.W. and Gershenfeld, M.K. (2003). Groups: Theory and Experience (7th edn). Boston, MA: Houghton-Mifflin.

Nel, A., Valchev, V.H., Rothmann, S., Van de Vijver, F.J.R., Meiring, D. and De Bruin, G.P. (2012). Exploring the personality structure in the 11 languages of South Africa. *Journal of Personality*, 80(4), 915–948.

Nelson, D. and Cooper, C. (2007). *Positive Organizational Behaviour*. London: Sage.

Nelson, D.L. and Simmons, B.L. (2003). 'Health psychology and work stress: A more positive approach'. In: J.C. Quick and L.E. Tetrick (eds), *Handbook of Occupational Health Psychology*. Washington, DC: American Psychological Association, 97–119.

Nemetz, P.L. and Christensen, L. (1996). The challenge of cultural diversity: Harnessing a diversity of views to understand multiculturalism. *Academy of Management Review*, 21, 434–462.

Northouse, P. (2001). *Leadership: Theory and Practice* (2nd edn). London: Sage.

Notelaers, G., Einarsen, S., De Witte, H. and Vermunt, J.K. (2006). Measuring exposure to bullying at work: The validity and advantages of the latent class cluster approach. *Work and Stress*, 20, 289–302.

Oakland, T. (2004). Use of educational and psychological tests internationally. *Applied Psychology: An International Review*, 53, 157–172.

Odiorne, G.S. (1965). *Management by Objectives*. New York: Pitman.

Palmer, I., Dunford, R. and Akin, G. (2006). *Managing Organizational Change*. New York: McGraw Hill.

Paterson, T.T. (1972). *Job Evaluation*. London: Business Books, Vols 1 and 2.

Pervin, L.A. and John, O.P. (2001). *Personality: Theory and Research* (8th edn). New York: Wiley.

Peterson, C. and Seligman, M.E.P. (2004). *Character Strengths and Virtues: A Handbook and Classification*. Oxford: Oxford University Press.

Peterson, S. J., Luthans, F., Avolio, B.J., Walumbwa, F.O. and Zhang, Z. (2011). Psychological capital and employee performance: A latent growth modeling approach. *Personnel Psychology*, 64, 427–440.

Porath, C., Spreitzer, G., Gibson, C. and Garnett, F. G. (2012). Thriving at work: Toward its measurement, construct validation, and theoretical refinement. *Journal of Organizational Behavior*, 33 , 250–275.

Porter, L. and Lawler, E. (1968). *Managerial Attitudes and Performance*. Homewood, IL: Dorsey Press.

Putnam, L.L. (1988). 'Understanding the unique characteristics of groups within organizations'. In: R.S. Cathcart and L.A. Samovar (eds), *Small Group Communication*. Dubuque, IO: Wm. C. Brown, 76–85.

Rahim, A.M. and Psenicka C. (1996). A structural equations model of stress, locus of control, social support, psychiatric symptoms, and propensity to leave a job. *The Journal of Social Psychology*, 136(1), 69–84.

Randall, P. (1997). *Adult Bullying: Perpetrators and Victims*. London: Routledge.

Raudsepp, E. (1992). Are you properly assertive? *Supervision*, 53, 17–18.

Rayner, C. (1997). The incidence of workplace bullying. *Journal of Community and Applied Social Psychology*, 7, 199–208.

Reynolds, P.D. (1984). Leaders never quit: Talking, silence and influence in interpersonal groups. *Small Group Behaviour*, 15, 404–413.

Rich, B.L. Lepine, J.A. and Crawford, E.R. (2010). Job engagement: Antecedents and effects on job performance. *Academy of Management Journal*, 53, 617–635.

Robbins, S.P. and Judge, T.A. (2013). *Organizational Behavior: Global Edition* (15th edn). Boston, MA: Pearson.

Roberts, G.E. (1998). Perspectives in enduring and emerging issues in performance appraisal. *Public Personnel Management*, 27, 301–320.

Roe, R.A. and Ester, P. (1999). Values and work: Empirical findings and theoretical perspective. *Applied Psychology: An International Review*, 48(1), 1–21.

Rokeach, M. (1973). *The Nature of Human Values*. New York: Free Press.

Rosenfeld, P., Giacolone, R. and Riordan, C. (2002). *Impression Management*. London: Thomson Publishing.

Rothmann, S. (2013). 'From happiness to flourishing at work: A southern African perspective'. In M.P. Wissing (ed.), *Well-being Research in South Africa: Cross-cultural Advances in Positive Psychology*, Vol. 4. Dordrecht, The Netherlands: Springer, 123–152.

Rothmann, S. (2014a). 'Flourishing in work and careers'. In: M. Coetzee (ed.), *Psycho-social Career Meta-capacities: Dynamics of Contemporary Career Development*. Dordrecht: Springer International Publishing, 203–220.

Rothmann, S. (2014b). 'Positive institutions'. In: M.P. Wissing, J.C. Potgieter, L. Nel, I.P. Khumalo and T.Guse (eds), *Towards Flourishing: Contextualising Positive Psychology*. Pretoria: Van Schaik Publishers.

Rothmann, S. and Welsh, C. (2013). Employee engagement in Namibia: The role of psychological conditions. *Management Dynamics*, 22(1), 14–25.

Rothmann, S., Diedericks, E. and Swart, J.P. (2013). Manager relations, psychological need satisfaction and intention to leave in the agricultural sector. *South African Journal of Industrial Psychology*, 39(2), 11 pages. doi: 10.4102/sajip.v39i2.1129.

Rotter, J.B. (1966). Generalised expectancies for internal versus external control of reinforcement. *Psychological Monographs*, 80, 1–28.

Ryan, A.M. (2003). Defining ourselves: I/O psychology's identity quest. *The Industrial–Organizational Psychologist*, 41, 21–33.

Ryan, R.M. and Deci, E.L. (2002). 'Overview of self-determination theory: An organismic-dialectical perspective'. In: E.L. Deci and R.M. Ryan (eds), *Handbook of Self-determination Research*. Rochester, NY: University of Rochester Press, 3–33.

Ryan, R.M., Huta, V. and Deci, E.L. (2008). Living well: A self-determination theory perspective on eudaimonia. *Journal of Happiness Studies*, 9, 139–170.

Ryff, C.D. and Singer, B. (1998). The contours of positive human health. *Psychological Inquiry*, 9, 1–28.

Rynes, S.L., Gerhart, B. and Parks, L. (2005). Personnel psychology: Performance evaluation and pay for performance. *Annual Review of Psychology*, 56, 571–600.

Salas, E., Stagl, K. and Burke, C. (2004). '25 years of team effectiveness in organizations'. In: C. Cooper, and I.T. Robertson (eds), *International Review of Industrial and Organizational Psychology*. Chichester: Wiley, 47–93.

Salgado, J.F. (1997). The five factor model of personality and job performance in the European Community. *Journal of Applied Psychology*, 82, 30–43.

Salovey, P. and Mayer, J. (1990). Emotional intelligence. *Imagination, Cognition, and Personality*, 9, 185–211.

Saucier, G. (2003). An alternative multi-language structure for personality attributes. *European Journal of Personality*, 17, 179–205.

Schabracq, M. (2005). 'Well-being and health: What HRM can do about it'. In: R. Burke and C. Cooper (eds), *Reinventing HRM: Challenges and New Directions*. London: Routledge, 187–206.

Schaufeli, W.B. (2003). Past performance and future perspectives of burnout research. *South African Journal of Industrial Psychology*, 29(4), 1–15.

Schaufeli, W.B. and Bakker, A.B. (2004). Job demands, job resources and their relationship with burnout and engagement: A multi-sample study. *Journal of Organizational Behavior*, 25, 293–315.

Schaufeli, W.B. and Enzmann, D. (1998). *The Burnout Companion to Study and Practice: A Critical Analysis*. London: Taylor & Francis.

Schein, E.H. (1969). *Process Consultation*. Reading, MA: Addison Wesley, Vol. 1.

Schein, E.H. (1985). *Organisation Culture and Leadership*. San Francisco, CA: Jossey-Bass.

Schein, E.H. (1990). Organizational culture. *American Psychologist*, 45, 109–119.

Schiffrin, H.H. and Nelson, K.S. (2010). Stressed and happy? Investigating the relationship between happiness and perceived stress. *Journal of Happiness Studies*, 11, 33–39.

Schmidt, F.L. and Hunter, J.E. (1981). Employment testing: Old theories and new research findings. *American Psychologist*, 36, 1128–1137.

Schmidt, F.L. and Hunter, J.E. (1998). The validity and utility of selection methods in personnel psychology: Practical and theoretical implications of 85 years of research findings. *Psychological Bulletin*, 124, 262–274.

Schneider, B., Goldstein, H.W. and Smith, D.B. (1995). The ASA framework: An update. *Personnel Psychology*, 48, 747–773.

Schneider, K.T., Swan, S. and Fitzgerald, L.F. (1997). Job-related and psychological effects of sexual harassment in the workplace: Empirical evidence from two organizations. *Journal of Applied Psychology*, 82, 401–415.

Schultz, D. and Schultz, S.E. (2014). *Psychology and Work Today*. Essex: Pearson Education.

Schutz, W.C. (1978). *FIRO Awareness Scales Manual*. Palo Alto, CA: Consulting Psychologists Press.

Schwartz, S.H. (1994). *Packet for Participation in Cross-Cultural Research on Values*. Department of Psychology, The Hebrew University: Jerusalem.

Schwartz, S.H. (1999). A theory of cultural values and some implications for work. *Applied Psychology: An International Review*, 48, 23–47.

Searle, S.J. (1997). 'Sickness absence: Facts and misconceptions'. In: H.A. Waldron and C. Edling (eds), *Occupational Health Practice*. Oxford: Butterworth-Heinemann, 112–113.

Seligman, M.E.P. (2002). *Authentic Happiness: Using the New Positive Psychology to Realize Your Potential for Lasting Fulfillment*. London: Nicholas Brealey.

Seligman, M.E.P. (2011). *Flourish*. New York: Simon & Schuster.

Seligman, M.E.P. and Csikszentmihalyi, M. (2000). Positive psychology: An introduction. *American Psychologist*, 55, 5–14.

Senge, P.M. (1990). *The Fifth Discipline: The Art and Practice of the Learning Organisation*. New York: Doubleday/Currencey.

Singh, B., Winkel, D.E. and Selvarajan, T.T. (2013). Managing diversity at work: Does psychological safety hold the key to racial differences in employee performance? *Journal of Occupational and Organizational Psychology*, 86, 242–263.

Smith, P., Fischer, R. and Sale, N. (2001). 'Cross-cultural industrial/organizational psychology'. In: C.L. Cooper and I.T. Robertson (eds), *International Review of Industrial and Organisational Psychology*. Chichester: Wiley, Vol. 16, Ch. 5.

Smith, P.B. and Bond, M.H. (1993). *Social Psychology Across Cultures*. Cambridge: Harvester Wheatsheaf.

Snyman, J.R. and Sommers, De K. (1999). *Mims Disease Review*. Pretoria: MIMS.

Sonnentag, S., Niessen, C. and Ohly, S. (2004). 'Learning at work: Training and development'. In: C. Cooper and I. Robertson (eds), *International Review of Industrial and Organizational Psychology*. Chichester: Wiley, 249–289.

Spreitzer, G.M. (1995). Psychological empowerment in the workplace: Dimensions, measurement, and validation. *Academy of Management Journal*, 38, 1442–1465.

Staw, B.M. and Ross, J. (1985). Stability in the midst of change: A dispositional approach to job attitudes. *Journal of Applied Psychology*, 70, 469–480.

Sternberg, R. (1994). *In Search of the Human Mind*. New York: Harcourt Brace.

Swart, J.J. and Rothmann, S. (2012). Authentic happiness of managers, and individual and organisational outcomes. *SA Journal of Psychology*, 42(4), 492–508.

Tannenbaum, R. and Schmidt, W.H. (1958). How to choose a leadership pattern. *Harvard Business Review*, 36, 95–101.

Tellegen, A. and Waller, N.G. (1995). 'Exploring personality through test construction: Development of the multidimensional personality questionnaire'. In: S.R. Briggs and J.M. Cheek (eds), *Personality Measures, Development and Evaluation*. Greenwich, CT: JAI Press, Vol. 1, 23–42.

Tett, R.P., Jackson, D.N. and Rothstein, M. (1991). Personality measures as predictors of job performance: A meta-analytic review. *Personnel Psychology*, 44, 703–742.

Theobald, T. and Cooper, C. (2004). *Shut Up and Listen: How to Communicate at Work*. London: Kogan Page.

Thomas, R.R. (1996). *Redefining Diversity*. New York: Amacom.

Tierney, L.M., Mcphee, S.J. and Papadakis, M.A. (1999). *Current Medical Diagnosis and Treatment*, (38th edn). Stamford, CT: Appleton & Lange.

Timmerman, T. (2000). Racial diversity, age diversity, interdependence, and team performance. *Small Group Research*, 31, 592–606.

Tinsley, H.E.A. (2000). The congruence myth: An analysis of the efficacy of the person-environment fit model. *Journal of Vocational Behavior*, 56, 147–179.

Trist, E.H., Murray, B.J. and Pollack, A. (1963). *Organizational Choice*. London: Tavistock.

Trist, E.L. and Bamforth, K.W. (1951). Some social and psychological consequences of the long-wall method of goal-setting. *Human Relations*, 4, 3–38.

Trower, P. (1990). Situational analysis of the components and processes of behavior in socially skilled and unskilled patients. *Journal of Consulting and Clinical Psychology*, 48, 327–339.

Truss, C., Mankin, D. and Kelliher, C. (2012). *Strategic Human Resource Management*. New York: Oxford University Press.

Tuckman, B.W. and Jensen, M.A. (1977). Stages of small group development revisited. *Group and Organization Studies*, 2, 419–427.

Turner, N., Barling, J. and Zacharatos, A. (2002). 'Positive psychology at work'. In: C.R. Snyder and S.J. Lopez (eds), *Handbook of Positive Psychology*. Oxford: Oxford University Press, 715–728.

Valchev, V.H., Nel, J.A., Van de Vijver, F.J.R., Meiring, D., De Bruin, G.P. and Rothmann, S. (2013). Similarities and differences in implicit personality concepts across ethno-cultural groups in South Africa. *Journal of Cross-Cultural Psychology*, 44(3), 365–388.

Van den Broeck, A., Vansteenkiste, M., De Witte, H. and Lens, W. (2008). Explaining the relationships between job characteristics, burnout, and engagement: The role of basic psychological need satisfaction. *Work & Stress*, 22, 277–294.

Vroom, V.H. (1964). *Work and Motivation*. New York: Wiley.

Walumbwa, F.O., Peterson, S.J., Avolio, B.J. and Hartnell, C.A. (2010). An investigation of the relationships among leader and follower psychological capital, service climate job performance. *Personnel Psychology*, 634, 937–963.

Warr, P. (2002). 'Learning and training'. In: P. Warr (ed.), *Psychology at Work* (5th edn). London: Penguin Books, 153–177.

Watkins, M.L. (2001). Industrial psychology: An identity crises and future direction. *South African Journal of Industrial Psychology*, 27, 8–13.

Wechsler, D. (1944). *The Measurement of Adult Intelligence* (3rd edn). Baltimore, MD: Williams & Wilkins.

Weick, K.E. (1985). 'The significance of corporate culture'. In: P.J. Frost, L.F. Moore, M.R. Louis, C.C. Lundberg and J. Martin (eds), *Organizational Culture*. Beverly Hills, CA: Sage, 381–390.

Weick, K.E. (2000). 'Emergent change as a universal in organizations.' In: M. Beer and N. Nohria (eds), *Breaking the Code of Change*. Boston, MA: HBS Press, 223–224.

Weinberg, A. and Cooper, C. (2007). *Surviving the Workplace: A Guide to Emotional Well-being*. London: Thomson.

Weiss, H.M. (2002). Deconstructing job satisfaction: Separating evaluations, beliefs and affective experiences. *Human Resource Management Review*, 12, 173–194.

Werner, J.M. and Bolino, M.C. (1997). Explaining US courts of appeals decisions involving performance appraisal: Accuracy, fairness, and validation. *Personnel Psychology*, 50, 1–24.

Wexley, K.N. and Latham, G.P. (2002). *Developing and Training Human Resources in Organizations* (3rd edn). Englewood Cliffs, NJ: Prentice Hall.

Wiggam, A.E. (1931). 'The biology of leadership'. In: H.C. Metcalf (ed.), *Business Leadership*. New York: Pitman.

Wood, R.E. and Bandura, A. (1989). Impact of conceptions of ability on self-regulatory mechanisms and complex decision-making. *Journal of Personality and Social Psychology*, 56, 407–415.

Worrall, L. and Cooper, C.L. (2014). The effect of the recession on the quality of working life of UK managers: An empirical study. *International Journal of Management Practice*.

Wright, G.E. and Multon, K.D. (1995). Employer's perceptions on nonverbal communication in job interviews for persons with disabilities. *Journal of Vocational Behavior*, 47, 214–227.

Wright, P.L. (1996). *Managerial Leadership*. London: Routledge.

Wright, T.A. (2003). Positive organizational behavior: An idea whose time has truly come. *Journal of Organizational Behavior*, 24, 437–442.

Wright, T.A. and Cropanzano, R. (2000). The role of organizational behaviour in occupational health psychology: A view as we approach the millennium. *Journal of Occupational Health Psychology*, 5, 5–10.

Wright, T.A. and Wright, V.P. (2002). Organizational researcher values, ethical responsibility, and the committed to participant perspective. *Journal of Management Inquiry*, 11, 173–185.

Wrzesniewski, A. (2012). 'Callings'. In: K.S. Cameron and G.M. Spreitzer (eds), *The Oxford Handbook of Positive Organizational Scholarship*. New York: Oxford University Press, 45–55.

Xanthopoulou, D., Bakker, A.B., Demerouti, E. and Schaufeli, W.B. (2009). Reciprocal relationships between job resources, personal resources, and work engagement. *Journal of Vocational Behavior*, 74, 235–244.

Zaleznik, A. (1993). 'Managers and leaders: Are they different?' In: W.E. Rosenbach and R.L. Taylor (eds), *Contemporary Issues in Leadership*. Oxford: Westview Press, 36–56.

Zamahani, M., Ghorbani, V. and Rezaei, F. (2011). Impact of authentic leadership and psychological capital on followers' trust and performance. *Australian Journal of Basic and Applied Sciences*, 5, 658–667.

Zapf, D. (1999). Organisational, work group related and personal causes of mobbing/bullying at work. *International Journal of Manpower*, 20(1–2), 70–85.

Index

Relevant and further reading

Chapter 1

(1) Holloway, E. (1995) *Clinical Supervision: A Systems Approach*. Thousand Oaks, CA: Sage.
(2) Corey, M.S. and Corey, G. (1992) *Groups: Process and Practice*. Pacific Grove, CA: Brooks/Cole.

Chapter 2

(1) Bernard, J.M. and Goodyear, R.K. (1998) *Fundamentals of Clinical Supervision* (2nd edition). Boston, MA: Allyn and Bacon.
(2) Bion, W. (1961) *Experiences in Groups*. New York: Basic Books.
(3) Yalom, I. (1970) *The Theory and Practice of Group Psychotherapy*. New York: Basic Books.
(4) Carroll, M. (1996) *Counselling Supervision: Theory, Skills and Practice*. London: Cassell.
(5) Inskipp, F. and Proctor, B. (1993) *The Arts, Crafts and Tasks of Counselling Supervision. Part 1. Making the Most of Supervision*. Middlesex: Cascade Publications.
(6) Holloway, E.L. and Johnston, R. (1985) 'Group supervision: widely practised but poorly understood', *Counselor Education and Supervision*, 24: 332–40.
(7) Prieto, L.R. (1996) 'Group supervision: still widely practised but poorly understood', *Counselor Education and Supervision*, 35: 295–307.
(8) Lammers, W. (1999) 'Training in group and team supervision', in E. Holloway and M. Carroll (eds), *Training Counsellor Supervisors: Strategies, Models and Methods*. London: Sage.

Chapter 3

(1) Holloway, E.L. and Johnston, R. (1985) 'Group supervision: widely practised but poorly understood', *Counselor Education and Supervision*, 24: 332–40.
(2) Lammers, W. (1999) 'Training in group and team supervision', in E. Holloway and M. Carroll (eds), *Training Counsellor Supervisors: Strategies, Models and Methods*. London: Sage.
(3) Goldberg, C. (1981) 'The peer supervision group: an examination of its purpose and process', *Groups*, 5: 27–40.
(4) Hawkins, P. and Shohet, R. (1989) *Supervision in the Helping Professions*. Buckinghamshire: Open University Press.
(5) Borders, D. and Leddick, G. (1987) *Handbook of Counseling Supervision*. Alexandria, VA: ACES.

(6) Rogers, C. (1961) *On Becoming a Person*. London: Constable.
(7) Patterson, C.H. (1982) 'A client-centred approach to supervision', *Counselling Psychologist*, 11: 21–6.
(8) Berne, E. (1961, reprinted 1993) *Transactional Analysis in Psychotherapy*. Souvenir Press.

Chapter 4

(1) Kadushin, A. (1985) *Supervision in Social Work* (2nd edition). New York: Columbia University Press.
(2) Holloway, E. (1995) *Clinical Supervision: A Systems Approach*. Thousand Oaks, CA: Sage.
(3) Proctor, B. (1998) 'Contracting in supervision', in C. Sills (ed.), *Contracts in Counselling*. London: Sage.
(4) Hewson, J. (1995) 'Training supervisors to contract in supervision', in E. Holloway, *Clinical Supervision: A Systems Approach*. Thousand Oaks, CA: Sage.
(5) Association for Counselor Education and Supervision (ACES) (1993) *Ethical Guidelines for Counseling Supervisors*. Alexandria, VA: ACES.
(6) British Association for Counselling (BAC) (1995) *Code of Ethics and Practice for Supervisors*. Rugby: BAC.
(7) Corey, M.S. and Corey, G. (1992) *Groups: Process and Practice*. Pacific Grove, CA: Brooks/Cole.
(8) Bordin, E.S. (1983) 'A working-alliance based model of supervision', *Counseling Psychologist*, 11 (1): 35–43.

Chapter 5

(1) Yalom, I. (1970) *The Theory and Practice of Group Psychotherapy*. New York: Basic Books.
(2) Corey, M.S. and Corey, G. (1992) *Groups: Process and Practice*. Pacific Grove, CA: Brooks/Cole.
(3) Truax, C. and Carkhuff, R. (1967) *Towards Effective Counseling and Psychotherapy*. Chicago: Aldine.
(4) Ivey, A.E. (1971) *Micro-counseling; Innovations in Interviewing Training*. Springfield, IL: Chas. C. Thomas
(5) Neufeldt, S. (1999) 'Training in reflective processes in supervision', in E. Holloway and M. Carroll (eds), *Training Counsellor Supervisors: Strategies, Models and Methods*. London: Sage.
(6) Schon, D.A. (1983) *The Reflective Practitioner*. New York: Basic Books.
(7) Inskipp, F. and Proctor, B. (1995) *The Arts, Crafts and Tasks of Counselling Supervision. Part 2. Becoming a Supervisor*. Middlesex: Cascade Publications.
(8) Inskipp, F. (1999) 'Training supervisees to use supervision', in E. Holloway and M. Carroll (eds), *Training Counsellor Supervisors: Strategies, Models and Methods*. London: Sage.

Chapter 6

(1) Lammers, W. (1999) 'Training in group and team supervision', in E. Holloway and M. Carroll (eds), *Training Counsellor Supervisors: Strategies, Models and Methods*. London: Sage.
(2) Tuckman, B.W. (1965) 'Developmental sequences in small groups', *Psychological Bulletin*, 63 (6): 384–99.
(3) Schulz, W.C. (1989) *Joy*. Berkeley, CA: Ten Speed Press.

Chapter 7

(1) Doehrman, M.J. (1976) 'Parallel process in supervision and psychotherapy', *Bulletin of the Menninger Clinic*, 40 (1): 1–104.
(2) Houston, G. (1984) *The Red Book of Groups*. London: Rochester Foundation.
(3) Carroll, M. and Holloway, E. (eds) (1998) *Supervision in Context*. London: Sage.
(4) Sue, D.W. and Sue, D. (1990) *Counseling the Culturally Different*. New York: John Wiley.
(5) Gilbert, M. and Sills, C. (1999) 'Training for supervision evaluation', in E. Holloway and M. Carroll (eds), *Training Counsellor Supervisors: Strategies, Models and Methods*. London: Sage.
(6) Holloway, E. (1995) *Clinical Supervision: A Systems Approach*. Thousand Oaks, CA: Sage.
(7) Inskipp, F. and Proctor, B. (1995) *The Arts, Crafts and Tasks of Counselling Supervision. Part 2. Becoming a Supervisor*. Middlesex: Cascade Publications.
(8) Carroll, M. (1996) *Counselling Supervision: Theory, Skills and Practice*. London: Cassell.
(9) Bernard, J.M. and Goodyear, R.K. (1998) *Fundamentals of Clinical Supervision* (2nd edition). Boston, MA: Allyn and Bacon.

Chapter 8

(1) Goldberg, C. (1981) 'The peer supervision group: an examination of its purpose and process', *Groups*, 5: 27–40.
(2) Nobler, H.A. (1980) 'A peer group for the therapists', *International Journal of Group Psychotherapy*, 30: 51–61.

Chapter 10

(1) Bandler, R. and Grinder, J. (1975/76) *The Structure of Magic*, 1 and 2. Palo Alto, CA: Science and Behavior Books.
(2) Dilts, R., Badler, R. and Grinder, J. (1980) *Neurolinguistic Programming*, Vol. 1. USA: CA: Meta Publications.
(3) Holloway, E. (1995) *Clinical Supervision: A Systems Approach*. Thousand Oaks, CA: Sage.

Chapter 11

(1) Hess, A.K. (1986) 'Growth in supervision: stages of supervisor and supervisee development', *Clinical Supervisor*, 4 (2): 51–67.
(2) Carroll, M. (1996) *Counselling Supervision: Theory, Skills and Practice*. London: Cassell.
(3) British Association for Counselling (BAC) (1995) *Code of Ethics and Practice for Supervisors*. Rugby: BAC.
(4) British Association for Counselling (BAC) (1990) *Code of Ethics and Practice for Counsellors*. Rugby: BAC.
(5) Association for Counselor Education and Supervision (ACES) (1993) *Ethical Guidelines for Counseling Supervisors*. Alexandria, VA: ACES.
(6) Hellman, S. (1999) 'Supervision of school counsellors in Israel: setting up a network of supervision', in M. Carroll and E. Holloway (eds), *Supervision in Context*. London: Sage.

Further reading in group supervision

Cheston, S.E. (1992) 'A case presentation paradigm: a model for efficient use of small group or individual counselor supervision', *Clinical Supervisor*, 9: 149–59.
Cooper, L. and Gustafson, J.P. (1985) 'Supervision in a group: an application of group theory', *Clinical Supervisor*, 3: 7–25.
Garrett, K.J. and Barretta-Herman, A. (1995) 'Moving from supervision to professional development', *Clinical Supervisor*, 13: 97–110.
Hillerbrand, E. (1989) 'Cognitive differences between experts and novices: implications for group supervision', *Journal of Counseling and Development*, 67: 293–6.
Kruger, L.J., Cherniss, C., Maher, C.A. and Leichtman, H.M. (1988) 'A behavior observation system for group supervision', *Counselor Education and Supervision*, 87: 331–43.
Pistole, M.C. (1995) 'The genogram in group supervision of novice counselors: draw them a picture', *Clinical Supervisor*, 13: 133–43.
Remley, T.P., Jr., Benshoff, J.M. and Mowbray, C.A. (1987) 'Postgraduate peer supervision: a proposed model of peer supervision', *Counselor Education and Supervision*, 27: 53–60.
Riva, M.T. and Erickson Cornish, J.A. (1995) 'Group supervision practices at psychology predoctoral internship programs: a national survey', *Professional Psychology: Research and Practice*, 26: 523–5.
Savickas, M.L., Marquart, C.D. and Supinski, C.R. (1986) 'Effective supervision in groups', *Counselor Education and Supervision*, 26: 17–25.
Sharpe, M. (ed.) (1995) *Supervision of Analytic Groups*. London: Routledge.
Tebb, S., Manning, D.W. and Klaumann, T.K. (1996) 'A renaissance of group supervision in practicum', *Clinical Supervisor*, 14: 39–51.
Westwood, M.J. (1989) 'Group supervision for counsellors-in-training', *Canadian Journal of Counselling/Revue Canadienne de Counseling*, 23: 348–53.
Wilbur, M.P., Roberts-Wilbur, J., Hart, G.M., Morris, J.R. and Betz, R.L. (1994) 'Structured group supervision (SGS): a pilot study', *Counselor Education and Supervision*, 33: 262–79.

Index